A DOUBLE SINGLENESS

A Double Singleness

Gender and the Writings of
Charles and Mary Lamb

JANE AARON

CLARENDON PRESS · OXFORD
1991

Oxford University Press, Walton Street, Oxford OX2 6DP

Oxford New York Toronto
Delhi Bombay Calcutta Madras Karachi
Petaling Jaya Singapore Hong Kong Tokyo
Nairobi Dar es Salaam Cape Town
Melbourne Auckland
and associated companies in
Berlin Ibadan

Oxford is a trade mark of Oxford University Press

Published in the United States
by Oxford University Press, New York

British Library Cataloguing in Publication Data
Aaron, Jane
A double singleness : gender and the writings of Charles
and Mary Lamb.
1. essays in English. Lamb, Charles, 1775–1834
I. Title
824.7
ISBN 0–19–812890–8

Library of Congress Cataloging in Publication Data
Aaron, Jane.
A double singleness : gender and the writings of Charles and Mary
Lamb / Jane Aaron.
p. cm.
Includes bibliographical references (p.   ) and index.
1. Lamb, Charles, 1775–1834—Criticism and interpretation.
2. Lamb, Mary, 1764–1847—Criticism and interpretation.
3. Feminism and literature—England—History—19th century.
4. Brothers and sisters—England—History—19th century.
5. Psychoanalysis and literature. 6. Authorship—Collaboration.
7. Sex role in literature. I. Title.
PR4864.A2   1991   824'.7—dc20   90–27142
ISBN 0–19–812890–8

Typeset by Hope Services (Abingdon) Ltd.
Printed in Great Britain by
Courier International Ltd.
Tiptree, Essex

ER COF AM
MARGARET IOLA MORGAN

Acknowledgements

The main debts I have incurred in writing this book are to Susan Sellers and Barry Palmer, who read through the whole manuscript with meticulous care, and made a great many useful suggestions for amendments; I am very grateful to them both. I should also like to thank Mary Lynne Ellis, Kelvin Everest, and Philip Dodd for their helpful comments on various parts of the manuscript.

The book owes its origins to my earlier doctoral dissertation on Charles Lamb, and I should like to thank St Anne's College, Oxford, for appointing me to the research fellowship which enabled me to complete that project. I am also grateful to Kathryn Sutherland and Roy Park for their help and encouragement with that early research.

Though they have since been revised, parts of this book have appeared in earlier publications. A section from the Introduction was published as 'Charles and Mary Lamb: The Critical Heritage' in the July 1987 issue of the *Charles Lamb Bulletin*; parts of Chapters 2 and 3 were first published as '"On Needle-Work": Protest and Contradiction in Mary Lamb's Essay' in September 1987 in *Prose Studies*; and a part of Chapter 5 was published as 'Charles Lamb, The Apostate: 1796–1798' in January 1978 in the *Charles Lamb Bulletin*. Passages from the Introduction and Chapter 1 were also published in my essay '"Double Singleness": Gender Role Mergence in the Autobiographical Writings of Charles and Mary Lamb' in Susan Groag Bell and Marilyn Yalom (eds.), *Revealing Lives: Autobiography, Biography and Gender* (Albany, NY: State Univ. of New York Press, 1990). All of this material is used here by permission of the publishers.

Contents

List of Abbreviations   x

Introduction   1

1. Rank and Gender   20
2. Work and Time   51
3. 'We are in a manner *marked*'   97
4. A Modern Electra   115
5. 'The impertinence of manhood'   133
6. 'Bridget and I should be ever playing'   167

Bibliography   208

Index   215

List of Abbreviations

Works, ed. Lucas   Charles Lamb and Mary Lamb, *The Works of Charles and Mary Lamb*, ed. E. V. Lucas, 7 vols. (London: Methuen, 1903–5). All references in the text to the Lambs' works are from this edition.

Letters, ed. Marrs   *The Letters of Charles and Mary Anne Lamb*, ed. Edwin W. Marrs, Jr., 3 vols. (Ithaca, NY and London: Cornell University Press, 1975–8).

Letters, ed. Lucas   *The Letters of Charles Lamb: To which are added those of his sister Mary Lamb*, ed. E. V. Lucas, 3 vols. (London: Dent and Methuen, 1935).

Introduction

I

In May 1833 an Edmonton schoolmistress noticed that her neighbours, the Waldens, had acquired two new lodgers; as Mr Walden, formerly an asylum keeper, let lodgings to the mentally ill, 'the reputation of insanity', not surprisingly, attached itself in the schoolmistress's mind to both of the newcomers.[1] In fact, of the two new lodgers, Charles and Mary Lamb, only Mary suffered from attacks of what has subsequently been categorized by their biographers as a manic depressive disorder.[2] Her brother chose to live with her at the Waldens because he believed that the strain of moving to and fro from their own home to an asylum whenever she became ill was increasing the frequency of Mary's attacks, and he could not tolerate the thought of their living permanently apart. As he wrote to a correspondent at that time:

It is no new thing for me to be left to my sister. When she is not violent her rambling chat is better to me than the sense and sanity of this world. . . . I could be nowhere happier than under the same roof with her.[3]

His sister's company was indeed no new experience for Charles Lamb; ten years his elder, Mary had been in childhood his nurse and in adolescence his closest friend. In 1796, when Mary, then 31, in a sudden and very violent attack of insanity, took her mother's life, her brother pledged himself to be responsible for her care, thus sparing her from threatened incarceration in Bedlam. From then until his death in 1834 they were separated only by the recurring pattern of her periodic madness; 'wedded'

---

[1] H. F. Cox, 'Charles Lamb at Edmonton', *Globe* (1875), quoted E. V. Lucas, *The Life of Charles Lamb*, 2 vols. (London: Methuen, 1905), ii. 253.
[2] See D. G. Wilson, 'Charles Lamb and Bloomsbury', *Charles Lamb Bulletin*, 4 (1979), 21; and Winifred F. Courtney, *Young Charles Lamb: 1775–1802* (London and Basingstoke: Macmillan, 1982), pp. 236 and 370 n. 3.
[3] *Letters*, ed. Lucas, iii. 401.

in an intense sibling bond, they lived together, wrote together, 'writing on one table', according to Mary, 'like an old literary Darby and Joan',[4] and were rarely seen apart. Their friends and contemporaries often commented upon their inseparability. According to Thomas De Quincey, for example:

As, amongst certain classes of birds, if you have one you are sure of the other, so, with respect to the Lambs . . . seeing or hearing the brother, you knew that the sister could not be far off.[5]

Bachelor and spinster, they shared together what Charles in his Elia essays was to describe as 'a sort of double singleness'.[6]

One of the aims of this book is to explore the unique relationship between the Lambs, and its effects upon their writings. Unusual at any time, the reciprocity of their sibling bond seems particularly distinctive in the context of its immediate historical period. As recent socio-historical accounts of gender relations during the first decades of the nineteenth century have shown, the Lambs' times were ones in which the more flexible arrangements of the eighteenth century, with its characteristically companionate marriage pattern, shifted under the pressure of reactionary ideological change, hardening towards the strongly polarized gender system typical of the Victorian period.[7] Male domination and female dependency were taken for granted during this period in sibling relations as much as in marital ones. Harriet Martineau in her *Autobiography*, lamenting the lack of reciprocity in her relationship with her youngest brother for whom she had felt the 'strongest passion' of her life, presents it as a universal, if painful, truth that 'brothers are to sisters what sisters can never be to brothers as objects of engrossing and devoted affection'.[8] But the Lambs had no such one-sided relationship. On the contrary, despite

---

[4] *Letters*, ed. Marrs, ii. 228–9. (Marrs is still in the process of publishing a new and definitive edition of the Lambs' letters, hence the reference to two editions.)

[5] *The Collected Writings of Thomas de Quincey*, ed. David Masson, 14 vols. (Edinburgh: Adam & Charles Black, 1889–90), iii. 58.

[6] *Works*, ed. Lucas, ii. 75.

[7] See e.g Leonore Davidoff and Catherine Hall, *Family Fortunes: Men and Women of the English Middle Class, 1750–1850* (London: Hutchinson, 1987) and Lawrence Stone, *The Family, Sex and Marriage in England 1500–1800* (London: Weidenfeld & Nicolson, 1977).

[8] *Harriet Martineau's Autobiography* (London: Virago repr. of 1877 edn., 1983), i. 99.

his legal position as Mary's guardian after 1796, it was Charles who, of the two, most frequently expressed in his writings his reliance upon their union. When his sister was absent in hospital he was desolate, feeling that 'my daily & hourly prop has fallen from me. I totter and stagger with weakness, for nobody can supply her place to me'.[9] 'I am a widow'd thing, now thou art gone!' he exclaims in a 1797 poem to his absent sister (v. 22). Many of their contemporary acquaintances also testify to the mutuality of the emotional tie between them, and, indeed, to Charles's greater reliance upon it. Robert Southey, for example, on hearing of Charles's death in 1834, commented:

Forlorn as his poor sister will feel herself . . . it is better that she should be the survivor. Her happiness, such as it was, depended less upon him than his upon her.[10]

This atypical merging of gender roles, in which both partners appear to have functioned alternately as caretaker and cared for, bore unusual fruit in their writings as well as in the day to day patterns of their existence. Culturally as well as socially, theirs was an age of transition, from the cults of sensibility and gothic writing characteristic of the second half of the eighteenth century, with their particular appeal to a new generation of women readers, to a more patriarchal aesthetic in which the popular styles of the earlier epoch were dismissed as unmanly.[11] One consequence of the British establishment's reaction to the terror of the French Revolution was the widespread adoption of new paternalistic and evangelical value-systems, which accorded well with the ideological needs of an emerging middle class. Many of the Lambs' Romantic contemporaries, responding to such pressures, had, by the 1820s, eschewed their earlier radical allegiances, and adopted literary tones and themes more suited to the new ethos. Coleridge, for example, in his *Aids to Reflection in the Formation of a Manly Character* (1825), condemns the lack of manliness in the eighteenth-century sentimental writing

---

[9] *Letters*, ed. Marrs, i. 203–4.
[10] *Selections from the Letters of Robert Southey*, ed. John Wood Warter, 4 vols. (London: Longman, 1856), iv. 394.
[11] For an account of the transition from the point of view of women writers, see Mary Poovey, *The Proper Lady and the Woman Writer: Ideology & Style in the Works of Mary Wollstonecraft, Mary Shelley, and Jane Austen* (Chicago and London: Univ. of Chicago Press, 1984), pp. 3–47.

which he had earlier admired and imitated. His treatise *On the Constitution of the Church and State* (1829) deplores the 'emasculation' of the nation and stresses the need for a revival of paternalistic powers, ideally to be embodied in the nation's clerisy.[12] Poems characteristic of Wordsworth's later works, such as his 'Ode to Duty' and the 'Character of the Happy Warrior', function as moral guides to the formation of an orderly, responsible, and authoritarian male identity. In 'Ode to Duty' a manly 'Law' and 'Light' are presented as mature virtues to which the poet is gladly prepared to sacrifice the 'unchartered freedom' and 'chance-desires' of his youth, which he now experiences as dangerously debilitating.[13] Both he and Coleridge assume for themselves as speakers the roles and tones of social responsibility and leadership which their writing seeks to inculcate in their readers, whom they appear to envisage as predominantly male and upper class.

But the Lambs never identify with the voice of authority or leadership. The ethos of paternalism does surface occasionally in Charles's writings, but when it does, he, unlike his contemporaries, associates himself not with those in authority but with those under it, with the governed rather than the governor. His voice at such times is that of the obedient child, the faithful servant, or the admiring disciple, rather than that of the patriarchal master or teacher figure. At other times, often in the same piece of writing, a very different note predominates, and Charles, through his characteristic use of the first person pronoun, identifies himself with those voices which puncture and subvert the paternalistic rhetoric—with the ironist, the jester, or the trickster, and with drunkards, sluggards, liars, and felons. Occasional indicators in Charles's writings suggest that he was aware of their unmasculine, or, indeed, anti-masculine, cast. Whether playing the gentle servant or the subversive

---

[12] See Samuel Taylor Coleridge, *On the Constitution of the Church and State,* ed. John Colmer (The Collected Works of Samuel Taylor Coleridge, gen. ed. Kathleen Coburn, x) (Princeton, NY: Princeton Univ. Press, 1976), pp. 48 and 72–6. For a detailed account of the relation of paternalism to the English Romantic poets, see David Roberts, *Paternalism in Early Victorian England* (London: Croom Helm, 1979), pp. 25–74.

[13] Wordsworth, 'Ode to Duty', *The Poetical Works of William Wordsworth,* ed. Ernest de Selincourt and Helen Darbishire, 5 vols. (Oxford: Clarendon Press, 1940–9), iv. 85–6.

trickster, he frequently draws his reader's attention to the prevalence in these roles of characteristics usually regarded as female or childlike. The Elia essay 'Old China', for example, begins 'I have an almost feminine partiality for old china' (ii. 247), and in the mock-elegiac 'Preface, by a Friend of the late Elia' he accounts for the Elia persona's intense horror of appearing 'important' or 'respectable', or in any way approximating to the required model of manly identity, by explaining that 'the impressions of infancy had burnt into him, and he resented the impertinence of manhood' (ii. 153).

Mary's essay 'On Needle-Work' is similarly marked by internal contradiction; in an attempt to retain her readers' sympathies her stance shifts from feminist protest to an apparent acceptance of the prevailing social roles then allotted to women. Her writing, like her brother's, avoids the least hint of an authoritarian, dominating voice; her tone suggests always, even in her writing for children, a concern for the reader as an equal or a friend, and an anxiety with regard to any influence her position as writer may give her. Critics of her children's books have recognized her pronounced capacity to merge with her characters, and identify with the lives she describes;[14] her letters reveal the same ability. Such tendencies have recently been identified as the psychological consequence for women of the conventional allocation by gender of child care and mothering. It is argued that because women mother, girls, identifying with their mothers, develop a subjectivity which is more continuous with that of others and more permeable in its ego boundaries than a boy's more detached and separate sense of himself.[15] This book will demonstrate, however, that in the Lambs' case, the brother also, closely bound as he was to his sister throughout his life, reveals in his writings that he shared in her unusually pronounced capacity to identify with others. But the prevalence of an accommodating voice in both their writings made it difficult for them to wage war outright upon the increasingly masculinist ideologies of

---

[14] See Joseph E. Riehl, *Charles Lamb's Children's Literature*, ed. James Hogg, Salzburg Studies in English Literature, 94 (Salzburg: Univ. of Salzburg Press, 1980), p. 103.

[15] See Nancy Chodorow, *The Reproduction of Mothering: Psychoanalysis and the Sociology of Gender* (Berkeley, Calif.: Univ. of California Press, 1978).

their period. The characteristic swerves and slippages of their language are a consequence of the contradictory impulses at work within the texts: the wish to merge their interests with those of the reader conflicts with the need to attack those aspects of the prevailing ideology which, through the implementation of rigid social roles, would limit the potential fluidity and multiplicity of the subject, its very capacity to recognize within itself a number of apparently contradictory positions.

The existence of such conflicting voices within the Lambs' texts would appear to make them appropriate subjects of study for critics influenced by the contemporary interest in the intertextuality of writing and its inclusion of multiple voices or points of view. But, with the exception of one recent essay by Mary Jacobus,[16] their work has aroused little critical involvement of this kind. Had Charles Lamb been a Frenchman, his writings might today be better known. As it is, Charles's literary reputation in Britain has waned considerably since the heyday of his popularity in the late Victorian and Edwardian periods. The oscillations in the reception of his work cast an interesting light upon the processes and trends of English literary criticism generally, during the late nineteenth and twentieth centuries. As they also illuminate some of the covert effects of gender bias in constructing and deconstructing literary reputations, I provide in the next section a brief account of the critical heritage on the Lambs, before proceeding further to introduce the issues arising from my own interest in their work.

II

During his lifetime and afterwards, criticisms of Charles Lamb's work were energized to an unusual extent by strong emotive responses to his personality. His literary contemporaries tended to respond to his unconventionality with an affectionate but at times patronizing protectiveness. Defending Charles from a reviewer's criticisms, Southey, for example, in a poem entitled 'To Charles Lamb, On the Review of his "Album Verses" in the *Literary Gazette*' (1830), writes more as if Charles

[16] Mary Jacobus, *Romanticism, Writing, and Sexual Difference: Essays on* The Prelude (Oxford: Clarendon Press, 1989), pp. 142–7, 154–8.

were the beloved child of his friends than their adult contemporary:

> To us who have admired and loved thee long,
> It is a proud as well as pleasant thing
> To hear thy good report.[17]

Charles's puns and witticisms appealed to his friends as the whimsical manifestations of a perpetual 'child of impulse',[18] a Peter Pan figure who refused to age. He features as a 'fantastic' or 'wild-eyed' 'boy',[19] even in late manhood, in the reminiscences of the many of his close acquaints. 'How Lamb confirms the remark of the childlikeness of genius', Henry Crabb Robinson muses in his 1816 diaries.[20] For Coleridge he was, to Lamb's chagrin, 'my gentle-hearted Charles';[21] for Wordsworth, 'the frolic and the gentle'.[22] After his death, Thomas Talfourd's disclosure, in his *Final Memorials of Charles Lamb* (1848), of the history of Mary's madness and her brother's devotion to her, unleashed a proliferation of personal testimonies to the worth of Charles's character: consequently, his writings came to be appreciated increasingly for the light they threw upon an exemplary individual whose personality was assuming mythic proportions. Charles himself took his allegiance to his sister for granted; had the sexes been reversed and the sister rather than the brother been afforded the opportunity to manifest such devotion, no doubt others also would have

[17] Robert Southey, 'To Charles Lamb, On the Review of his "Album Verses" in the *Literary Gazette*', *The Times* (6 Aug. 1830).

[18] Charles Lloyd, from verses on Lamb given in Thomas Allsop, *Letters, Conversations and Recollections of S. T. Coleridge*, 2 vols. (London: Moxon, 1836), i. 204.

[19] Coleridge, 'To a Friend', *The Poetical Works of Samuel Taylor Coleridge*, ed. Ernest Hartley Coleridge (London: OUP, 1912), p. 159; and Bryan Waller Procter ['Barry Cornwall'], in the dedication to his poem 'The Fall of Saturn', *The Poetical Works of Milman, Bowles, Wilson and Barry Cornwall* (Paris: Galignani. 1829), p. 128.

[20] Henry Crabb Robinson, *Henry Crabb Robinson on Books and their Writers*, ed. Edith J. Morley, 3 vols. (London: Dent, 1938), i. 185.

[21] Coleridge, 'This Lime-Tree Bower my Prison', *Poetical Works*, p. 179; Charles asked Coleridge 'please to blot out *gentle hearted*, and substitute drunken dog, ragged-head, seld-shaven, odd-ey'd, stuttering, or any other epithet which truly and properly belongs to the Gentleman in question' (*Letters* ed. Marrs, i. 224.)

[22] Wordsworth, 'Extempore Effusion on the Death of James Hogg', *Poetical Works*, iv. 277.

accepted the relationship as a 'natural', if commendable, example of feminine self-sacrifice. But as it was, his combination of selflessness and maleness led to the secular canonization of 'Saint Charles', as Thackeray called him.[23] The pet-Lamb cult served to distance Charles's behaviour from that required of the average male. As a saint, an innocent, a holy fool, his image could be cherished as one comfortably set apart, in its sweet domestic niche, from the self-assertive public world of the nineteenth-century middle-class male. Like the Victorian icon of the ideal female as the 'Angel in the House', Saint Charles featured as the 'heart of a heartless world' in the writings of most of his Victorian and Edwardian commentators.

The cult of his personality became inextricably intertwined for his admirers with their assessment of his writing, in a manner that discouraged objective analysis. Augustine Birrell, for example, refused to accept as an admirer of Charles Lamb any reader not thoroughly acquainted with the life:

I run no great risk in asserting that, of all English authors, Charles Lamb is the one loved most warmly and emotionally by his admirers, amongst whom I reckon only those who are as familiar with the four volumes of his 'Life and Letters' as with Elia.[24]

The importance of the life was also stressed by Charles's most vociferous and enthusiastic Victorian idolater, Swinburne. Swinburne attempts very little straightforward criticism of his 'best beloved', presenting instead a justification for not doing so which would invalidate further critical studies of Charles Lamb altogether:

No good criticism of Lamb, strictly speaking, can ever be written; because nobody can do justice to his work who does not love it too well to feel himself capable of giving judgement on it.

Loving Lamb became a moral touchstone for Swinburne; he asserts that 'All men worthy to know him would seem always to have loved him in proportion to their worthiness.'[25] Similarly, Arthur Symons maintained that 'to read Lamb makes a man

---

[23] See *Letters*, ed. Lucas, ii. 448, for an account of Thackeray pressing one of Charles Lamb's letters to his forehead, with the remark: 'Saint Charles!'.

[24] Augustine Birrell, *Obiter Dicta* (London: Elliot Stock, 1884), pp. 102–3.

[25] Algernon Charles Swinburne, *Miscellanies* (London: Chatto & Windus, 1886), pp. 157 and 195.

more human' and 'incites to every natural piety'.[26] Charles's
childlikeness continued to be stressed in tandem with his
saintliness; for the 'Agnists', Elia, as they liked to call Lamb,
was 'the grown-up child of letters', who preserved throughout
life 'a spirit of youth in everything'.[27] The frequently rebarbative
ironies in Charles's writings were indulged as the frolics of a
whimsical child rather than accorded any substantial significance.
Altogether, Charles Lamb's image seems to have functioned to
such potent effect during the years bridging the nineteenth and
twentieth centuries because it incorporated in one figure two
apparently disparate ideals, both of which the age found
particularly compelling: firstly, the devoted allegiance to familial
duty and domestic responsibility of a male equivalent of the
'Angel in the House'; secondly, the blithe, childlike freedom of
a Never-Never Land or Wonderland, with its mischievous
dodging of the values of a conventional grown-up world.

But Charles also had his detractors, who were more inclined
to denounce him for unmanly degeneracy than soften to the
popular appeal of his pet-Lamb image. Thomas Carlyle's
meeting with the Lambs in 1831 aroused in him a horrified
disgust for the brother, which he recorded in his diaries with
characteristic vigour:

A more pitiful, ricketty, gasping, staggering, stammering Tom fool I do
not know. . . . His speech wriggles hither and thither with an incessant
painful fluctuation; not an opinion in it or a fact or a phrase that you
can thank him for: more like a convulsion fit than natural systole and
diastole.—Besides he is now a confirmed shameless drunkard . . . Poor
Lamb! Poor England where such a despicable abortion is named
genius![28]

Charles's popularity is similarly perceived as a threat to the
manly health of the British nation in an article from the early
twentieth-century periodical *The New Age*. J. M. Kennedy, a
self-professed Nietzschean, finds Elia drastically lacking in 'the
will to power', and all too representative of 'the flaccid,
shrinking degenerative period of romanticism'. 'The prime

[26] Arthur Symons, *Figures of Several Centuries* (London: Constable, 1916),
p. 29.
[27] Ibid., 18 and 20.
[28] Carlyle, *The Notebooks of Thomas Carlyle*, ed. Charles Eliot Norton (New
York: The Grotier Club, 1898), pp. 217–19.

test', according to Kennedy, 'is a man's strength': 'does he command, or does he obey?' The 'weak, timorous essayist' dismally fails this test, and the popularity of his 'nauseating twaddle' is seen as indicative of a national loss of fighting spirit, that 'ancient British virtue'. 'Can we wonder that weak spines should now be so common,' Kennedy asks, 'that boxing matches should be frowned upon—that there should be temperance reformers?'[29] Ludicrous as it would appear—Charles Lamb would have been the last to welcome temperance reformers —the *New Age* article, which must have seemed an oddity when it was published in 1909 at the height of Charles's popularity, was to prove prophetic of twentieth-century attitudes towards Lamb. The enthusiastic spate of anthologies and semi-fictional biographies published by Charles's admirers to mark the centenary of his death in 1935 brought him to the attention of F. R. Leavis's critical journal *Scrutiny*, and, in the furtherance of its self-imposed duties as the rigorous watch-dog of literary values, *Scrutiny* very effectively damned him.

Denys Thompson, one of Leavis's followers, in an article entitled 'Our Debt to Lamb', found the 'extravagant eulogy' accorded to Charles Lamb 'preposterous and so unrelated to fact, that one can hardly take it seriously or find a point to engage in controversy'. Instead, he stated his own reactions categorically, with characteristic Leavisite downrightness: Charles Lamb's was a 'regressive mind, shrinking from full consciousness'; 'Elia has been a Bad Influence'. According to Thompson, Charles's work does not require its reader to 're-orientate' himself, and provides no salutary 'shock to self-satisfaction'; consequently, it represents a falling away from the more rigorous eighteenth-century essay which attempted to improve the reader's 'spiritual manners' by disturbing his complacency. That the essay of his own day was a 'profitable channel for vulgarity, "low-brow" propaganda and a studied irresponsibility' Thompson attributed to his contemporaries' debt to Charles Lamb.[30] Thompson's *Scrutiny* article was collected in the volume *Determinations*, edited by Leavis and published in 1934; in the same year the first edition of Thompson's *Reading and Discrimination* appeared. The manner in which

---

[29] J. M. Kennedy, in *New Age* (7 Jan. 1909), p. 226.
[30] Denys Thompson, 'Our Debt to Lamb', in F. R. Leavis (ed.), *Determinations: Critical Essays* (London: Chatto & Windus, 1934), pp. 201–17.

Charles Lamb is referred to in this practical criticism guide for schools did him in all probability more effective harm than the *Scrutiny* essay itself. The professed intention of *Reading and Discrimination* is to train its students to discriminate for themselves between good and bad literature, but, in fact, its commentary on the extracts it supplies, the choice of extracts, and the guidance implicit in the order in which they are placed, make up altogether a didactic and domineering overview of the texts which it would take an unusually independent-minded student to resist. In the section 'The Essayist—Then and Now' an extract from the Elia essay 'The Praise of Chimney-Sweepers' is placed between an extract from an Addison *Spectator* essay and a verbose twentieth-century advertisement. The commentary informs the student or teacher that in the eighteenth century the essay was a medium for serious writers but 'Lamb reduced it to a vehicle for charming whimsies'. The Elia extract is described as 'remarkable for its offensive affectedness, a pseudo-literary style unvitalized by living speech'. Its 'pretentiousness' and 'Bad Influence' have resulted in the 'undesirable' style of the advertisement which follows it, according to Thompson, and he goes on to deplore that Lamb's work should be distributed as 'literature' in schools at all.[31] A revised edition of *Reading and Discrimination* appeared in 1954 in which the section on Lamb remained substantially the same as in the 1934 edition, but when a 'New edition, completely rewritten' was published in 1979 it contained no mention of Lamb whatsoever. Thompson's diatribes have had their effect: Charles Lamb is no longer generally taught in schools, and it is exceptional to find his name on university syllabuses.

The Leavisite school of criticism thus succeeded in severely damaging Charles Lamb's reputation within the framework of academic studies of English literature. But the reasons for the attack, and for its success, need to be understood in the light of the general purposes of Leavis and his followers with regard to the development of 'English' as a new discipline in higher education during the first half of this century. In order to further its aim of establishing English as a strenuous branch of academic study, the intellectual equivalent of scientific subjects,

[31] Id., *Reading and Discrimination* (London: Chatto and Windus, 1934), pp. 40–1.

Scrutiny set itself against what it saw as the hitherto 'gentlemanly' mode of English teaching, which encouraged, as they saw it, an effeminate or dilettante sense of the subject. The concept of studying 'English' was to be reformed as an arduous activity, more capable than any other discipline of strengthening the manly moral and intellectual fibre of its practitioners.[32] A new canon of the 'Great Tradition' of English writers was established, in which a writer such as Charles Lamb, whose appeal was considered to apply generally to the emotions, and who had no underlying didactic moral mission to pursue, could have little place. Since the 1960s other authors damned by *Scrutiny*, such as Sterne and Shelley, have been rehabilitated, but Elia's equivocal reputation still seems too embarrassing for the British educational institutions to countenance him.

Nor is his status much higher in the United States. Although his fame in America never underwent the same swooping oscillation from high praise to detraction as it did in Britain, and does not seem to have been associated to such an extent with anxieties regarding the possible effeminacy of reading literature, the 'New Critics' disparaged his critical works as lacking in the objectivity proper to the literary analyst. In the 1930s Charles had been acclaimed as 'the chief of critics', but René Wellek, W. K. Wimsatt, and Cleanth Brooks found his commentaries upon texts too personal and lacking in detachment to be of worth.[33] In the annotations to his *Specimens of English Dramatic Poets*, commenting upon the scene from *The Revenger's Tragedy* in which Vindici and Hippolito tempt their mother, Charles had written:

The reality and life of this Dialogue passes any scenical illusion I ever felt. I never read it but my ears tingle, and I feel a hot blush spread my cheeks, as if I were presently about to 'proclaim' such 'malefactions' of myself, as the Brothers here rebuke in their unnatural parent. (iv. 160)

---

[32] See Brian Doyle, 'The Hidden History of English Studies', in Peter Widdowson (ed.), *Re-Reading English* (London: Methuen, 1982), pp. 24–8, for a similar account of the reshaping of English studies.

[33] See René Wellek, *The Romantic Age: A History of Modern Criticism 1750–1950* (London: Jonathan Cape, 1955), ii. 191–5; and W. K. Wimsatt and Cleanth Brooks, *Literary Criticism: A Short History* (New York: Alfred A. Knopf, 1957), p. 494.

Wellek, in his volume on *The Romantic Age* for the series *A History of Modern Criticism*, isolates this passage for particular disapprobation: while for him the notes to the *Specimens* as a whole are 'little more than exclamation marks, mere assertions of enthusiasm', this particular comment reaches the pits of 'personal unargued criticism' of obvious 'irrelevance to the text'.[34] But given the present stress, in both feminist and poststructuralist criticism, on acknowledging the wholeness of the reader's involvement in the 'pleasure of the text', the way in which the play of signs affects the body as well as the mind, it should now be possible to see Lamb's criticism, as well as his work generally, in a less dismissive light.

If Charles's writings have suffered recent neglect, Mary's have been consistently ignored. Kennedy's dismissal of her at the close of his *New Age* article—'Mary Lamb is of little importance'—is representative of her critical non-status. Originally, her neglect was in part the consequence of her own inclination to preserve her anonymity, and to publish only under a pseudonym or under her brother's name, but the eventual recognition of her authorship of much of the literature for children initially produced under Charles's name led to little further critical attention. During the years of her brother's popularity, she commonly featured in his admirers' commentaries as the ominous shadow which thwarted his happiness, as the cross he had to bear which proved his saintliness. Since his fall from critical grace, his few remaining defenders tend to blame Mary for her brother's apparent limitations: his relatively slender output, for example, is attributed to the burden of maintaining his sister, and the extremes of his whimsicality are held to be the consequence of his close and debilitating involvement with her madness. The critics' difficulty in coming to terms with Mary is projected on to her brother; F. V. Morley, in his *Lamb before Elia* maintains that it would have been 'inhuman' of Charles not to fear Mary, and attributes Elia's attack upon misogynistic attitudes in his essay 'Modern Gallantry' to an 'extreme' over-compensation for his repressed hatred of his sister.[35] Thomas McFarland, in his recent reappraisal of Charles, represents Mary as nothing but a monstrous and

---

[34] Wellek, *The Romantic Age*, p. 193.
[35] F. V. Morley, *Lamb before Elia* (London: Jonathan Cape, 1932), pp. 249–50.

'smothering burden' upon her brother, with apparently no sufferings of her own.. While Charles struggled in an abyss of her making, Mary heartlessly 'survived, and survived, and survived', a malignant incubus, sucking the life-blood from her brother's frail but courageous form.[36]

For the contemporaries who knew them both, however, Mary's personality, as much as if not more than Charles's, was haloed by the 'mystery of goodness', rendered the more poignant in her case by her periodic plunges into madness. According to Talfourd, for example,

Miss Lamb would have been remarkable for the sweetness of her disposition, the clearness of her understanding, and the gentle wisdom of all her acts and words, even if these qualities had not been presented in marvellous contrast with the distraction under which she suffered for weeks, latterly for months, in every year. There was no tinge of insanity discernible in her manner to the most observant eye.

'She was enabled', he continues, 'by a temper more placid, a spirit of enjoyment more serene' than her brother's, 'to guide, to counsel, to cheer him; and to protect him on the verge of that mysterious calamity, from the depths of which she rose so often unruffled to his side'.[37] Charles frequently referred to Mary as his 'guardian angel',[38] and their friends not only endorse the appellation but make it clear in their writing that they also benefited from Mary's nurturing protectiveness. Mary Cowden Clarke, in the *Recollections of Writers* which she published with her husband, remembers Mary as having

a mind at once nobly-toned and practical, making her ever a chosen source of confidence among her friends, who turned to her for consolation, confirmation, and advice, in matters of nicest moment, always secure of deriving from her both aid and solace.[39]

'With her I can unbosom myself cordially,' Crabb Robinson remarks of Mary in his 1824 diaries.[40] Thomas Allsop, in his

---

[36] Thomas McFarland, *Romantic Cruxes: The English Essayists and the Spirit of the Age* (Oxford: Clarendon Press, 1987), pp. 26 and 27.

[37] Thomas Noon Talfourd, *Final Memorials of Charles Lamb; Consisting Chiefly of his Letters not before Published, with Sketches of some of his Companions*, 2 vols. (London: Moxon, 1848), ii. 226 and 227. [38] See, e.g. *Letters*, ed. Lucas, ii. 407.

[39] Charles Cowden Clarke and Mary Cowden Clarke, *Recollections of Writers* (London: Sampson Low, 1878), p. 177.

[40] *Henry Crabb Robinson on Books and their Writers*, i. 301.

Letters, Conversations and Recollections of S. T. Coleridge, gives an instance of her aid on one occasion when he confided to his friends his fears with regard to his future prospects: 'I have a clear recollection of Miss Lamb's addressing me in *a tone* acting *at once* as a solace and support, and *after* as a stimulus, to which I owe more perhaps, than to the more extended *arguments* of the others.'[41] A passage from one of Mary's letters to her closest friend, Sarah Stoddart, provides some illumination as to why Mary could function so effectively as a counsellor. Mary describes

a knack I know I have of looking into peoples real characters, and never expecting them to act out of it—never expecting another to do as I would do in the same case. When you leave your Mother and say if you never shall see her again you shall feel no remorse . . . all this gives me no offence, because it is your nature, and your temper, and I do not expect or want you to be otherwise than you are, I love you for the good that is in you, and look for no change.[42]

Of course Mary suffered profoundly, as we shall see, from her madness and the way in which it brought about the death of the mother to whom she was devoted, but she was able not only to live with the knowledge of the darker aspects of her own nature, but to extend the same spirit of unjudgemental acceptance to others. Her capacity for loving concern is manifest in her few published writings, as well as her correspondence. The time seems more than ripe for a renewal of critical interest in her own writings, as well as those of her brother.

III

There were times during the writing of this book when I felt inclined to abandon my material on Charles Lamb and concentrate wholly on his sister. Yet aspects of his life and writings seemed as interesting, from a feminist's point of view, as anything I could say about Mary. The primary focus of the book increasingly became the manner in which many of Charles Lamb's characteristics as a writer accord more closely to

[41] Allsop, *Letters, Conversations and Recollections of S. T. Coleridge*, ii. 226.
[42] *Letters*, ed. Marrs, ii. 124.

what have recently been considered to be 'feminine' sensibilities and styles as opposed to 'masculine' ones. As I shall argue, his work seems to me to demonstrate how differences generally attributed to gender are the consequence not of biological sex but of social patterning, and in particular of each subject's relation to the sources of power in his or her society.

Foremost amongst the social determinants which affected the Lambs must have been their position as the children of domestic servants. Charles's biographers, for all their apparently inexhaustible interest in every aspect of his life, generally pay little attention to this detail, passing without comment over the facts of his parentage, or ignoring them entirely. In my first chapter I explore the manner in which the Lambs' ambiguous social ranking, and the ideology of service in which they grew up, affected their depiction of the power relations in their society. Identification with the dispossessed made it impossible for them to adopt the tones of patronage, even while a history of dependence limited their capacity to condemn systems of social privilege and hierarchy outright. The Lambs' story provides a telling example of the way in which, as feminist historians have recently put it, 'gender and class always operate together', 'consciousness of class always takes a gendered form'.[43] I explore the consequences for the formation of gender identity of an upbringing like that of the Lambs, in which the source of all financial and social power within the family lay not so much with the parents themselves as with their employers. When a father is socially designated his master's man and only subversively operates as a man in his own right, when a mother's first nurturative allegiance is to her employer rather than her children, then modern concepts of gender construction based essentially upon middle-class paternal relations are less likely to be relevant. The Lambs' own occupations also, as needlewoman and clerk respectively, saw them still placed in an indeterminate social ranking, which had its effects on their concept of gender; the second chapter of the book investigates their responses to their employment.

But the close tie between Charles Lamb and the sister who had largely been responsible for him as a child must also have

---

[43] Davidoff and Hall, *Family Fortunes*, p. 13.

affected his gender orientation, intensified as the tie was by his reactions to his mother's death. Charles's sympathy with his sister during this trauma may well have been in part due to his own previous experience of mental illness; he too on one occasion had been confined for madness. Mary's act of matricide, and her brother's subsequent identification with her, condemned them both to a marginal and sometimes persecuted position on the fringes of respectability, and added to their experience of themselves as a pair at odds with their society. As recent feminist critics have shown, the treatment of the mad during this period relates interestingly to the treatment of women;[44] just as it is difficult to distinguish between the powerlessness which is the consequence of class stratification and that which results from a system of gender difference, so, in the Lambs' case, the perception of the mad as 'Other' also played its part in their experience of alienation. At the same time, the fear of drawing too much public attention to lives marked by the stigma of madness, limited their capacity to speak out publicly and openly upon such issues. The two central chapters of this book look at the effect upon both their writings of the manner of their mother's death and their association with madness, an investigation obstructed by the fact that both sought to suppress open reference to these aspects of their lives. Yet, as we shall see, mothers, madness, and social ostracism feature so frequently as subtexts in their writings, particularly Mary's, and seem so central an aspect of the tie which bound them, that the attempt to decipher as far as possible what they made of their position with regard to these concerns seems very necessary.

The final chapters analyse the manner in which Charles's writings encode his resistance to the cult of manliness prevalent during his period. In Chapter 5 I begin by assessing his critical attitude towards manifestations of the 'egotistical sublime' in the writings of his contemporary Romantics, largely through an account of his correspondence with Coleridge and Wordsworth, then turn, in the second part of the chapter, to an examination of his own pre-Elian writing. The last chapter, on Elia, emphasizes the element of play in his essays, presenting Elia as a chameleon writer, who through his manifold disguises and personae,

---

[44] See Elaine Showalter, *The Female Malady: Women, Madness and English Culture, 1830–1980* (London: Virago, 1987), pp. 1–50.

discloses the multiplicity of the human subject, and coaxes his readers too into a playful involvement with the text, which increases their own awareness of their subjective plurality. The Elia essays thus become a vehicle for communicating what may be interpreted as feminine, as much as masculine, responses to experience.

In that it deals largely with what is indirectly or unconsciously revealed through the nuances of language, such an analysis requires a change in methodological direction from the 'new history' of the book's first chapters to an approach more informed by recent developments in poststructuralist and psychoanalytic textual criticism. As feminist theorists are currently stressing, a consideration of the functions of gender in writing, or, indeed in the history of human society generally, requires a methodological combination of both approaches in order to achieve anything like a full appreciation of the complexities involved.[45] On the one hand, the particular functioning of gender difference in the work of historical figures cannot be adequately assessed without exploring its ideological relation to the prevalent attitudes in the society which informed it. But, on the other, a purely materialistic investigation of the determining pressures upon individual formation limits itself, when it comes to an analysis of the power relations at work in the gender system, if it fails to appreciate the manner in which the unconscious, as much as the conscious mind, is constructed by socio-economic, as well as sexual-familial, pressures. A psychoanalytically informed deconstruction of the ambiguities at play in language can provide a demystifying route into the experience of gender, and of power relations generally, in a given subject. The Lambs' characteristic writing, with its tensions and contradictions, invites such an approach, but in so far as it also reflects their involvement with a changing society it calls too for a socio-

[45] See, e.g. Rosalind Coward and John Ellis, *Language and Materialism: Developments in Semiology and the Theory of the Subject* (London: Routledge & Kegan Paul, 1977), pp. 1–11; Cora Kaplan, 'Pandora's Box: Subjectivity, Class and Sexuality in Socialist Feminist Criticism', in Gayle Greene and Coppélia Kahn (eds.), *Making a Difference: Feminist Literary Criticism* (London: Methuen, 1985), pp. 146–76; and Joan Kelly, 'The Doubled Vision of Feminist Theory', in Judith L. Newton, Mary P. Ryan, and Judith R. Walkowitz (eds.), *Sex and Class in Women's History* (London: Routledge & Kegan Paul, 1983), pp. 259–70.

historical alertness, if the issues at play are to be thoroughly explored. Throughout the book my underlying concern is not solely with the Lambs as individuals, but also with their representative function as emblems of other more hidden lives, equally affected by gender and class discrimination, and by the label of madness.

1

Rank and Gender

I

One Sunday morning in 1809 Charles Lamb found himself set in the stocks at Barnet for disturbing the peace of the Sabbath, or, as he termed it in a pseudonymous essay describing the incident, for 'timing my Saturnalia amiss' (i. 210).[1] Although this was the only instance in his life in which his occasional intemperance brought him into quite such public disrepute, nevertheless it serves to illustrate the degree to which he and his times were ill-attuned. The decades bridging the eighteenth and nineteenth centuries witnessed a period of social change in Britain which has been described as more drastically revolutionary than any since the prehistoric agricultural communities saw the passing away of the old hunter-gatherer way of life.[2] In order to man the accumulating machinery of the industrial revolution, Georgian capitalists and entrepreneurs found it necessary to bring what forces they could to bear upon the disciplining of a rural or barely urbanized work-force; a proletariat had to be created capable of accepting and enduring the regular hours and mechanized labour of the factory system. Self-control, and the repression of that hedonism which was considered a characteristic of the eighteenth-century mob, now became important virtues to be inculcated. The evangelical and methodist religious revivals, widespread in Britain during the last quarter of the eighteenth century, served usefully, from the industrialist's point of view, to promote a secular as well as spiritual law-abiding propriety, and to encourage the lower ranks of society to look for the rewards of a lifetime's self-

[1] See E. V. Lucas, *The Life of Charles Lamb* 2 vols. (London: Methuen, 1905) ii. 144.
[2] See Harold Perkin, *The Origins of Modern English Society 1780–1880* (London: Routledge & Kegan Paul, 1969), p. 4.

subordination in the hereafter.[3] Caught drunkenly carousing on a Sunday, Charles had violated a central tenet of the new code of behaviour. In 1787 George III had issued a Proclamation condemning 'excessive drinking, blasphemy, profane swearing and cursing, profanation of the Lord's day, and other dissolute, immoral or disorderly practices';[4] later, at the turn of the century, William Wilberforce's and John Bowdler's Society for the Suppression of Vice and Encouragement of Religion successfully prosecuted 623 Sabbath-breakers in 1801 to 1802 alone, as part of their general campaign to cleanse and regulate their erring brethren.[5]

But Charles's spell in the stocks, as well as demonstrating his inability or refusal to internalize the new mores, also serves to indicate the equivocal nature of his social position. The new regulations brought in by the evangelical moralists generally restricted diversions characteristic of the poor rather than the rich: legislation was passed against 'two-penny hops and gingerbread fairs', for example, but Bowdler's attempt to make adultery punishable by imprisonment failed to get through the House of Commons.[6] In 1809 Sydney Smith, querying the bias of the new laws, commented that the Society for the Suppression of Vice should more properly call themselves 'a Society for suppressing the vices of persons whose income does not exceed £500 a year'.[7] The concept and terminology of class in its modern, post-Marxist sense had not as yet matured into full consciousness;[8] but the punishment which Charles received, along with the crime for which it was deemed fitting, would suggest that his general demeanour was such as to mark him

[3] See ibid., 89–90; E. P. Thompson, 'Time, Work-Discipline, and Industrial Capitalism', in M. W. Flinn and T. C. Smout (eds.), *Essays in Social History* (Oxford: Clarendon Press, 1974), pp. 62–4; and Leonore Davidoff and Catherine Hall, *Family Fortunes: Men and Women of the English Middle Class, 1750–1850* (London: Hutchinson, 1987), pp. 93–5.

[4] See Lawrence Stone, *The Family, Sex and Marriage in England 1500–1800* (London: Weidenfeld & Nicholson, 1977), p. 666.

[5] See E. P. Thompson, *The Making of the English Working Class* (Harmondsworth: Penguin, 1968), p. 442.

[6] Ibid., 443.

[7] *Edinburgh Review*, 13 (1809), 342, quoted Stone, *The Family, Sex and Marriage in England*, p. 667.

[8] See Asa Briggs, 'The Language of "Class" in Early Nineteenth-Century England', in Asa Briggs and John Saville (eds.), *Essays in Labour History* (London: Macmillan, 1960), pp. 43–73.

out, at least on this occasion, as belonging more to the unruly mob than to the middle or upper ranks of his society. It is difficult to imagine many of his literary acquaintances, Wordsworth, say, or Coleridge, caught in quite such a plebeian predicament.

And yet, by 1809, not only his fellow Romantic writers but also such noteworthy figures of his day as the statistician John Rickman, later to organize the first national Census, and Thomas Manning, the Cambridge mathematician and orientalist, who became the first white man to enter Lhasa and meet the Dalai Lama, counted Charles amongst their closest friends. His social status, however, remained throughout his life, from a disinterested observer's point of view, a lowly one. At least one of his superiors at the East India Company was later to dismiss Elia's claims to fame on the grounds that 'an individual, whose official status was never very high, and who did not rise to the receipt of more than £600 a year' could hardly be credited with much significance.[9] In fact, it is clear from Charles's correspondence with Manning that his failure to gain promotion at work was largely a matter of choice. In 1808 Manning, then travelling through China, made the acquaintance of visitors to the East India Company's factory in Canton who could have secured his friend's promotion. He repeatedly assures Charles in his letters of his new friends' 'good interest at the India House', asking him 'what will you have?' but his correspondent insists that there is 'nothing to be done' for him, and that he wishes for no preferment.[10] Earlier, in 1798, John May, a friend of Robert Southey's, had similarly offered to secure Charles's promotion through the interests of his friends in the East India Company, but in a letter to Southey Charles refused the offer on his own behalf, asking instead whether something could not be done for an unemployed acquaintance of his.[11] It appears to have been his preference deliberately to maintain both himself, and also, necessarily, given the dependent position of women during their day, his sister, in an indeterminate social grouping;

[9] William Carew Hazlitt, *The Lambs: Their Lives, Their Friends and Their Correspondence* (London: Elkin Mathews, 1897), pp. 53–4.
[10] See *The Letters of Thomas Manning to Charles Lamb*, ed. G. A. Anderson (London: Martin Secker, 1925), pp. 101 and 105.
[11] *Letters*, ed. Marrs, i. 154.

he refuses, in effect, to adopt the full status and authority of a middle-class nineteenth-century gentleman, not only in his written work but also in the practical realities of his daily life. Indications as to his and Mary's understanding and experience of class, or of 'rank' as they would have termed the social divisions of their society, emerge from an investigation of their earliest familial circumstances.

II

As with every individual history, the patterns and processes of their lives and writings developed in response to interacting public and private pressures; their personal domestic history and the social and cultural context of their times worked together to establish the framework of their lives, and direct their understanding of it. The Lambs' was by no means a privileged background, or, at least, not in the customary sense: privileges featured largely in their childhood, but more as patronage bestowed than as an unquestioning inheritance of riches. The cramped set of Inner Temple chambers in which they were born, Mary in 1764 and Charles eleven years later, were rented by their father's employer, Samuel Salt, a barrister of the Temple and a Whig member of Parliament. Their father, John Lamb, after a period of early employment as a footman in Bath, had established himself as a waiter at the Inner Temple Hall, and had become Salt's personal 'man', his valet and secretarial assistant. Salt had probably to some degree been an agent in his servant's marriage, for John Lamb's wife Elizabeth was the daughter of a housekeeper to one of his master's friends and colleagues at Westminster, William Plumer; Elizabeth probably assisted in the housekeeping of Salt's establishment after her marriage.[12] On both sides of the family, therefore, the Lambs were born into the upper servant classes, and the strongest and most influential component in their ideological inheritance was the ethos of domestic service.

In the eighteenth century, the ideal, if not the practice, of master/servant relations still retained many of the characteristics

---

[12] See Lucas, *Life of Charles Lamb*, i. 1–6; and Winifred F. Courtney, *Young Charles Lamb: 1775–1802* (London and Basingstoke: Macmillan, 1982), pp. 4–8.

of the old feudal system.[13] Conduct books written for servants during this period stressed the need for an entire self-subordination on the part of the servant to the requirements of his role. A servant's identity was considered as merged with that of his employer, as if he possessed no independent existence; 'you will be known by your master's rank and fortune', the anonymous author of the *Servants Pocket-Book* (1761) declares.[14] Complete obedience and deference was due to the master, as to a patriarchal parent. Anthony Heasel's *Servants Book of Knowledge* (1773), for example, reminded those in service that 'as we are commanded to honour our parents, so it is necessarily implied that we also honour and respect all those who have authority over us'.[15] For the offspring of male servants the consequence of this power relation must have been, from a post-Freudian point of view, a curious one in terms of gender role models; inside the family unit itself the ultimate patriarch and the source of the family's social status and identity was not the biological father but his master, in relation to whom all members of the family were in a position of dependence.[16] During their childhood, and well into their adult years, the paternalistic source of material power in the Lamb children's lives was not John Lamb but Samuel Salt, the benevolent master. Salt's income supported the family; Salt's influence secured for the two Lamb boys places at the charity school Christ's Hospital, and procured employment as trading-house clerks for them afterwards; Salt's library provided for Mary and Charles an early introduction to English literature, thereby doing much to enhance Mary's otherwise very limited dame's school education. Yet these advantages were due purely to the charitable interest of their father's employer: the death of Salt in 1792 thrust the family into sudden poverty and resulted in the loss of all their former privileges.

In the Elia essay 'The Old Benchers of the Inner Temple', Charles describes the relationship between John Lamb and Salt

[13] See J. Jean Hecht, *The Domestic Servant Class in Eighteenth-Century England* (London: Routledge & Kegan Paul, 1956), p. 71.

[14] Quoted ibid., p. 37.   [15] Ibid., p. 75.

[16] For a theoretical discussion of this power relation, see Judy Lown, 'Not so much a Factory, More a Form of Patriarchy: Gender and Class during Industrialization', in Eva Gamarnikow, *et al.* (eds.), *Gender, Class and Work* (London: Heinemann, 1983), pp. 29–33.

as he witnessed it in his boyhood. His father, called 'Lovel' in the essay, is portrayed as the perfect helpmate, one who 'took care of everything' and was at once his master's 'clerk, his good servant, his dresser, his friend, his "flapper", his guide, stop-watch, auditor, treasurer' (ii. 87).[17] Salt was apparently utterly dependent on the nurturing capacities of his servant. Even the name Charles gives his father in the essay suggests the quality of caring affection he emphasized in portraying his father's performance of the servant role. The values he saw his father as embodying, and with which, as a son, he might be expected to identify, were quite opposite to those qualities of authority, dominance, and control typical of the nineteenth-century paterfamilias figure; on the contrary, his father plays an essentially motherly, or wifely, role in his relationship with his master. It is true that the indolently inclined Salt is presented in the essay as very dependent for the running of his daily affairs upon the practical resourcefulness of his competent servant, but the nature of that dependence, as part of a social system, suggests to the contemporary mind more the conventional relation of men to women, in the various stereotyped roles of husband/wife or employer/secretary, than that of men to men. That a similar connection between the two relations of husband/wife and master/servant existed also in the ideological structures of the Lambs' own time is clear from the tone and content of such popular conduct tracts as William Fleetwood's *The Relative Duties of Parents and Children, Husbands and Wives, Masters and Servants*, in which the moral necessity for the docile subordination of servant and wife is in both cases stressed and justified by biblical quotation. Fleetwood reminds his readers that for a servant to kill his master, and for a wife to kill her husband, were equally considered crimes of treason, more heinous than murder, because they broke the bonds of 'Faith and Allegiance' owed to the superior in both cases.[18] The early feminist writer Mary Lee, Lady Chudleigh, in 1713, similarly compares the

[17] The term 'flapper', referring as it does to the Laputa servants in Swift's *Gulliver's Travels* who carried bladders with which to 'flap' their employers, if their minds wandered, and return them to their immediate surroundings, here suggests Salt's absent-mindedness, and his reliance on his servant's practical good sense.

[18] William Fleetwood, *The Relative Duties of Parents and Children, Husbands and Wives, Masters and Servants* (2nd edn., London: John Hooke, 1716), p. 294.

servant's lot to that of the wife, complaining in her address 'To the Ladies' that

> Wife and Servant are the same,
> But only differ in the Name.

Servants and wives, she writes, are equally 'govern'd by a Nod' and compelled to fear their 'master' as a 'God'.[19]

Lovel, however, is not presented by his son as entirely docile and submissive: one of the anecdotes included in the 'Old Benchers' essay shows him as having once, at least, turned upon his 'betters'. Elia records of him that:

In the cause of the oppressed he never considered inequalities, or calculated the number of his opponents. He once wrested a sword out of the hand of a man of quality that had drawn upon him; and pommelled him severely with the hilt of it. The swordsman had offered insult to a female—an occasion upon which no odds against him could have prevented the interference of Lovel.

Once the heat of the moment is passed, however, the claims of social deference come into play once more; the anecdote proceeds:

He would stand next day bare-headed to the same person, modestly to excuse his interference—for L. never forgot rank, where something better was not concerned. (ii. 87–8)

Lovel's paradoxical behaviour—for why should the passing of one day obliterate the transgression?—appears to be recorded approvingly by Elia. One moment the father ardently defends from dishonour victims of the hierarchical system under which he lived, the next he subordinates his own self-respect, and the maintenance of his principles in an abstract form, to the demands of rank; and the son, in recounting the tale with an apparent acceptance of the paradox, seems to recreate the ideological contradiction.

But it was a contradiction which the servant could not have confronted without running the risk of self-alienation: if he questioned his master's authority, or that of his 'betters' who shared his master's rank, then in effect he questioned his own

---

[19] Mary Lee, Lady Chudleigh, *Poems on Several Occasions, Together with The Song of the Three Children, paraphras'd* (London: Bernard Lintott, 1703), p. 40.

identity and the meaning of his life as a whole. As with the dependent wife in an unequal marriage, his own status and sense of self was enmeshed with that of the master; in honouring the master, he also paradoxically increases his own prestige, even as he subordinates his individuality and perhaps betrays his personal convictions and capacities. Collusion with the power of the master, at least on a formal, specious level, becomes part of the role for those trapped in the dependent position in the hierarchies of personalized power relations. And yet a necessary surface deference on the part of the subordinate might, in many cases, act but as a formal veneer to an underlying sharp awareness of the weaknesses of authority figures, an awareness likely to find open expression in the group privacy of the servants' quarters, or their equivalent. In John Lamb's case, it is clear from the few available records of his own accounts of a servant's life that in fact he credited his 'betters' with very little in the way of true superiority. As all three of his children were subsequently to do, John Lamb published verses, originally composed in his case for the servants' Friendly Society of which he was a member, and printed under the title *Poetical Pieces on Several Occasions* (1777?). Many of his rhymes are based upon his experiences in service, and all give an unflattering picture of those whom he served. The poem 'The Lady's Footman', for example, describes the footman's mistress as perpetually querulous in her relation with her servants, uncharitable to the poor, in debt with her tradesmen, and only prevented from making her footman's life a misery by his own easy and cheerful disobedience to her injunctions.[20] In another poem, a servant satirizes the behaviour and mores not only of his masters but of the upper orders generally: using culinary metaphors, he accuses the Church, the Law, and the medical establishment of cooking the books, and does not spare members of parliament either:

> Our worthy representatives
> Do promise us rich Broth;
> But when their bounty we do taste,
> We find it Wind and Froth.[21]

[20] See Lucas, *Life of Charles Lamb*, ii. 339; Lucas included John Lamb's poems as an appendix to his volume.
[21] Ibid., 345.

Yet John Lamb remained loyally bound to his position of service, although he was provided, on at least one occasion, with the opportunity of moving out of it. According to Elia, he was once offered a post in the Temple's treasury, a lucrative promotion which would have raised him above the condition of a domestic servant, but, like his son after him, he turned down the opportunity to leave behind the social grouping of which he was originally a member.[22] In the eighteenth century, with its developing humanist sense of the importance of individuality and autonomy, for a man to be a servant had come to be considered demeaning; one correspondent to the *London Chronicle* in 1757 insists that 'I consider an Englishman in Livery, as a kind of Monster. He is a Person born free, with the obvious badge of Servility.'[23] A scene from 'The Lady's Footman', in which the servant is sneered at by a passing pedestrian when he attempts to clear a way for his mistress, shows that John Lamb, like his fellow servants, must have been made aware of the stigma attached to service; nevertheless he chose to retain his original occupation.[24] The 'bonds of attachment', to his master, to his colleagues in service, and to the system of deference and rank itself and his ordained place in it, must have formed together too convoluted and involved a loyalty for him to think himself free of it. But in his verse he finds a subversive vent for an antagonism directed against the power figures in his life.

Elia mentions Lovel's 'fine turn for humorous poetry' in 'The Old Benchers' (ii. 88), but he forbears to detail the characteristic topics and themes of his verse. However, in depicting the personalities of the old Temple lawyers in the essay, particularly that of Salt, he himself carries out a process of subtle belittlement of these gods of his childhood, or at any rate of frank rather than deferential appraisal of their characteristics, similar to that found in the father's verse. Salt is presented as a man of little intrinsic merit, a king wearing no clothes, and

[22] See *Works*, ed. Lucas, ii. 368–9; the passage from the original essay in the *London Magazine* (Sept. 1821), describing Lovel's refusal of promotion, was left out of the collected edition of the *Essays of Elia*, but is included by Lucas in the notes to his edition.

[23] *London Chronicle*, 2 (1757), 468; quoted Hecht, *The Domestic Servant Class*, p. 179.

[24] See Lucas, *Life of Charles Lamb*, ii. 341.

certainly as no hero to his valet. His reputation as a lawyer relies heavily upon the quick-wittedness of his servant; according to Elia:

When a case of difficult disposition of money, testamentary or otherwise, came before him, he ordinarily handed it over with a few instructions to his man Lovel, who was a quick little fellow, and would despatch it out of hand by the light of natural understanding, of which he had an uncommon share. (ii. 86)

Salt, in contrast to his servant, is 'indolent and procrastinating to the last degree'; 'a child might pose him in a minute':

He did nothing without consulting Lovel, or failed in any thing without expecting and fearing his admonishing. . . . He resigned his title almost to respect as a master, if L. could ever have forgotten for a moment that he was a servant. (ii. 87)

What is stressed in this description of the master/servant relation is the virtue and wholeheartedness of the servant's commitment to the relationship rather than the worth of the master. Elia continues: 'I knew this Lovel. He was a man of an incorrigible and losing honesty. A good fellow withal, and "would strike".' The reference is to the last act of *King Lear*, to the scene in which the Duke of Kent attempts to disclose to the dying king the double role he has played. Reminded of his servant Caius, Lear responds:

> He's a good fellow, I can tell you that;
> He'll strike, and quickly too.   (v. iii. 285–6)

The figure of Kent/Caius and the ideal of self-abnegating, voluntary service which he represented was an immensely appealing one for Charles. Later, in his 'Table-Talk' in the *Athenaeum*, he was to describe Kent as the 'noblest feature' of the conceptions of Shakespeare's mind:

The old dying king partially catching at the truth, and immediately lapsing into obliviousness, with the high-minded carelessness of the other to have his services appreciated, as one that

> —served not for gain,
> Or follow'd out of form,

are among the most judicious, not to say heart-touching, strokes in Shakespeare. (i. 345)

Through connecting Lovel's image with that of Kent, Charles is adding to his portrait of his father a dignity and freedom which it may have had in spirit but could not have had materially: John Lamb, along with his family, was dependent upon Salt's financial support and patronage. Yet Lovel's cheerful acceptance of a circumscribed role, and one in which his multiple talents only served to further another's reputation and not his own, can seem to point to an attitude of self-abnegation equivalent to Kent's. For his son, at least, his life appears to have served as a potent emblem of the highest type of nobility, a nobility embodied in acts of voluntary and self-sacrificing dedication, which Charles associated particularly with the subordinate's role in an unequally balanced power relationship.

One of Charles's last essays, 'Barrenness of the Imaginative Faculty in the Productions of Modern Art' ends with an account of the relationship between the squire Sancho Panza and his master Don Quixote, that 'errant Star of Knighthood, made more tender by eclipse', as Charles calls him (ii. 233). He maintains that it is to Sancho's persistent, if bemused, loyalty that his master owes much of his appeal and dignity in the First Adventures: 'From the moment Sancho loses his reverence, Don Quixote is become a—treatable lunatic' (ii. 234). The rhythms of this sentence, as well as its conceptual connotations, are evocative of a text which in Charles's time represented the apotheosis of conservative rhetoric, Burke's *Reflections on the Revolution in France* (1790), with its condemnation of those irreverent revolutionary acts which stripped away the nobility of rank, and reduced even queens to animals 'not of the highest order'.[25] Certainly there is much in Charles's writings which would appear to convey an ideological concurrence with Burke's praise of 'that subordination of the heart, which kept alive, even in servitude itself, the spirit of an exalted freedom',[26] and retained hierarchical systems in their full splendour. But unlike Burke he never lost himself in rapturous admiration of the glamour and power of the privileged; on the contrary, figures of authority, or those with any pretensions to social prestige, were generally mocked by Charles, in both his

[25] Edmund Burke, *Reflections on the Revolution in France*, ed. C. C. O'Brien (Harmondsworth: Penguin, 1969), p. 171.
[26] Ibid., p. 170

writings and his daily life.[27] He concentrates upon bringing to light the unheroic virtue of the subordinate: what strength the master has is given to him by the persistent devotion of his loving servant.

A similar response to patterns of privilege is manifest in Charles's occasional comments upon the distribution of power in gender relations. In one of his pre-Elian critical essays, 'On the Genius and Character of Hogarth', the figure of Kent is introduced once more, but this time his relation to Lear is compared not with that of a servant and his master but with a woman devoted to her lover. Describing the central figures in the last print of Hogarth's series *The Rake's Progress*, Charles comments,

> Is it carrying the spirit of comparison to excess to remark, that in the poor kneeling weeping female, who accompanies her seducer in his sad decay, there is something analogous to Kent, or Caius, as he delights rather to be called, in *Lear*,—the noblest pattern of virtue which even Shakespeare has conceived,—who follows his royal master in banishment, that has pronounced *his* banishment, and forgetful at once of his wrongs and dignities, taking on himself the disguise of a menial, retains his fidelity to the figure, his loyalty to the carcass, the shadow, the shell and empty husk of Lear? (i. 72)

What seems significant here is not only the fact that Charles appreciated the connection between the systems of rank and gender operant in his society, but also the overt stress he lays upon the unworthiness of the object of devotion. The 'master' figure is an 'empty husk', who seduces and entraps his devotee in part by preying upon her better nature and her capacity for self-sacrificial love, that 'servitude above freedom, the gentle mind's religion', as Charles describes it in one of the notes to his *Specimens of English Dramatic Poets* (iv. 53). A similarly intense recognition of the unworthiness of the objects of female devotion seems to have excited Charles when in 1819 he saw Fanny Kelly's performance as Yarico in George Colman's tragedy *Inkle and Yarico*; in his review he comments that:

---

[27] See, e.g. his explanation to the Wordsworths as to why he 'so strangely coiled up from' a Stamp office official encountered at a party at Haydon's: 'I think I had an instinct that he was the head of an office. I hate all such people' (*Letters*, ed. Lucas, ii. 228).

To see her leaning upon that wretched reed, her lover—the very
exhibition of whose character would be a moral offence, but for her
clinging and noble credulity—to see her lean upon that flint, and by
the strong workings of passion imagine it a god—is one of the most
afflicting lessons of the yearnings of the human heart and its sad
mistakes, that ever was read upon a stage. (i. 185–6)

The pain, amounting to masochism, implicit from the loving
subordinate's point of view in embracing ties which bring
about his or her self-abnegation surface vividly in these
depictions of women's devotion; the object can never be
worthy of such sacrifice, and if it is accepted as a right a 'moral
offence' is committed, and yet the devotion itself remains in
Charles's eyes one of the highest examples of human virtue.

Nowhere in Charles's works is this recurring connection
between male service and female gender roles more apparent
and striking than in one of his rare pieces of fictional work, the
story 'Arabella Hardy' which formed a part of his contribution
to what was essentially a literary project of his sister's. In 1806
William Godwin commissioned Mary to produce a volume of
Tales from Shakespear for his new venture, the Juvenile Library.
Charles assisted her to complete that work, and they subsequently co-authored further volumes for the series. *Mrs Leicester's
School*, published in 1808, the one original fiction they produced
together, was probably influenced in its structure by Sarah
Fielding's *The Governess or, Little Female Academy* (1749),
although it differs markedly in tone and content from the earlier
work. A consignment of new pupils arrive at Mrs Leicester's
school for girls, and, in order that they should not 'look so
unsociably upon each other' (iii. 274), she suggests that they
spend their first evening together relating to each other the
histories of their past lives. Most of the tales were the work of
Mary rather than of her brother, but his 'Arabella Hardy' forms
the last chapter of the volume. In it a nurturing male becomes
the hero of a narrative which is centrally concerned with the
arbitrary nature of conventional gender-role differentiation,
and the limiting prejudices the system creates. Arabella, a
colonial orphan, travels alone on a long sea voyage, despatched
to England by her relatives to be educated. During the journey
she is very effectively mothered by Atkinson, one of the sailors,
whose 'gentleness of manner' and 'pale feminine cast of face'

has earned him the nickname 'Betsy' from the rest of the ship's crew. 'Betsy' comforts, entertains, and educates the child, and imaginatively sympathizes with her isolation, alleviating her fears. Arabella recalls, for example, that

when I have looked around with a mournful face at seeing all *men* about me, he would enter into my thoughts, and tell me pretty stories of his mother and his sisters . . . and with these images of women and females which he raised in my fancy, he quietened me. (iii. 333)

Thanks to his guidance, the sea becomes a home for her, she learns to think of the tossing of the ship in a storm as the rocking of a cradle in the hand of a loving parent, and is reconciled to her position. But before the voyage is over 'Betsy' dies of a lingering illness. The tale closes with Arabella's account of how she later met his family and heard more of her mother-substitute's history:

I have learned passages of his former life, and this in particular, that the illness of which he died was brought on by a wound of which he never quite recovered, which he got in the desperate attempt, when he was quite a boy, to defend his captain against a superior force of the enemy which had boarded him, and which, by his premature valour inspiriting the men, they finally succeeded in repulsing. This was that Atkinson, who, from his pale and female appearance, was called Betsy. This was he whose womanly care of me got him the name of a woman, who, with more than feminine attention, condescended to play the hand-maid to a little unaccompanied orphan, that fortune had cast upon the care of a rough sea captain, and his rougher crew. (iii. 335)

Into this lyrical passage, charged with an emotional rhetoric uncharacteristic of most of the stoic narratives of *Mrs Leicester's School*, Charles appears to have compressed much of his ambivalence concerning the question of gender roles and authority. Atkinson's history has all the qualities of the typical boys' adventure story—a fight at sea, a boy's courage inspiring the troops, the saving of the captain's life—yet it also subverts conventional notions of leadership. In the tale, the actual figure of authority, the captain, seems to have little power over the men; they respond not to orders and exhortations but to example alone. And when the boy who provided that example grows to manhood he makes no attempt to assume the leadership roles for which his courageous manliness would appear to qualify him. Instead, he takes upon himself the offices of a servant, and a female servant at that, a 'hand-maid', to the lowliest of beings, a female orphan, and employs his fortitude in resisting the consequent jeers of his fellows. Like Lovel and Kent, he is tied by bonds of deep respect and allegiance to those above him in the hierarchical structure, but he pays no heed to his own status and will serve the humblest for love. Such portrayals exemplify Charles's tendency to glorify self-sacrificial life patterns, which involve not so much a rebellion against the injustices of a system as an attempt to redeem the suffering and humiliation they entail through refusing to adopt dominant roles, and accepting subordinate ones voluntarily, in the name of love.

Inheriting an ideology commonly more impressed upon women and children than upon the male author, Charles finds in positions of humility, devoted service, and passive endurance of suffering, the highest moral ideal. And yet at the same time his persistent refusal to accord any worth to leadership figures as such, apart from the quality of devotion they may incite in their followers, suggests the existence of a subversive and rebellious subtext beneath the surface romance of allegiance. Real power in his favoured relationships becomes the property of the devotee rather than the object of devotion, of the servant rather than the served; the servant acts freely, giving out of devotion, but the master is presented as accepting out of need, dependent upon the other's care. That he should, in describing the final downfall of Hogarth's Rake, have linked the servant's self-subordinating fidelity with the female role in heterosexual partnership is not surprising given the gender-based differentiations of his day, and the social and familial conditioning into nurturing roles to which most women would have been subject. Unregarded generally, or thought of as a 'natural', instinctive characteristic of women, female service is, by means of the Kent analogy, here given the quality of an intentional act of a higher moral value than any which the dominant power figure can perform. Charles refuses to allot any strength to the conventional adult male role, and insists, on the contrary, on valuing most highly amongst males those capable of adopting the so-called female attributes of nurturing care, involving the sacrifice of personal identity, particularly in cases where the object of that care has no intrinsic power to command apart from the urgency of its need. Hierarchical systems may perpetuate themselves through exploiting, to a perverse extent, capacities for devotion and loyalty in the subordinated, but only the subordinated, not the system itself or those who benefit in terms of social privilege from it, are redeemed in Charles's view by such a configuration.

III

Charles Lamb's atypical representation of gender roles cannot, however, be attributed unproblematically merely to his father's station in life, and to the system of values he inherited from him. His older brother John appears to have been entirely unaffected by the father's role model and the ethos of self-abnegating service which so impressed his sibling; he seems in all respects to have differed very greatly in character from both his brother and his sister. John Lamb junior did not inherit his father's reluctance to rise in the world, but made full use of the opportunities for upward social mobility provided by his clerical post at the South Sea Company, acquiring the positions first of Deputy Accountant and then of Accountant within that company. On Salt's death he dissociated himself from his impoverished family, and did nothing to aid them in the difficult financial circumstances in which they then found themselves; nevertheless when, in 1796, he received a leg injury he returned to the cramped family lodgings to be nursed, and both Charles and Mary were required to give up their free hours, and the expectation of a rare holiday, to wait upon their brother.[28] He clearly enjoyed a very different position in the family constellation from either of his younger siblings. Elizabeth Lamb, their mother, was extremely attached to her eldest son, who had inherited her handsome, statuesque physique and commanding presence;[29] the two younger children

---

[28] *Letters*, ed. Marrs, i. 17: Charles writes to Coleridge on 8 June 1796, 'let me thank you again & again in my own name & my sister's name for your invitations. Nothing could give us more pleasure than to come, but . . . while my Brother's leg is so bad it is out of the question. . . . We are necessarily confined with him the afternoon & evening till very late, so that I am stealing a few minutes to write to you.'   [29] Lucas, *Life of Charles Lamb*, i. 6.

were physically more like their small-framed father. According to Charles in the Elia essay 'Dream-Children', the spirited manliness of her oldest grandchild also made him the maternal grandmother's favourite as well as the mother's (ii. 102). In her letters Mary refers very rarely to her parents, but from Charles's correspondence it would appear that his mother's manner towards her two younger children lacked the tender nurturing care he saw in his father's relation to his master. He does not complain of her conduct towards him, but he felt her neglect of Mary strongly. In describing their upbringing to Coleridge he records that his mother could never accept her daughter's love,

but met her caresses, her protestations of filial affection, too frequently with coldness & repulse . . . she would always love my brother above Mary, who was not worthy of one tenth of that affection, which Mary had a right to claim.[30]

In the autobiographical Elia essay 'Mackery End, in Hertford-shire', he presents Mary, or 'Bridget Elia' as she becomes in the essays, as one who suffered neglect in childhood: her 'education in youth was not much attended to' and she 'missed all that train of female garniture' with which an affectionate mother might have been expected to adorn her daughter (ii. 76).

   Charles suffered from a stammer throughout his life, and his recent biographers, working on the understanding that a childhood stammer is often the consequence of harsh or critical parenting, have tended to see in Elizabeth Lamb the type of parent who might induce the handicap.[31] His mother appears to have been the dominant figure within the family power structure. Contrary to the commonly accepted figure of the subordinate at work who becomes a petty tyrant at home, John Lamb does not seem to have taken advantage of his position as a husband, or to have established in his immediate domestic circle a pattern of marital or paternal superiority to compensate for his role as Salt's 'man'. His verse suggests that his was in all domestic situations the mildest of dispositions. A poem entitled 'Matrimony', for example, advocates familial self-restraint and gentleness:

[30] *Letters*, ed. Marrs, i. 52.
[31] See Courtney, *Young Charles Lamb*, pp. 8 and 347–8.

> At home let's be chearful, good-natur'd, and kind,
> When troubles attend us, be ever resign'd.[32]

One of the few family anecdotes recorded in Mary's later correspondence suggests that he may well indeed have found occasion to exercise such resignation, and conveys the impression that the tensions which seem to have developed between the maternal and paternal sides of the family may have been related to issues of rank and social prestige. Throughout her own and her brother's childhood, John Lamb's sister, Sarah, lived with them in Salt's Inner Temple lodgings, and the relation between the sisters-in-law was fraught. According to Mary:

They made each other miserable for full twenty years of their lives— my Mother was a perfect gentlewoman, my Aunty as unlike a gentlewoman as you can possibly imagine a good old woman to be, so that my dear Mother . . . used to distress and weary her with incessant & unceasing attentions, and politeness to gain her affection. The Old woman could not return this in kind, and did not know what to make of it—thought it all deceit, and used to hate my Mother with a bitter hatred, which of course was soon returned with interest.[33]

Her account interestingly suggests that the hierarchies of rank operated within the family as well as outside it, to divisive effect. The mother's claim to a higher state of gentility than that of her sister-in-law seems surprising at first given that Elizabeth Lamb was the daughter of servants, and was also servicing Salt's needs along with her husband. But the structures of rank within the domestic servant class were as severe in their categorization as that of any other hierarchically organized group; 'we are delicate, nice in our distinctions', a servant comments in a late eighteenth-century comedy, 'for a valet moves in a sphere, and lives in a stile as superior to a footman, as a Pall-mall groom porter to the marker of a tennis court'.[34] Mary Field, the Lambs' maternal grandmother, as the house-keeper in charge of her employers' Jacobean mansion in Hertfordshire, could consider herself a member of the highest echelons of domestic service, and took great pride in her situation and in the family she served. Her grandson records of

---

[32] Lucas, *Life of Charles Lamb*, ii. 337. [33] Ibid., ii. 123–4.
[34] John O'Keeffe, *Tony Lumpkin in Town* (1782), quoted Hecht, *The Domestic Servant Class*, p. 36.

her that 'if she had one failing 'twas that she respected her
master's family too much',[35] and in the largely autobiographical
essay 'Dream Children' he describes her as living in the great
house, deserted by its owners, 'in a manner as if it had been her
own' (ii. 101). It appears, from Mary Lamb's letter, that her
grandmother passed on to her daughter Elizabeth the manner,
if not the material attributes, of gentility, but that the Lamb side
of the family had no such pretensions. John Lamb came from
Lincolnshire agricultural labouring stock; Charles claims his
forefathers were shepherds (ii. 156 and v. 41), though this may
be a conjecture, based on an association of ideas with the family
name, rather than a historical fact. For all the father's artistic
and poetic talents, the mother seems to have acquired the
position of arbitrator of manners in the home, but from
Charles's account it would appear that she soon gave up the
task of attempting to impress upon a daughter very different in
personality from herself the 'female garniture' and genteel
patterns of behaviour in which she herself was reared. In adult
life, at any rate, Mary appears to have been entirely without any
ladylike pretensions; according to Mary Cowden Clarke, for
example, who was taught by Mary as a child and later became
her friend, 'her manner was easy, almost homely, so quiet,
unaffected and perfectly unpretending was it'.[36] She appears to
have influenced her younger brother in this respect; in her
correspondence she teases him for even jocularly attempting to
adopt an air of gentility. 'Charles Lamb commencing gentleman!'
she mocked, on one occasion when he lay claim to such a title.[37]

One obvious differential in the pattern of Charles's upbringing
as distinct from his older brother's was that he had from infancy
been left very much to the care of this sister, ten years his
senior; many of his autobiographical writings record the details
of Mary's caretaking role in their childhood, always with deep
affection and gratitude. In the Elia essay 'Mackery End, in
Hertfordshire', for example, he testifies that 'I have obligations
to Bridget, extending beyond the period of memory . . . in the
days of weakling infancy I was her tender charge' (ii. 75 and 79).

---

[35] *Letters*, ed. Marrs, i. 30.
[36] Charles Cowden Clarke and Mary Cowden Clarke, *Recollections of Writers*
(London: Sampson Low, 1878), p. 177.
[37] *Letters*, ed. Marrs, iii. 194.

Little has been written on the psychological consequence for the developing subject of sibling nurturance, as opposed to parental care. The customary concentration in psychoanalytic writings on the mother–child relationship, virtually to the exclusion of all other formative bonds, is blinkered according to the few commentators who have examined cross-cultural modes of child-rearing.[38] In primitive communities, and, historically, in western societies too, before the development of the typical post-industrial nuclear family, that a child should largely be cared for by one or more of its older siblings throughout most of its dependent years was common practice. Recent attempts at evolving an analytic understanding of the effects of such practice suggest that, for both the younger and older children involved, it resulted in interdependent co-operative behaviour and a responsible and nurturant orientation towards others, particularly towards the peer-group.[39] According to the anthropologist Thomas S. Weisner, sibling rivalry, and the development of possessive and aggressive characteristics, feature less in the ego construction of children reared under child caretaking conditions than they do within the more intensively parented childhoods of modern western culture.[40] A child reared by a sibling develops less strong bonds with its mother, and characteristically resembles that sibling more closely than it does its parents. He or she also apparently acquires at an early age the ability to change roles, from, for example, a nurtured role to a nurturing one, according to its position within the family community which changes with the birth of each new offspring.[41]

Charles Lamb's personality appears to have included many of the qualities described as characteristic of sibling-reared subjects: he too, formed his strongest loyalties within his peer-group, and throughout his life functioned best when working co-operatively as part of a team, in his joint compositions with

[38] See Thomas S. Weisner and Ronald Gallimore, 'My Brother's Keeper: Child and Sibling Caretaking', *Current Anthropology*, 18 (1977), 171.

[39] Ibid., 178–80.

[40] Thomas S. Weisner, 'Sibling Interdependence and Child Caretaking: A Cross-Cultural View', in Michael E. Lamb and Brian Sutton-Smith (eds.), *Sibling Relationships: Their Nature and Significance across the Lifespan* (Hillsdale: Lawrence Erlbaum Associates, 1983), p. 325.

[41] Ibid., 309.

Mary, for example, or in the closely bonded group of *London Magazine* contributors, rather than when engaged on a more individualistic venture. His readiness to accept responsibility for his sister after their mother's death, and his inability to see his actions at the time of the 1796 family crisis as in any way self-sacrificial or unusually virtuous, provides a clear illustration of his tendency to identify with the sibling who had reared him rather than with the parent, and to accept that nurturing roles should be shared between them, as the need arose. The comparatively less self-centred orientation of the developing subject in societies in which children serve as sibling caretakers also has interesting gender-role implications; it is said to encourage, in boys as well as girls, that development of more permeable ego boundaries which in western culture is seen as a predominantly female characteristic.[42] According to recent feminist theory, the psychological consequence of the conventional allocation of child care to the biological mother has a significant part to play in the formation of attitudinal gender difference. Nancy Chodorow claims that

because women mother, the early experience and preoedipal relationship differ for boys and girls. Girls retain more concern with early childhood issues in relation to their mother, and a sense of self involved with these issues. . . . The greater length and different nature of their preoedipal experience, and their continuing preoccupation with the issues of this period, mean that women's sense of self is continuous with others and that they retain capacities for primary identification . . . In men, these qualities have been curtailed, both because they are early treated as an opposite by their mother and because their later attachment to her must be repressed. The relational basis for mothering is thus extended in women, and inhibited in men, who experience themselves as more separate and distinct from others.[43]

Through gender identification with the caretaking mother a girl is conditioned to adopt her nurturative traits, while a boy, on the contrary, is required to differentiate himself from them. But it may be that a pre-adolescent girl rearing a male sibling would not yet have acquired that experience of gender which would

---

[42] Weisner and Gallimore, 'My Brother's Keeper', p. 178.

[43] Nancy Chodorow, *The Reproduction of Mothering: Psychoanalysis and the Sociology of Gender* (Berkeley, Calif.: Univ. of California Press, 1978), p. 207.

unconsciously have led her to impose a distancing difference between herself and the infant. Relatively unencumbered, due to her mother's neglect, by the trappings of an acquired femininity, Mary Lamb may well have gleaned little sense of any necessity to treat her brother 'as an opposite'. In her familial isolation, she seems to have knitted together her own developing life and that of her infant brother, to an extent which neither of the pair afterwards cared to unravel. A 1795 sonnet addressed to his sister expresses Charles's deep appreciation of 'the mighty debt of love I owe, | Mary, to thee, my sister and my friend' (v. 8).

Mary's correspondence frequently indicates her marked propensity towards identification with others. In a letter of 1814, for example, she writes to Barbara Betham, a 14-year-old who had visited the Lambs three years previously:

You wish for London news . . . I have been endeavouring to recollect who you might have seen here, and what may have happened to them since, and this effort has only brought the image of little Barbara Betham, unconnected with any other person, so strongly before my eyes, that I seem as if I had no other subject to write upon. Now I think I see you with your feet propped upon the fender, your two hands spread out upon your knees—an attitude you always chose when we were in familiar confidential conversation together—telling me long stories of your own home . . . I remember your quiet steady face bent over your book.[44]

Here Mary Lamb's empathic capacity to mirror the remembered life of the child until it lives again in her representation of it exemplifies her readiness to merge her interests, and even her very sense of being, with those of others. Some of her verses for the volume *Poetry for Children* which she published with Charles in 1809 also show her entering into the ways of seeing not only of other persons but of the least of living creatures; the poem 'Breakfast', for example, describes a fly in a sugar bowl as clambering over 'rocky cliffs of sweet delight' (iii. 397), vividly conveying the insect's-eye view. But while Mary thus appears to have experienced in extreme form that characteristic permeability of the female ego attributed by Chodorow to the consequences for women of female child-rearing, in the Lambs'

[44] *Letters*, ed. Marrs, iii. 116.

case the brother manifested these tendencies as well, and shared in his sister's unusually pronounced capacity to identify with others. In a letter of 1824, for example, he complains of a compulsive, unwilled tendency to empathize with others' afflictions, and to lose his sense of a separate existence of his own in the process.[45]

Charles's early bond with Mary as opposed to his mother may, then, have much to do with the difference in personality traits between him and his older brother. Both Charles and Mary apparently shared a tendency to ameliorate any warring forces in their immediate environment. When describing to Sarah Stoddart the rift between her mother and aunt, Mary adds that she and Charles when they grew older succeeded in reconciling the conflicting parties;[46] in later life, part of the popular appeal of the social 'evenings' they held on a regular basis during the 1810s and 1820s lay in the hosts' ability to harmonize a disparate company. 'The beauty of these evenings', according to Procter in his memoir of Charles, 'was that everyone was placed upon an easy level. No one out-topped the others'.[47] Mary's writings also indicate that she felt sharply the antagonism between social groups effected by the large-scale divisions of power at work in her society. She appears to have responded with particular sensitivity to the iniquities of social hierarchies and of rank, both in terms of her own experience and in sympathy with others. The death of Salt and the removal of the Lamb family from the Temple in 1792 cannot but have brought with it many anxieties for her;[48] as an unmarried woman her prospects were more closely tied up with those of her parents than her brothers were, and she also bore the responsibility for their physical care in comparative poverty. Denied the Christ's Hospital education which provided the Lamb boys with the opportunity to achieve social mobility, Mary must have seen herself trapped in the 'uncomfortable circumstances' in which, in the winter of 1794–5, Robert

---

[45] *Letters*, ed. Lucas, ii. 447.   [46] *Letters*, ed. Marrs, ii. 124.

[47] Bryan Waller Procter ['Barry Cornwall'], *Charles Lamb: A Memoir* (London: Edward Moxon, 1866), p. 146.

[48] See Katharine Anthony, *The Lambs: A Study of Pre-Victorian England* (London: Hammond, Hammond & Co., 1948), p. 30; and Leslie Joan Friedman, 'Mary Lamb: Sister, Seamstress, Murderer, Writer', Ph.D. thesis (Stanford, Calif., 1976), pp. 1–2, 8 and 93.

Southey remembers first meeting the family.[49] Their grandmother's death, which also occurred in 1792, brought to an
abrupt close the Lamb children's former frequent visits to
Blakesware, the Plumers' stately mansion, narrowing their
horizons down even further to their cramped and impoverished
London lodgings. In a manner which appears to reflect her
experiences of the sudden loss of privileges bestowed benevolently rather than through inheritable right, much of Mary's
semi-autobiographical writings illustrate a preoccupation with
the social vulnerabilities entailed by the 'accidents' of birth,
and by abrupt changes of fortune over which the protagonists
have no control.

In those tales, by far the majority, which form Mary's
contribution to *Mrs Leicester's School*, narratives of social
displacement abound; their overriding tone is one of childhood
desolation, brought about by too early a forced recognition of
the vulnerabilities of the individual caught up within the
complexities of a rigid and arbitrarily differentiating hierarchical
social system. Virtually all of Mary's protagonists suffer from
material insecurity, and her tales show a vivid awareness of the
significance of social status, and the effects of its loss. In
'Charlotte Wilmot: The Merchant's Daughter', for example,
Charlotte, formerly proud of her family's wealth and social
position, is mortified when her father's sudden bankruptcy
leaves her temporarily abandoned to the mercy of a clerk from
his counting-house and his family, whom she had previously
regarded as her inferiors and treated with a patronizing
contempt. During her first night at the clerk's dwelling she
dreams that Maria, the clerk's daughter, 'was ordering me to
fetch her something; and on my refusal, she said I must obey
her, for I was now her servant' (iii. 325–6). In fact, she awakens
to a very different world, in which Maria treats her with great
sympathy and courtesy, offering her assistance as if no change
had taken place in their relative social positions. The message of
the tale is similar to that in much of Charles's writings, that true
virtue is manifested in playing the faithful servant's role when
no power enforces it apart from the neediness of those served.
What Charlotte Wilmot's story conveys most vividly, however,

[49] *The Life and Correspondence of Robert Southey*, ed. C. C. Southey, 6 vols.
(London: Longman, 1850), vi. 286.

is the confusion and shame of the merchant's daughter when not only the arbitrary nature of her former social superiority but also the moral and emotional inferiority of her attitudes with regard to rank are chasteningly revealed to her by Maria's behaviour. It illustrates empathically the pain of a sudden change in fortune, and the manner in which it confounds former notions of the world and one's own place in it. Mary Lamb's sympathy is extended more to the misguided Charlotte, whose earlier pride is shown to be the consequence of her upbringing, than to the virtuous Maria, for all the biographical piquancy of the latter's position as the daughter of a counting-house clerk. The moral subtext of the tale is that any divisive pretensions to over-top others are founded on false conscious-ness, but sympathy is shown towards the erring 'élite' who are tempted into such self-inflations.

In another tale, 'The Young Mahometan', Margaret Green, the narrator, is the daughter of a distressed gentlewoman forced through the threat of penury to take employment as the companion of a great house's ageing proprietor. As the portrayal of the house constitutes a replica in detail of the Blakesware mansion familiar to Mary from childhood, it has been assumed by the Lambs' biographers that the relation of child, mother, and mistress in the tale is similar to that of Mary, her grandmother Mary Field, and old Mrs Plumer, who died when Mary was 13.[50] In the tale, Margaret is grievously neglected by her mother, who, following the practice of her employer, has 'wholly discontinued talking' to her (iii. 308). During her lonely explorations of the house, she identifies, in her isolation, with the Old Testament images of Hagar and Ishmael that she discovers on its tapestried walls, pitying their 'forlorn state' as outcasts 'in the wilderness', dispossessed of any claims to inheritance, just as she is dispossessed of any role or status in the large house in which she is virtually a non-person. Mary's use of her memories of Blakesware in this tale compares interestingly with Charles's reconstruction of his childhood visits to the Plumers' mansion in the Elia essay 'Blakesmoor in H——shire'. By the time Charles became familiar with Blakesware, old Mrs Plumer had died and the

---

[50] See Lucas, *Life of Charles Lamb*, i. 25–7 and Courtney, *Young Charles Lamb*, pp. 16–17.

house, abandoned by the younger members of the family, had been left in his grandmother's care. For Charles, as a child, the Plumer family's absence seems to have effected a process of imaginative displacement in which he experienced himself, in his passion for the aesthetic appeal of the old house, as its more rightful inheritor. Concerned by the thought that the antiquities he admired had been garnered at the expense of the peasant class to which his own family originally belonged, he attempted to bring about an imaginative reversal of the historical imbalance by using the aesthetic pleasure he imbibed as a weapon to redeem the earlier humiliations of his actual forefathers. Describing a seventeenth-century coat of arms, he asks:

And what if my ancestor at that date was some Damœtas—feeding flocks, not his own, upon the hills of Lincoln—did I in less earnest vindicate to myself the family trappings of this once proud Ægon?—repaying by a backward triumph the insults he might possibly have heaped in his life-time upon my poor pastoral progenitor. (ii. 156)

In his childhood imagination, the property became his own, as he was its sole appreciator: he repeatedly insists that

mine . . . BLAKESMOOR, was thy noble Marble Hall . . . Mine, too—whose else—thy costly fruit-garden . . . Mine was that gallery of good old family portraits, which as I have gone over, giving them in my fancy my own family name, one—and then another—would seem to smile, reaching forward from the canvas, to recognize the new relationship. (ii. 156–7)

'The claims of birth are ideal merely', he suggests, 'and what herald shall go about to strip me of an idea?' Returning to the estate in adulthood, however, he is forcibly reminded of the tenuousness of his attempt to take imaginative possession of it, for the Plumers' lack of interest in their ancestral residence has resulted in its demolition. The reality of their control over the property has been unequivocally manifested in its destruction, but at the same time his lament, in that it recreates the mansion's past glories, embodies his imaginative repossession of it. Both brother and sister, in these representations of their past relation with Blakesware, are similarly exploring the confusions and contradictions induced by a childhood lived in the midst of wealth and privilege, which exercised their influence over the children's sensibility, but over which neither they nor their relations ever in fact held any proprietorial rights.

Mary's tales in *Mrs Leicester's School* also explore the way in which oscillations in social rank also affect parents' relations with their children. In 'The Young Mahometan' and 'The Merchant's Daughter', good mothering seems to depend upon a secure social identity. It is after Margaret Green's mother has been forced into service through poverty that she begins to neglect her little daughter, and it is after their sudden bankruptcy that Charlotte Wilmot's parents abandon her to her fate with the clerk's family. If Mary is to be seen as encoding autobiographical experience in these tales and exploring through them the rift between herself and her mother, then she appears to be laying the blame for the neglect she suffered in childhood more upon the social situation in which her mother found herself than upon any of her individual traits. No doubt Elizabeth Lamb's housekeeping obligations kept her from her daughter, just as Margaret Green's mother was too preoccupied by her new duties to attend to hers. There is also an interesting suggestion in 'The Young Mahometan' that the mother becomes distanced from her child because she has to adapt her personality to fit that of her new mistress; it is her mistress's initial practice that she follows in not speaking to Margaret, and she also discovers a readiness to involve herself with her mistress's obsession with needlework, and to inflict this taste upon her reluctant, book-loving daughter (iii. 308 and 306). The self-abnegation of service roles, as they were understood in the eighteenth and early nineteenth centuries, entailed a subjection of the servant's authentic individuality; the acquired propensity to adopt readily an inauthentic role might lead to some difficulty in understanding a child or relative not easily moulded into the required pattern.

The relations between the roles of servant and mother are further explored by Mary in perhaps the most painful of all her tales in *Mrs Leicester's School*, that of 'Ann Withers: The Changeling'. The opening of the tale immediately thrusts the narrator's audience into the confusion of identity she had herself experienced:

My name you know is Withers, but as I once thought I was the daughter of sir Edward and lady Harriot Lesley, I shall speak of myself as miss Lesley, and call sir Edward and lady Harriot my father and mother during the period I supposed them entitled to those beloved names. (iii. 288–9)

The confusion persists throughout the telling of Ann's forlorn history of dispossession. When she was a month old, her biological mother, a previous servant of the Lesleys, was summoned to act as wet nurse for their new baby girl, Harriot. Called upon to desert her own child, she found herself unable to do so:

she looked on me, and then on the little lady-babe, and she wept over me to think she was obliged to leave me to the charge of a careless girl, debarred from my own natural food, while she was nursing another person's child.

The laced cap and the fine cambric robe of the little Harriot were lying on the table ready to be put on: in these she dressed me, only just to see how pretty her own dear baby would look in missy's fine clothes. When she saw me thus adorned, she said to me, 'O, my dear Ann, you look as like missy as any thing can be. I am sure my lady herself . . . would not know the difference.' (iii. 290–1)

The change once accomplished, no difference is indeed perceived; the nurse's biological child grows up accepted by all as Sir Edward's daughter, until her friendship with her old nurse's daughter, the real Harriot, leads to her discovery of the secret. Thrilled by the dramatic potential of the story, and without realizing fully its significance from her own point of view, she brings about her own downfall inadvertently by disclosing all, Hamlet-like, in a children's play. The nurse confesses the truth in a fit of hysterical remorse, when she sees her own child enacting her part and exchanging the babies. Ann Withers loses in the catastrophe 'my own name' and all her former social privileges: 'all my rank and consequence in the world fled from me for ever' (iii. 294). She is now required to teach the new Miss Lesley, her former patronized inferior, the necessary role of gentility, which she had herself previously played with an unquestioned competence; at the same time she must relinquish her own right to the status of the nobly born, and learn to adjust to her new, biologically determined role as the child of her former parents' dependant. But it is the emotional change which finally proves too much for her, and

leads to her arrival at Mrs Leicester's school. She has difficulty
loving her biological mother and is tortured with envy as she
witnesses a close relationship developing between Lady Harriot
and her new-found real daughter, who has inherited her
mother's musical ability: 'Nothing makes the heart ache with
such a hopeless, heavy pain, as envy. . . . All day long the notes
of the harp or the piano spoke sad sounds to me, of the loss of a
loved mother's heart' (iii. 301).

It is difficult not to see in such passages Mary's attempt at
exorcizing the pain of her own lonely childhood before
Charles's birth, when the two figures who seem to have
mattered most to her, her mother and maternal grandmother,
openly favoured her brother John. But what is also of interest
in 'Ann Withers' is the manner in which it intertwines
maternal love, and the image of a 'good' mother, with social
status, and shows both as lost through a daughter's impetuous
intelligence. Ann's play reveals her real mother as 'bad',
as one who played a deceiving part; it also brings about
the eternal loss of the 'good' mother, of high rank. Her
intelligence inadvertently strips away the veil of her true
mother's deception and shows the reality of the situation as it
is, but the emotional loss entailed by that denouement is more
than she can bear. As such, 'The Changeling' may mirror
Mary's recognition of the deceptions in her own position,
brought up to identify herself entirely with powers and
properties which could never be her own, and the distance that
realization effected between herself and the mother who always
insisted upon behaving like a 'perfect gentlewoman'. The
sudden loss of all the family's privileges in 1792, at Salt's and
grandmother Field's deaths, may have brought about the
realization, or its roots may have laid deeper in Mary's
recognition of the situation in her earlier years. In her adult life,
at any rate, her attitude towards social roles in general,
including those of gender, seems to have been one of quiet
cynicism; the poses played out with regard to both rank and
gender she saw as parts which could be learned and acted to
suit the occasion. In 1805, the brother of her friend Sarah
Stoddart apparently wrote to Mary with the request that she
help his impulsive sister to acquire a more decorous ladylike
demeanour. After initially mocking his wish, and the suggestion

that she herself should know anything of 'nicely correct maidenly manners', she goes on in a letter to Sarah to tell her that if she would indeed find such a change useful then it could easily enough be accomplished:

believe me Sarah it is not so difficult a matter as one is sometimes apt to imagine—. I have observed many a demure Lady who passes muster admirably well who I think we could easily learn to imitate in a wee[k or two].[51]

Such passing comments present the social order as a theatre in which the actors con their parts and play them out according to their circumstances or needs rather than any intrinsic suitability for the role.

According to Samuel Johnson, English society in the eighteenth century was characterized by 'the fixed, invariable external rules of distinction of rank, which create no jealousy, as they are allowed to be accidental'.[52] An individual's social ranking, apparent in every detail of his or her mode of work, dress, manner, and conduct, was a determinant to be accepted as part of a divinely ordained social plan. But what Mary appears to be exploring in such tales as 'The Changeling' is the irony of such arbitrary but all too real differentiations. In her brother's essays also, the 'accident of birth' is not accepted, but exposed as an absurdist system, in which human potential is imprisoned and distorted. The Lambs' personal experience constituted the forcing-ground from which these perceptions arose: through Samuel Salt's easy benevolence they enjoyed such privileges that they must to some degree have experienced themselves as the children of their master rather than of their master's servant, until the death of Salt suddenly brought that illusion to a close. The late eighteenth century in England is regarded, in general, as a transitional period, in which, due to the rapid growth of industrialization, the old master/servant relation, with its traditions of patronage, deference, and dependence, was swiftly eroded as an essentially capitalist, employer/employee structure, based on contractual employment, took its place. The Lambs, as

---

[51] *Letters*, ed. Marrs, ii. 184.
[52] James Boswell, *London Journal 1762–1763*, ed. Frederick A. Pottle (London: Heinemann, 1950), p. 320; quoted Perkin, *Origins of Modern English Society*, p. 25.

the children of servants, were caught in the maelstrom of this all-encompassing social change. That they should retain some deferential loyalties pertaining to the older order, and affecting their ability to criticize its injustices directly, is a consequence of their ideological inheritance. But their own work roles also, as well as those of their parents, contributed significantly to their experience of rank and gender; in the next chapter I examine the influence of their adult employment upon their representation of social power and its relation to gender roles.

2

Work and Time

I

In a manner entirely in accord with the system of sex discrimination at work during her period, Mary Lamb received a very different education from that of her brothers, one governed by very different expectations as to her subsequent social position. After a few years at a very basic dame's school, she was apprenticed in her teens to a mantua-maker, a maker of the short cloaks then fashionable for women. Her parents need not necessarily have intended to secure for her a career outside domestic service by this move, for an apprenticeship as a needlewoman was commonly considered suitable preparation for a post as a lady's maid at that time. And even a successful mantua-maker, who by unusual good fortune managed to retain an independent position within that precarious profession, was not eligible for middle-class status. In Mary Wollstonecraft's novel *The Wrongs of Woman: or Maria, A Fragment* (1798), Maria, lamenting her difficulties in trying to assist her impoverished sisters to situations of gainful employment, draws a line 'at the name of milliner or mantua-maker as degrading to a gentlewoman'.[1] The Lamb boys, on the other hand, once enrolled at Christ's Hospital, had every opportunity to progress towards careers of middle-class status, such as the Accountant's position which John Lamb eventually secured. In 1815, under the pseudonym 'Sempronia',[2] Mary published a

[1] Mary Wollstonecraft, *The Wrongs of Woman: or, Maria. A Fragment* in *Mary, A Fiction and The Wrongs of Woman* (London: OUP, 1976), p. 148.

[2] Mary Lamb probably took her pseudonym from the name of a fictional character in Mary Hays's *Letters and Essays, Moral and Miscellaneous*; see Katharine M. Rogers, 'The Contribution of Mary Hays', *Prose Studies*, 10 (1987), 135–6.

letter on the situation of needleworkers in the new *British Ladies' Magazine*. The letter illustrates her acute awareness of the disadvantages accruing to women from their deficient education. Needlework is represented as one of the few professions open to them, not because they lack the capacity for acquiring new skills, or the robustness for furthering them, but because they have never been in any way trained or educated for other tasks. She argues that if parents could but foresee their daughters' prospects in the marriage market and the possibility of their remaining single, they would exert themselves to provide for girls as well as for boys the training in self-discipline and confidence necessary for career success. Her letter also interestingly demonstrates her awareness of the central significance for gender role formation of the differential value attributed to male and female time, a difference instilled and internalized in both sexes through education, or the lack of it. A man is taught to control his time, make conscious productive use of it, and value himself accordingly, while a woman is conditioned to think of hers as inevitably consumed by 'the minutiae which compose the sum of a woman's daily employment'. 'Nay,' 'Sempronia' adds,

many a lady who allows not herself one quarter of an hour's positive leisure during her waking hours, considers her own husband as the most industrious of men, if he steadily pursue his occupation till the hour of dinner, and will be perpetually lamenting her own idleness. (i. 177)

Whether they belong to the struggling or more affluent classes, women's time, unlike men's, is never in fact experienced as self-validatingly their own.

This chapter explores the growing significance of internalized time-awareness as a feature of gender discrimination during the Lambs' period by means of an investigation of Charles's and Mary's differing educational and work experience. Unlike his brother, Charles, as we have seen, did not choose to make use of the opportunities for social mobility afforded to him by his education, and remained within the lowlier ranks of his office hierarchy. The final section of the chapter investigates the implications of his refusal. Historically, the clerical profession has had an interesting role to play in the socialization of gender difference. During the course of the nineteenth century its originally entirely male work-force was transmuted into one which increasingly offered employment opportunities to women. In the Lambs' time, embryonic suspicions as to its suitability as employment for men seem to have pervaded the ideology of the profession, rendering it one in which it became difficult to achieve and maintain an authoritative masculine identity. Promotion to a managerial position seems to have provided the only clerical route both to secure middle-class status and to masculine self-respect, and yet such promotion was paradoxically only achieved by those who conformed with particular propriety to a behavioural pattern of self-subordinating deference to hierarchical authority and to the work ethic. The patterns of the Lambs' employment experiences provide telling examples of the way in which gender and class differentials are intertwined.

II

Charles and his older brother must have been amongst the first members of their family to experience that long period of dependency and special status which is now taken for granted as constituting childhood. Prior to the development of a general recognition of the need for schooling, children were expected to make a quick transition from the state of infancy to one of miniature adulthood, being dressed, equipped, and generally treated as adults as soon as the initial period of absolute dependency had passed.[3] Before the nineteenth century, most children, particularly those from the lower social ranks, learnt their social roles through being thrust willy-nilly into them. It was not until the reformative Factory Acts of the 1830s and 1850s, debarring children from industrial work, and the Education Act of 1870 which made primary schooling compulsory, that working-class children finally gained access to the full privileges of a status socially separated from that of adults. But these changes also reflected new stratifications in the concept of segregated social roles generally, and were part of a general movement to establish separate spheres for the child, the

---

[3] See Philippe Ariès, *Centuries of Childhood* (Harmondsworth: Penguin, 1973).

female, and the male. The woman's world and that of the child's came more and more to belong to a domestic sphere now set apart from the man's world of work and business; the old eighteenth-century way of life, in which work and leisure had both taken place within the home and involved the combined activities of all members of the family, rapidly disappeared as economic changes in the structure of an increasingly industrialized society brought about a division of material production from domestic life, and, consequently, a new polarization of social roles.[4] According to Leonore Davidoff and Catherine Hall, in their seminal study *Family Fortunes: Men and Women of the English Middle Class 1780–1850*, this developing segregation had become entrenched by the 1830s; 'it was recognized that men would be preoccupied with business and domesticity had become the "woman's sphere" rather than . . . a way of living for both men and women'.[5] In her book *The Proper Lady and the Woman Writer*, Mary Poovey, discussing the same polarization, argues that it was strengthened and in part brought about by the need to retain a sacrosanct area of personal relationship within increasingly impersonalized methods of production: 'As competition and confrontation replaced the old paternalistic alliances of responsibilities and dependences, women . . . as exemplars of paternalistic virtues . . . were being asked to preserve the remnants of the old society within the private sphere of the home'.[6] The nineteenth-century middle-class child, like its mother, belonged to this sharply demarcated domestic sphere, which only the male child was educated to outgrow.

Much of Charles's writings can be seen as a protest against this new demarcation and separation of child, male, and female roles. He experienced his own childhood, which ended when he became a clerk in 1790 in his fifteenth year, as a numinous,

[4] For a historical survey of gender role changes during the early nineteenth century, see Dorothy Thompson, 'Women, Work and Politics in Nineteenth-Century England: The Problem of Authority', in Jane Randall (ed.), *Equal or Different: Women's Politics 1800–1914* (Oxford: Blackwell, 1987), pp. 57–64.

[5] Leonore Davidoff and Catherine Hall, *Family Fortunes: Men and Women of the English Middle Class, 1750–1850* (London: Hutchinson, 1987), p. 181.

[6] Mary Poovey, *The Proper Lady and the Woman Writer: Ideology as Style in the Works of Mary Wollstonecraft, Mary Shelley, and Jane Austen* (Chicago and London: Univ. of Chicago Press, 1984), p. xv.

golden age, and resisted the ideological pressure to view it as a sphere of leisure and affectionate warmth sharply divided from the rest of his adult life. Many of his Elia essays are organized around a central core of childhood reminiscence, a factor which probably featured largely amongst the reasons for their popularity during the late Victorian and Edwardian era, with its character-istic predilection for the wonderland of a prolonged childhood. Contemporary readers, seeing the Elia essays through the prism of a critical heritage, are unavoidably affected by the Peter Pan characteristics with which the Edwardian image of Elia is nostalgically imbued. But when read in the immediate historical context of his times, many of Charles's essays which deal with childhood can be seen as a subtle attack upon the new insistence on a male role dedicated to industriousness, competi-tiveness, and self-control. The essay 'The Old Benchers of the Inner Temple', for example, begins with a eulogy to the child-delighting furniture of the Temple gardens as Charles knew them in his early years, and develops into a lament at the changes that a new set of 'mannish' utilitarian values have brought about in his old haunts. The loss of the old sundials in favour of the more efficient and businesslike clock is particularly mourned:

What a dead thing is a clock, with its ponderous embowelments of lead and brass, its pert or solemn dulness of communication, compared with the simple altar-like structure, and silent heart-language of the old dial! . . . Why is it almost every where vanished? If its business-use be superseded by more elaborate inventions, its moral uses, its beauty, might have pleaded for its continuance. It spoke of moderate labours, of pleasures not protracted after sun-set, of temperance, and good-hours. It was the primitive clock, the horologe of the first world. (ii. 83)

The antagonism with which Charles regards the popular technology of his age, and his sense of the relation between its introduction and larger changes in the social and economic climate of his day, bears comparison with Dickens's similar association in *Hard Times* of Thomas Gradgrind's 'deadly statistical clock' with the utilitarian principles of its possessor. Rather than interpreting 'The Old Benchers' as a typically Romantic, aesthetic lament for the passing of an idealized childhood, 'scattering clouds of glory', Charles's complaint may also be read as a social criticism, levelled against contemporary forces bent upon transforming the more leisurely eighteenth-century way of life into an efficient, industrial, and time-conscious world. E. P. Thompson has detailed, in an important essay, the relentless drumming of the need for time-thrift and discipline into a recalcitrant work-force which was in process during the Lambs' period, and the changes it wrought in the common experience of life.[7] The passing of the peasant communities, whose work was not valued by the hour but according to their completion of a cycle of daily and seasonal tasks, resulted in a harsher division between work and leisure than had prevailed earlier, and a greater alienation from the machine-driven and less humanly comprehensible industrial work requirement.[8] The rapid spread of ownership of clocks with minute hands throughout the late eighteenth-century populace is evidence of the new pressurized awareness of the value of time, and of the need for its precise measurement. For Charles, lamenting the sundials, England's burgeoning production figures during this period in no way compensated for the loss of the 'good-hours' and relaxed leisureliness of pre-industrial society. During an era in which the wearing of a watch was a practice taken for granted amongst the better off, and a 'certain indication of prosperity and of personal respectability on the part of the working man',[9] Charles Lamb never wore one. According to the reminiscences of one of his colleagues at work, at least one attempt was made to remedy this omission:

A friend observing the absence of the usual adjunct of a business man's attire, presented him with a new gold watch which he accepted and carried for one day only. A colleague asked Lamb what had become of it. "Pawned," was the reply. He had actually pawned the watch finding it a useless encumbrance.[10]

---

[7] E. P. Thompson, 'Time, Work–Discipline, and Industrial Capitalism', in M. W. Flinn and T. C. Smout (eds.), *Essays in Social History* (Oxford: Clarendon Press, 1974), pp. 39–77.

[8] Ibid., 60; and see also Francis Hearn, *Domination, Legitimation, and Resistance: The Incorporation of the Nineteenth-Century English Working Class* (Westport, Conn.: Greenwood Press, 1978), pp. 77–9.

[9] J. R. Porter, *The Progress of the Nation* (1843), iii. 5, quoted Thompson, 'Time, Work-Discipline and Industrial Capitalism', p. 73.

[10] Algernon Black, *Macmillans Magazine*, 39 (Mar. 1879), 431.

Unlike the majority of men of the middle rank, Charles consistently refused to internalize the new morality of time-thrift. From his first piece of published prose, a pastiche of Robert Burton's writings in praise of truths which only visit the empty, idle mind, to one of his last, an argument against the folly of 'rising with the lark', he mocks and opposes the doctrines of the popular tract-writers of his times, with their perpetual warnings that sloth and time-wasting were the instruments of Satan.[11] Moreover, he connects his resistance to the new time-consciousness with an antagonism towards related changes in the concept of sexual difference. In 'The Old Benchers of the Inner Temple', he sees the changes wrought in the Temple gardens as related to the ubiquity of a new and oppressive model of masculinity, involving the increased differentiation of goal-driven manhood from the more passive states seen as appropriate to the female state and to the new concept of childhood. 'Why must every thing smack of man, and mannish?' Elia asks (ii. 84), protesting against the Temple lawyers' condemnation of their old sundials and fountains as 'childish'. Amongst the middle ranks of society, adoption of the new time ethic was primarily a male prerogative, and as such it was one of the features which marked the growing sexual segregation between men's public worlds of industry, commerce, and politics, and the private domestic sphere of women. For the lower ranks also, the move away from task-orientated labour entailed the loss of some of the connections in life-style which had previously led to similar work-patterns for the sexes. In so far as women retained the conventional roles of mother and housewife, their time was still experienced in terms of the completion of necessary tasks, and tied to a cycle of human daily requirements rather than to the clock,[12] but men were caught up more rapidly and thoroughly in the rigours of industrialized time.

One of the major social institutions which was expected to inculcate in males an awareness of the value of time, and of the importance of developing a manly identity, was the school. 'Once within the school gates', according to Thompson, 'the

---

[11] See, e.g. John Wesley, *The Duty and Advantage of Early Rising* (1786), quoted Thompson, 'Time, Work-Discipline and Industrial Capitalism', p. 62.
[12] Ibid., 55.

child entered the new universe of disciplined time'; the inflexible regime of the school day was in part intended to habituate the pupils to order, regularity, and industry.[13] In boys' schools physical hardships, and frequent resort to corporal punishment and institutionalized bullying, were considered a necessary part of the process of 'awakening the man in the child' and of forcing him to acquire the extreme self-control indispensable to the new ethos of manliness.[14] Maria Edgeworth, in her *Frank: A Sequel to 'Frank' in Early Lessons* (1822) shows a model father insisting that his son be sent away to school in order that he should be 'roughened about among boys, or he will never learn to be a man, and able to live among men'.[15] Charity schools in particular were established with an eye to 'forming' a pupil as much as to instructing him, and to instilling strict habits of self-discipline and obedience.[16] At the age of 7 Charles entered Christ's Hospital, a charity school initially founded by the boy king Edward VI in 1552 'to take out of the streets all fatherless children and other poor men's children' and house, educate, and form them, but, by Charles's time, more commonly attended by the children of middle rank, but financially distressed, families. The school's regime during his day was ascetic in the extreme; its pupils endured a meagre diet and frequent floggings, as well as the customary public school stress upon regimentation and self-control. Samuel Taylor Coleridge, one of Charles's contemporaries at the school, provides an anecdote recording its emotional repressiveness, inculcated in this instance by the school's senior mentor, and its most enthusiastic wielder of the rod, James Boyer:

The discipline at Christ's Hospital during my time was ultra-Spartan; all domestic ties were to be put aside. 'Boy!' I remember Bowyer [*sic*] saying to me once when I was crying the first day of my return after the holidays, 'Boy! the school is your father! Boy! the school is your

[13] Thompson, 'Time, Work-Discipline and Industrial Capitalism', p. 60.

[14] Ariès, *Centuries of Childhood*, pp. 254 and 257; and Lawrence Stone, *The Family, Sex and Marriage in England 1500–1800* (London: Weidenfeld & Nicolson, 1977), p.672.

[15] Maria Edgeworth, *Frank: A Sequel to 'Frank' in Early Lessons*, 3 vols. (1822), i. 55; quoted Norman Vance, *The Sinews of the Spirit: The Ideal of Christian Manliness in Victorian Literature and Religious Thought* (Cambridge: CUP, 1985), p. 11.

[16] See Ariès, *Centuries of Childhood*, pp. 290–1.

mother! Boy! the school is your brother! the school is your sister! the school is your first cousin, and your second cousin, and all the rest of your relations! Let's have no more crying![17]

And yet, though it signally failed to develop in Charles an admiration for either time-thrift or the heavily self-controlled model of masculinity, Christ's Hospital itself, and his school years as a whole, generally figure in his writings as a particularly joyous part of the halcyon golden age of his childhood, though at other times he does record its cruelties. Why this was so, what were the pressures behind his deliberate ambivalence and inconsistency when it came to describing his school-days, and in what way his attitude towards his school-days was related to his developing sense of gender identity, are issues which call for further exploration.

For both the Lamb boys, their Christ's Hospital education constituted the means by which they avoided following their father into a career in service, and became the most influential factor in their upward social mobility. Samuel Salt, as a member of the school's Board of Governors, provided the support and sponsorship necessary to gain entry to its halls. Both boys were enrolled in the classical branch of the school, as opposed to its more technical, vocational classes, and both did well, rising to the ranks of 'Deputy Grecians', second in status only to those destined for the universities, the 'Grecians'. In Charles's case, it was apparently only his stammer, and the resultant impossibility of his effectively taking holy orders, the expected outcome of a university education during his day, which debarred him, as a 'first student' amongst the Deputies, from that highest circle.[18] Although it no longer normally admitted the destitute boys for which it had originally been established, the school seems to have retained a strongly egalitarian ethos: school rank and status were acquired through academic merit or perseverance alone, rather than through any consideration of the social hierarchies which dominated the world outside its gates. That

---

[17] Coleridge, *Specimens of the Table Talk of Samuel Taylor Coleridge* (London, John Murray, 1874), p. 196.

[18] See Leigh Hunt, *The Autobiography of Leigh Hunt*, ed. J. E. Morpurgo (London: Cresset Press, 1949), p. 107, for an account of Charles's stammer, a disability from which Hunt himself also suffered, with the same consequences for his own Christ's Hospital career.

Charles much appreciated, in afterlife if not during his school years, the freedom this offered from the more constraining aspects of his ideological background is indicated in his first published account of the school, the essay 'Recollections of Christ's Hospital' (1813).

The 'Recollections' were initially composed as part of a contemporary argument concerning the principles of entry into Christ's Hospital. In 1808 the reformer Robert Waithman, in an open letter to the governors of Christ's Hospital, charged the school with 'favouritism and the undue distribution of influence' in its admission procedures (i. 436), and the accusation gave rise to a public controversy in which the school's literary 'old boys' took vociferous part. Leigh Hunt, for example, who had entered Christ's Hospital just as Charles left it, agreed with the charges: the school in his eyes had reneged on its duty to provide an education for the poorest children of the metropolis. According to his *Examiner*:

That hundreds of unfortunate objects have applied in vain for admission is sufficiently notorious; and that many persons with abundant means of educating and providing for their children and relatives have obtained their admission into the School is also equally well known.[19]

Hunt is here, though he may not have been aware of it, arguing against a change which was not unique to Christ's Hospital but was widespread amongst the oldest established charity schools generally during the seventeenth and eighteenth centuries. It was common for those charity institutions which offered a classical education superior to that provided by many of the traditional schools to become as popular with the well-to-do as the needy, and be inundated by children of the lower middle and middle ranks.[20] What is more, as the eighteenth century advanced, providing a good education for the children of the poor came to be regarded as something of a seditious act. It was seen as socially impolitic to educate a child 'out of its station'; new eighteenth-century charity schools taught little beyond the elementary rudiments of reading and writing.[21] Indeed, Isaac

---

[19] Id., *Examiner*, (25 Dec. 1808), quoted *Works*, ed. Lucas, i. 436.
[20] Ariès, *Centuries of Childhood*, pp. 293 and 321.
[21] Ibid., 296–301.

Watts in his *Essay Towards the Encouragement of Charity Schools* (1728) does not even consider writing a necessary acquirement for children of the labouring class, maintaining that 'I would not by any means have it made a necessary Part of a Charity-School, that the Children should be taught to write.'[22]

In the introduction to his 'Recollections' Charles, unlike Hunt, views the depleted contribution made by the older, more classically orientated, charity school to the education of the poor with little of the reformer's zeal. He finds no fault with the Christ's Hospital governors, writing, on the contrary, in support of their practice of admitting 'a sprinkling of the sons of respectable parents', on the grounds that it 'has an admirable tendency to liberalize the whole mass' (i. 435). The gulf between the education actually afforded to the poor in his day and that gained by the Christ's Hospital boy spanned so broad a class division, and one by which a child in Charles's situation gained so much in terms of social mobility, that, in writing the essay originally, he seems to have felt that he could not have afforded to see its distinctiveness blurred. Himself an appreciative recipient of Christ's Hospital's 'liberalizing' influence, he writes as if he would limit the access of lower-rank children, like himself, to the school in order to maintain what he saw as its proper function, that of providing a subsidized education for middle-class children whose families had fallen into reduced circumstances without taking them out of their original social station (i. 40). 'For the Christ's Hospital boy', he writes,

feels that he is no charity-boy; he feels it in the antiquity and regality of the foundation to which he belongs . . . he feels it in his education, in that measure of classical attainments, which every individual at that school, though not destined to a learned profession, has it in his power to procure, attainments which it would be worse than folly to put in the reach of the labouring classes to acquire: he feels it in the numberless comforts, and even magnificences, which surround him; in his old and awful cloisters, with their traditions . . . in his stately dining-hall, hung round with pictures by Verrio, Lely, and others . . . above all, in the very extent and magnitude of the body to which he belongs, and the consequent spirit, the intelligence, and public

---

[22] Isaac Watts, *An Essay towards the Encouragement of Charity Schools* (London, John Clark and Richard Hett, 1728), p. 30.

conscience, which is the result of so many various yet wonderfully combining members. (i. 140–1)

The recollection of his Christ's Hospital days seem to have had the same kind of significance for Charles as his memory of holidays at the Plumers' mansion, Blakesware: both scenes glittered similarly with the aesthetic charm of antiquity and nobility. When it came to his school-days, however, he could feel himself more legitimately an heir of those riches; as the housekeeper's grandson, his connection with Blakesware was tenuous, but he belonged unequivocally to the school, and took pride in that membership. As he saw it, the Bluecoat boy's special status saved him from acquiring either the 'servility' of the 'parish-boy' or the 'impudence' of the public schoolboy: 'His very garb, as it is antique and venerable, feeds his self-respect; as it is a badge of dependence, it restrains the natural petulance of that age from breaking out into overt-acts of insolence' (i. 141). In the 'Recollections' Charles attributes such sophisticated responses to all the Christ's Hospital boys, but one of his contemporaries at the school, Charles Valentine le Grice, later recalled them as having been very much Charles's own.[23] Both literally and in terms of his self-esteem Charles seems, in later life, to have considered himself as having been saved from servitude by Christ's Hospital, in part as a consequence of its questionable recruitment policies.

But when Charles included 'Recollections of Christ's Hospital' in the 1818 volume of his *Works*, he omitted both its opening paragraphs defending the school's governors and the later section on the contrast between the Christ's Hospital boy and the 'broken-down spirit' of the 'common orphan schools' or charity schools' boy (i. 436), leaving no reference to the original context of the piece. It may be simply that by 1818 he no longer considered the question of the school's entry procedures to be one of topical interest; it is also possible that he was by then no longer as whole-heartedly in support of the school's policies. Moreover, later recollections of his school-days, like his reconstructions of earlier childhood experience, are characterized by

---

[23] See Richard Madden, 'The Old Familiar Faces', *Charles Lamb Bulletin*, 1 (1974), 116–18, for a transcript of Charles Valentine Le Grice's letter to Thomas Talfourd after Lamb's death.

contradiction and ambivalence. Elia's first-person narrative is often employed to present dramatic monologues in which differing personae express opposing responses to the same subject. According to Coleridge, the Elia essay 'Christ's Hospital Five and Thirty Years Ago', published in 1820, was deliberately written to offset Charles's 'former panegyrical account of the same Institution'.[24] In it Elia, in the first part of the essay, recalls the school as seen through the lonely eyes of Coleridge as a child rather than those of the young Charles Lamb. Referring, with a characteristically self-referential whimsy, to 'Mr.Lamb's "Works" published a year or two since', Elia contradicts Mr Lamb's account of the school, claiming that his 'Recollections' contrived to show but half the truth. Presenting the other side of the picture, Elia proceeds to reveal the barbarities which the school's regulations instigated and condoned—young children beaten, branded with irons, fettered, scourged, and imprisoned in solitary confinement (ii. 12–14). Aspects of school life which Mr Lamb, or 'L.' as he is referred to in the essay, had singled out for praise are shown in an entirely different light by Elia. He describes, for example, the semi-starvation of the children, and the manner in which their school attendants openly purloined for themselves half of the boys' meagre meat rations, adding,

These things were daily practised in that magnificent apartment, which L. (grown connoisseur since, we presume) praises so highly for the grand paintings 'by Verrio, and others,' with which it is 'hung round and adorned.' But the sight of sleek well-fed blue-coat boys in pictures was, at that time, I believe, little consolatory to him, or us, the living ones, who saw the better part of our provisions carried away before our faces by harpies. (ii. 15)

The historical and aesthetic glamour of the school environment is now seen as mocking the actual deprivations of the boys caught in its mystifications.

Even the 'wholesome society' of equals, the 'pervading moral sense' of the 'common mass of that unpresumptuous assemblage of boys' which is presented as a panacea for all psychological ills in the 'Recollections' (i. 143) is shown to err in the later essay. Elia describes an incident in which a boy came to be

[24] *The Collected Letters of Samuel Taylor Coleridge,* ed. Earl Leslie Griggs, 6 vols. (Oxford: Clarendon Press, 1956–71), v. 125.

despised by his fellows because he was in the habit of collecting and secreting the scraps of fat left over after school meals, which the other boys had a superstitious dread of touching. As a 'gag-eater' the pilferer is beneath contempt, shamed and excommunicated by the whole school, until it is discovered that he is saving these fragments of food for his destitute, starving parents (ii. 15–16). Here, the shared rituals and common feeling which bind together a group of individuals are shown to be potentially heinous; they encourage the victimization of those beyond the ranks of brotherhood and an intolerance of any who break the group's established rules of behaviour. Abused for deviating from the expected pattern in order to nurture others, the sufferings of the little gag-eater are analogous to those of 'Betsy', the mothering sailor in *Mrs Leicester's School*, at the hands of his rough crew. For all Charles's gratitude to the school, the darker aspects of its *esprit de corps* are illustrated in such anecdotes; the treasured sense of belonging cannot unequivocally be celebrated, when the group ethos it promotes is recognized as a potential danger to the integrity and dignity of the individual.

Such deliberately contrary presentations serve to disclose Charles's ambivalence towards his old school and to indicate the extent of his resistance to its ideological mores. But certain circumstances peculiar to his particular position in the school tempered the harshness of its regime in his case. 'Christ's Hospital Five and Thirty Years Ago' may disclose the cruelty of the Grecians' tutor James Boyer but Charles's own tutor, Matthew Field, is presented as having played a very different role, and one which ran contrary to the prevailing disciplinarian ethos of the school life. Field was apparently an indolent and neglectful master who through default granted his pupils a freedom such 'as would have made the souls of Rousseau and John Locke chuckle to have seen us': 'the remembrance of Field comes back with all the soothing images of indolence, and summer slumbers, and work like play, and innocent idleness, and Elysian exemptions, and life itself a "playing holiday"' (ii. 19). Field's weaknesses as a teacher inadvertently provided the 'Deputy Grecians' under his care with the opportunity to develop unchecked according to their own impulses, in the manner prescribed in Rousseau's tract on education, *Émile*.

Charles's happy memories of his school-days, and the way in which, unusually for a Romantic, he can present them as integrated within a celebratory depiction of childhood and its imaginative creativity, rather than in lethal opposition to it, may owe much to Field's negligence. His stammer saved him from the sterner regime of Boyer, and also, consequently, from the cutting edge of the harsh disciplinary process by which a school such as Christ's Hospital imparted the ethos of self-restraining masculinity to its pupils. Valentine Le Grice, in his recollections of Charles at school, suggests that not only his stammer but also his general physical fragility spared him the rougher aspects of school life, and gave him a special place in it. According to Le Grice, Charles was

a quiet, gentle, studious boy, a looker on rather than a participator in the frolics of others. He enjoyed their mirth extremely, but his delicate frame, and his difficult utterance, which was increased by agitation, unfitted him for joining in the usual sports of boys. . . . I never heard his name mentioned without the addition of Charles, altho' as there was no other boy of a similar name the addition was unnecessary but there was an implied kindness in always so speaking of or addressing him.[25]

Both Le Grice in his letter and Charles himself in the Elia essay on Christ's Hospital also suggest that the proximity of Charles's home to his school, and the frequency of the visits he received there from his family, further protected him from the sterner astringencies of school discipline (ii. 12).

Charles's life at Christ's Hospital, then, constituted in many ways an atypical experience of male public schooling; apparently regarded with fondness as something of a school pet, one who was even exempt from the bluff public school use of the surname alone as appellation, he was spared the full pressure of enforced masculinization which would generally have been the lot of his contemporaries. He imbibed, as they did, an ideology which stressed the importance of hierarchical structure, but was fortunate enough to miss out on full indoctrination in those traits of manly self-assertion and self-discipline by means of which the highest ranks of the school were expected to acquire the authoritarian disposition which would prepare them for

[25] Madden, 'The Old Familiar Faces', pp. 116 and 117.

future roles as the leaders of their society. His place amongst the 'Deputy Grecians', and the nature of their mentor as opposed to that of the Grecians, enabled him to leave school with his propensity to position himself for preference amongst the subordinated rather than the socially dominant still intact, and indeed enhanced. 'Recollections of Christ's Hospital' records his early veneration of the 'Grecians', whose 'superior acquirements' 'drew the eyes of all' 'into a reverent observance and admiration' (i. 146–7). Half a century later, he was still clinging to his role in the schoolboy ranks; after Coleridge's death in 1834, Charles wrote of him as one who was

the proof and touchstone of all my cogitations. He was a Grecian (or in the first form) at Christ's Hospital, where I was a deputy Grecian; and the same subordination and deference to him I have preserved through a life-long acquaintance. (i. 351)

A letter written a few years earlier to another Christ's Hospital Grecian, George Dyer, contains a similar reminder of the old school hierarchies. Charles confesses:

I don't know how it is, but I keep my rank in fancy still since school-days. I can never forget I was a deputy Grecian! And writing to you, or to Coleridge, besides affection, I feel a reverential deference as to Grecians still.[26]

In its efforts to prepare its charity students for efficient and docile functioning in the world of work beyond its gates, Christ's Hospital, as Charles's essay of 1813 suggests, did attempt to inculcate a respect for hierarchical structures, and a self-restraining consciousness of dependence. Charles's upbringing and the family values he inherited made him particularly susceptible to such pressures. The Bluecoat ethos, with its rituals, regulations, and strict hierarchies, fostered and increased his tendencies towards hero-worship and self-subordination. But through his imaginative empathy with the greater hardships which many of his colleagues at the school endured, he did in later life come to appreciate and to portray the intransigence of the system in which he had been schooled, and to protest with some forcefulness against it.

[26] *Letters*, ed. Lucas, iii. 306.

III

An equivalent experience of the possibilities, for good or ill, afforded by school life was never extended to his sister Mary to the same degree; and although she like her brothers enjoyed their country holidays at their cousins' farm, Mackery End, there is little further evidence in her writings of happy childhood recollections. Childhood itself, as a state separate from infancy or adulthood, was a privilege granted to boys in advance of girls, who, largely because of the gender differentials in educational practices, were still in the late eighteenth century confused with women at an early age, and allotted little of an interim period.[27] In one of his contributions to William Hone's *Everyday Book* (1825), 'Captain Starkey', Charles does, however, record that his sister could look back nostalgically upon her brief period at a local dame's school; from about 1774 to 1778 she acquired the basic skills of literacy at William Bird's school, in which Starkey was the assistant master. She seems to have treasured these years primarily for the fleeting experience of childhood companionship they gave her (i. 301). Otherwise, she was left educationally very much to her own devices; throughout her life she was a voracious reader, a habit which no doubt began with the Lamb children's unsupervised access to Samuel Salt's library. In 1794, Coleridge testified to the erudition of his friend's sister; in a letter to Southey he describes Mary as one whose 'mind is elegantly stored—her Heart feeling'.[28] In later life, she taught herself Latin and Italian, and tutored her friends' children and the Lambs' own adopted daughter, Emma Isola, in classical and modern languages—this at a time when the acquirement of a 'learned language' was still commonly considered incompatible with a woman's 'nature and proper employments'.[29] Hazlitt, in his *Winterslow* essay 'Of persons one would wish to have seen', an account of an evening spent at the Lambs' lodgings during which the company entertained themselves by suggesting names from the past for reincarnation,

[27] Ariès, *Centuries of Childhood*, p. 56.
[28] Coleridge, *Collected Letters*, i. 147.
[29] See Hester Chapone, *Posthumous Works*, 3 vols. (London, John Murray, 1807), iii. 169.

interestingly reveals Mary's choice of the French seventeenth-
century courtesan Ninon de l'Enclos as the historic figure of
greatest appeal.[30] Renowned, according to Simone de Beauvoir
in *The Second Sex*, as 'the Frenchwoman whose independence
seems to us the most like that of a man', de l'Enclos had attained
'the rarest intellectual liberty';[31] Mary's choice illustrates her
admiration for women who defied social convention and
achieved thereby their full intellectual potential. But Mary was
afforded little leisure during her youth to pursue her own
autodidactic inclinations: soon after she left her dame's school,
her labours as a mantua-maker's apprentice began. After the
family's loss of Salt's protection, she seriously undermined her
physical and mental health in her twenties and early thirties
through her attempts to contribute to their meagre income by
her earnings, whilst carrying at the same time the domestic
burden of care for her ageing and disabled parents. She must,
none the less, have made some headway as a needlewoman, for
by 1796 she had herself acquired an apprentice. But the fact that
no apprenticeship records for this girl exist suggest that Mary's
assistant was a workhouse child, paid for by the parish, rather
than an independent prospective needlewoman, bound over by
her parents. The anonymity of her apprentice points to the
tenuousness of Mary's position in her profession.[32]

That she felt acutely the painful insecurities and unremitting
toil of the needlewoman's lot is indicated by her letter of 1815 to
the *British Ladies' Magazine*, the purpose of which is to beg the
magazine's affluent female readership no longer to take money
out of the mouths of their needy sisters, 'never in so much
distress for want of employment', by 'needle-work *done at home*'
(i. 176). Unusual for the directness with which it tackles the
economic situation of women, it also concerns itself with the
problematic issues of female aptitude for occupations conventionally pursued by men, of women's role in marriage, women's
education, and the value of a woman's time generally. And yet,

[30] *The Complete Works of William Hazlitt* ed. P. P. Howe, 21 vols. (London:
Dent, 1930–34), xvii. 133.

[31] Simone de Beauvoir, *The Second Sex* (Harmondsworth: Penguin, 1972),
pp. 580 and 581.

[32] For an account of the significance of the apprentice's anonymity, see Leslie
Joan Friedman, 'Mary Lamb: Sister, Seamstress, Murderer, Writer', Ph.D. thesis
(Stanford, Calif., 1976), p. 143.

for all the major changes in women's employment 'Sempronia' proposes, she also desires to bring about the necessary reforms 'without affronting the preconceived habits of society' (i. 178). A deferential decorum veils the anger of the piece, and muffles its protesting voice.

'Sempronia' begins her letter by informing the editor of the personal experience which provides her with the authority to speak on 'the state of needlework in this country': in her youth, she tells him, she passed eleven years 'in the exercise of my needle for a livelihood'. Now addressing readers 'among whom might perhaps be found some of the kind patronesses of my former humble labours', she is writing from a changed social position, one approximating more closely to parity with that of her earlier employers. Emphasis is laid upon the reality of this change, and therefore on her capacity to speak to the conditions of the upper classes as well as to those of the class of which she was originally part: 'among the present circle of my acquaintance,' she stresses, 'I am proud to rank many that may truly be called respectable.' But her loyalties, she confesses, still lie with the less fortunate group she has left, and her 'strongest motive' in writing the letter 'is to excite attention towards the industrious sisterhood to which I once belonged' (i. 176).

Nevertheless, the article concerns itself more with the daily lives of Britain's ladies than with that of its seamstresses, for 'Sempronia' wishes to persuade her readers that it would be in their interest, as well as in that of their labouring sisters, to desist from needlework *'done in the family'*. Her main argument is that time spent upon needlework is time lost from a new goal amongst upper- and middle-class women, that of 'intellectual progression': 'needlework and intellectual improvement', she asserts, 'are naturally in a state of warfare' (i. 176). She is writing to the *British Ladies' Magazine* precisely because it has allied itself to the cause of women's intellectual development. This progressive movement must have already, 'Sempronia' believes, done much to help needlewomen, in that it provided more affluent women with occupation other than the making of their own clothes. But its effects have not been far-reaching enough: needlewomen are still underemployed, and insufficiently remunerated for the work they do obtain, and women of the higher classes are still labouring under the intellectually impoverishing conviction that to fulfil their own and their family's sewing needs is their moral duty. Only if needlework were 'never practised but for a remuneration in money' might it become possible for women's lot to equal that of men 'as far as respects the mere enjoyment of life', 'Sempronia' would claim. 'As far as that goes', she adds, 'I believe it is every woman's opinion that the condition of men is far superior to her own'. And she presses home her argument with an extended account of the impoverishment of women's time, and therefore of their way of life, in comparison to that of men:

'They can do what they like,' we say. Do not these words generally mean, they have time to seek out whatever amusements suit their tastes? . . . *Real business* and *real leisure* make up the portions of men's time—two sources of happiness which we certainly partake of in a very inferior degree. To the execution of employment, in which the faculties of the body or mind are called into busy action, there must be a consoling importance attached, which feminine duties (that generic term for all our business) cannot aspire to (i. 177).

As an indictment of the early nineteenth-century English matron's situation, ceaselessly wasting her time on an array of undervalued, and in themselves trivial, tasks, in which needle-work figured obsessively, these paragraphs are painful and convincing. But they are immediately followed by one of the abrupt ideological swerves which characterize this text, as if the writer feared her protest had taken her too far. For in the very next paragraph, women's subordination to men is accepted as inevitable and even just, and accommodated as such within the writer's argument. 'Sempronia' goes on to proclaim that in the pursuance of these 'feminine duties' the highest praise women rightly look for is 'to be accounted the helpmates of *man*: who, in return for all he does for us, expects, and justly expects, us to do all in our power to soften and sweeten life.' And in the paragraphs that follow the intellectual improvement of a woman is now presented as a means for improving the home life of her husband rather than of herself: it is her duty to 'fit herself to become a conversational companion' for her husband, and laudably to exert herself in study not so much to develop her own mind as to contribute to the 'undisturbed relaxation of man'. The argument in favour of desisting from needlework is now that other tasks, in particular that of improving one's mind, will do more to fulfil a woman's fundamental duty of ensuring that her husband have no 'wish to pass his leisure hours at any fireside in preference to his own'. If she fulfil this function then she ought to have satisfied her sense of duty, and to be in a position cheerfully to lay aside her needle-book, contributing her part instead

to the slender gains of the corset-maker, the milliner, the dress-maker, the plain-worker, the embroidress, and all the numerous classifications of females supporting themselves by *needle-work*, that great stable commodity which is alone appropriated to the self-supporting part of our sex. (i. 178)

But as if in recognition here of the injustice inherent in the fact that needlework does indeed constitute one of the very few means of subsistence available to the unmarried woman, whose parents' income 'does not very much exceed the moderate', 'Sempronia', in accounting for this situation, is aroused to anger again. Echoing the arguments of Mary Wollstonecraft in her *Vindication of the Rights of Women* (1792), a book which Mary Lamb's biographers assume she must have read, she presents women's work opportunities as limited through the grievous inadequacy of their education,[33] and asserts that the male of the species, were he in the same deprived position, could fare no better:

Even where boys have gone through a laborious education, super-inducing habits of steady attention, accompanied with the entire conviction that the business which they learn is to be the source of their future distinction, may it not be affirmed that the persevering industry required to accomplish this desirable end causes many a hard struggle in the minds of young men, even of the most hopeful disposition? What then must be the disadvantages under which a very young woman is placed who is required to learn a trade, from which she can never expect to reap any profit, but at the expence of losing that place in society, to the possession of which she may reasonably look forward, inasmuch as it is by far the most *common lot*, namely, the condition of a *happy* English wife? (i. 179)

[33] See Mary Wollstonecraft, *Vindication of the Rights of Woman*, Miriam Brody Kramnick (Harmondsworth: Penguin, 1975), pp. 104–5. Katharine Anthony (*The Lambs: A Study of Pre-Victorian England* (London: Hammond, Hammond & Co., 1948), p. 164), insists that Mary Lamb must have read *Vindication*.

This elucidation of the importance of the psychological preparation for work which education, and social expectation, provides for men but denies to women, according to the nineteenth-century gender-role system, is striking and perceptive. Nevertheless, the author's stance in the essay as a whole prevents one from interpreting in an ironic light her concluding reference here to 'the *happy* English wife'. Although she argues that only their lack of education stops women from sharing in the occupations of men, and that as a result of this deprivation they suffer both materially and in terms of thwarted potential, yet 'Sempronia' would not have the *status quo* essentially changed. On the contrary she asks her reader 'to contribute all the assistance in her power to those of her own sex who may need it, in the employments they at present occupy, rather than to force them into situations now filled wholly by men.' No arguments sustain these reversals: they are interjected abruptly into the protesting body of the text, to be accounted for only by unspecific references to the writer's 'many years of observation and reflection'. The key to 'Sempronia's insistence upon such retrograde conclusions in an article which raises so many essentially radical issues lies in the circumstance of Mary's personal and social experience, her 'cultural locus', as Elaine Showalter would have it.[34]

Foremost of that undisclosed, yet relevant, experience upon which her 'years of observation and reflection' were based must have been the actual conditions of life under which she, as a former needlewoman, had laboured; she takes her readers' knowledge of the dire situation of nineteenth-century needlewomen for granted. Contemporary records did, in fact, draw the attention of the more affluent classes to the plight of 'thousands of young females of respectable parents' who, 'necessitated by the pecuniary misfortunes of their parents to earn a livelihood by needlework', found that employment so precarious and the profit so small that they were driven through 'sheer want' to resort 'to prostitution and its concomitants, misery, disease and death!'[35] And a needlewoman who managed

[34] Elaine Showalter, 'Feminist Criticism in the Wilderness', in ead. (ed.), *The New Feminist Criticism: Essays on Women, Literature and Theory* (London: Virago, 1986), p. 264.

[35] J. R. Pickmore, 'An Address to the Public on the Propriety of Midwives,

to survive on selling her labour rather than herself hardly seems to have enjoyed a less miserable, or healthier, existence. As an apprentice, learning her trade, she worked extortionately long hours for no pay, and once trained, a mantua-maker, attempting to make an independent living in a hopelessly overstocked and consequently under-priced market, could consider herself lucky to find work which kept her plying her needle from 9 a.m. to 11 p.m. for very little gain.[36] Given Mary's first-hand experience of the hazards of the trade, she may well have felt that to describe its conditions in more detail in her essay would have been to shatter the ostensible purpose of her plea completely. For if her affluent female audience had been reminded more graphically of the sufferings of those who earned their living by the needle they might well have preferred to force the penurious of their sex into situations 'filled wholly by men' rather than to perpetuate through their commissions the sweat-shop trade.

And yet Mary's sympathies clearly lie with the struggling needlewomen; why she chose to argue for so little real change in their apparently hopeless position, which was in fact rapidly to deteriorate even further as the century progressed, remains problematic. Her essay suggests that she did know of the proposals then being put forward that work opportunities for women be extended. A 'Ladies Committee for Promoting the Education and Employment of the Female Poor' had, for example, proposed in 1804 that women should at least be allowed to regain those occupations, such as midwifery and other branches of medical practice, which had formerly by tradition been theirs, but which had been wrested from them by the demand for more specialized training, not available to women.[37] Earlier, at the turn of the century, women writers politicized by the impact of the French Revolution upon British

instead of Surgeons, practising Midwifery', *Pamphleteer*, 28 (1827), 115–16; quoted Ivy Pinchbeck, *Women Workers and the Industrial Revolution 1750–1850* (1st edn. 1930; London: Virago, 1981), p. 315.

[36] See Pinchbeck, *Women Workers and the Industrial Revolution*, pp. 289 and 308–9, and Wanda Fraiken Neff, *Victorian Working Women: An Historical and Literary Study of Women in British Industries and Professions 1832–1850* (London: Allen & Unwin, 1929), pp. 116 and 129.

[37] 'Report of the Society for Bettering the Condition and Increasing the Comforts of the Poor' (1798–1808), iv. 182–92; quoted Pinchbeck, *Women Workers and the Industrial Revolution*, pp. 304–5.

radicals had protested against the lack of opportunity in female employment. Wollstonecraft, in the *Vindication*, deplored the fact that the few employments open to women were menial and humiliating; middle-class women's laudable attempts to earn their own subsistence lowered them in practice 'almost to the level of those poor abandoned creatures who live by prostitution', 'for are not milliners and mantua-makers', she asked, 'reckoned the next class?'.[38] Subsequently, Priscilla Wakefield, in her *Reflections on the Present Condition of the Female Sex* (1798) protested against the lack of equal pay for equal work for women in comparison with men;[39] and Mary Hays, an acquaintance of the Lambs, wrote an *Appeal to the Men of Great Britain in Behalf of Women* (1798) in which, in a development of Wollstonecraft's arguments, she listed the obstacles massed against the attempts by women of any class to gain independence through employment.[40]

Her apparent eagerness to promote the happiness of the English husband, as well as the welfare of his wife, by making that wife a more stimulating domestic companion, would appear to relegate Mary Lamb's protest to the ranks of the more conservative 'instrumental' feminists, those who argued for reform in the system of gender differentiation as a means towards general social amelioration rather than specifically towards the improvement of women's lot as such.[41] But her essay does also indicate an awareness of the relation between female employment and women's social position generally which is radical in its implications. She recognized that socially respectable and remunerative employment for women was necessary not only for pecuniary reasons but because it would have detracted from the prevalent concept of their labour, and consequently of their time, as essentially worthless by comparison with those of men. 'On Needle-Work' shows that Mary was sharply aware that the lack of female professions, and of

[38] Wollstonecraft, *Vindication*, p. 261.

[39] Priscilla Wakefield, *Reflections on the Present Condition of the Female Sex; with Suggestions for its Improvement* (London: J. Johnson and Darton & Harvey, 1798), pp. 151–5.

[40] Mary Hays [published anonymously], *Appeal to the Men of Great Britain in Behalf of Women* (New York: Garland, 1974), p. 278.

[41] See Alice Browne, *The Eighteenth Century Feminist Mind* (Brighton: Harvester, 1987), pp. 5–6, for her definition of 'instrumental feminism'.

training for women for those professions, meant that all women's labour, not only that of those forced to be self-supporting, brought them little reward and therefore no independent social status. Their occupations, such as they were, could not bring them the 'consoling importance' acquired by male labour but only either a precarious and unrespected subsistence or, at best, the approval of masculine protectors.

Whether they belonged to the struggling or more affluent classes, women's time was never in fact self-validatingly their own. Pointing to the distinction between men's *'real business'* and their *'real leisure'*, and recognizing it as a difference which did not exist for women, Mary is alerting her readers to the manner in which the male relation to time was, in her period, changing, while that of women remained static. Time consciousness, and the sharp division between work and leisure, was, as we have seen,[42] becoming all important for the male, but a woman's daily work remained task-orientated. A woman did not count her time in the manner in which a man was more and more being compelled to do, and the consequence was that a woman's time, as the correlation between time and money bit deeper, did not count. Mary also discerningly locates the development of this differing time consciousness in the differing patterns of male and female education; a boy's more strenuous education is seen in the essay as breaking down his resistance to control, and preparing him psychologically for the discipline of work ruled by the clock rather than the task. Before the end of the eighteenth century social commentators had begun to recognize and record a developing sex-gender system which more and more rigorously curtailed women to a private, domestic sphere, while men dominated the public domain.[43] Mary's account captures the reality of a woman's world caught in a time-warped situation in contrast with the accelerated pace of change then prevalent amongst her male contemporaries; in her world a woman could no longer credit herself with her own labour, for work within the home, within the sphere marked off for men as constituting 'leisure', could never acquire the dignity of 'real' work.[44]

[42] See pp. 55–7, above.
[43] Browne, *The Eighteenth Century Feminist Mind*, p. 136.
[44] See Joan Kelly, 'The Doubled Vision of Feminist Theory', in Judith L.

And yet, for all her perspicacity, Mary Lamb does not begin to propose any of the revolutions in the sex-gender role of nineteenth-century women which would be necessary to bring about any real amendment in the situation she describes. One indication of why she did not feel able to take this strategic step lies in her account in the essay of the likely consequence for the women of her era of an education which would prepare them adequately for the nineteenth-century entrepreneurial job market: a woman acquiring the necessary psychological training in competitiveness and time-consciousness would be endangering the possibility of her arriving at the condition 'of a *happy* English wife'. The essay accommodates itself to the unquestioned assumption that a woman's chance of marriage, as her best hope of happiness, is to be protected at all costs, even at the risk of her subsequent destitution were she to remain, like Mary herself and very many of her contemporaries, unwed, and even though her situation in that marriage has previously in the essay been forcefully shown to be much inferior to her husband's. The '*happy* English wife' of Mary's description is clearly a middle- or upper-class spouse, of the same social grouping as the readers she addresses; a working-class wife's lot would hardly be presented in such firmly positive terms. Historical studies of the period do indeed indicate that a practical education would have detracted from a woman's opportunities in the upper- and middle-class marriage market: to be trained for any profession would have entailed a loss in status and marital appeal in an age in which it was considered an 'affront against nature', and an indication of her 'moral and spiritual degradation', for a woman to earn her own wages.[45] Needlework, along with the one other occupation open to women of this class at the time, namely, the education of girls and small children, as a teacher or governess, were the only forms of remunerative employment for which a 'genteel' upbringing could have prepared a woman. Hence the glutting

---

Newton, Mary P. Ryan, and Judith R. Walkowitz (eds.), *Sex and Class in Women's History* (London: Routledge & Kegan Paul, 1983), p. 260, for a general account of the manner in which 'the separation of work (production) from leisure (consumption) really exists for men only', and entails the consequent mystification of women's work.

[45] Neff, *Victorian Working Women*, p. 37.

of the seamstresses' market with an endless supply of unfortunate daughters struggling to retain a foothold in the middle classes, and the possibility of marriage within that class, even though they were thus reduced to worse material circumstance than they would have endured had they sought factory employment or domestic service. The tragic irony of their situation was that the difficulty of ensuring a subsistence as a needlewoman meant that many were forced, through lack of employment, from the lower-middle-class status of an independent milliner or mantua-maker to the working-class position of a plain sewer or 'slop-worker' employed by a mistress, and often from thence, particularly in the middle years of the century, to prostitution, and its concomitant entire and irremediable loss, in their society's eyes, of all character and status. It is in the attempt to prevent this degradation of lower-middle-class needlewomen that Mary is writing her article.

And yet marriage, as the hoped-for goal towards which this deliberate curtailment of female potential was aimed, does not in itself ever seem to have had a very potent appeal for Mary. In her correspondence with her close friend, Sarah Stoddart, which often concerned itself with Sarah's frustrations in the marriage market, she generally attempts to tease Sarah out of her overriding preoccupation with finding herself a husband. In one letter of 1806, she invites Sarah, instead, to set up house with herself and her brother:

I think I should like to have you always to the end of our lives living with us, and I do not know any reason why that should not be expect for the great fancy you seem to have for marrying, which after all is but a hazardous kind of an affair . . . very few husbands have I ever wished was mine which is rather against the state in general that one never is disposed to envy wives their good husbands, So much for marrying— but however get married if you can.[46]

But the ideological pressure on upper- and middle-class women at this time to find in marriage the end of their existence, even though both their inclination and their perception of the condition of women inside marriage might be against it, was, of course, extraordinarily strong. The belief, held as established

[46] See *Letters*, ed. Marrs, ii. 229.

through religious doctrine, that Providence had created woman
as the helpmate and comfort of man, and by doing so had fully
indicated her function, served as a central foundation of the
patriarchal bourgeois social system. Mary, then, in accepting a
married woman's lot as unquestionably *'happy'* in 'On Needle-
Work', even though she has just previously described its
circumscriptions, is accommodating inside her argument the
established nostrums of her period.

But although the element of social protest in 'On Needle-
Work' may be ambivalent in terms of class relations, and in
terms of its assessment of the value of the bourgeois marriage,
both of these accommodations can be read as furthering the real
goal of the text, that of encouraging the solidarity of women as a
group in themselves, across the boundaries of class and marital
status. Given her class background, and the gender-role
vulnerabilities she shared with all nineteenth-century women,
it would have been in many ways far safer for Mary Lamb to
have forgotten that she ever knew at first hand the difficulties of
the self-supporting working woman. But in emphasizing, on
the contrary, the realities of her past experience in the text, she
presents her life as a mediating link between one group of
women and another, and asks the more affluent women she
addresses as her readers to realize through her their shared
sisterhood with the less privileged sector to which she originally
belonged. The last paragraph of the essay, in particular, challenges
middle-class women to demonstrate in practical terms their
female allegiance with needlewomen, in a manner which cuts
directly across the interests of their husbands. In it she suggests
that those of her readers who profess to enjoy their needlework
too much to relinquish it, though *'saving'* is not their object,
confine themselves to purely ornamental work,

> knitting, knotting, netting, carpet working, and the like ingenious
> pursuits—those so-often-praised but tedious works, which are so long
> in the operation, that purchasing the labour has seldom been thought
> good economy, yet, by a certain fascination, they have been found to
> chain down the great to a self-imposed slavery, from which they
> considerately, or haughtily, excuse the needy.

The function of needlework inside a system of upper-class
female subordination, fetishized and adopted as such even by

the women themselves, is tellingly indicated here. Furthermore, the last sentence of the letter continues:

But, if those works, more usually denominated useful, yield greater satisfaction, it might be a laudable scruple of conscience, and no bad test to herself of her own motive, if a lady, who had no absolute need, were to give the money so saved to poor needle-women belonging to those branches of employment from which she has borrowed these shares of pleasurable labour. (i. 180)

The significant word here is 'borrowed': the lady she addresses is not asked to give the needlewoman money as a gift of charity, in the conventional *noblesse oblige* fashion, but to give it to her as her right, as the rightful fruits of her labour, 'borrowed' from her by the ruling economic order. The money the gentlewoman is thus to pay back would not, of course, be likely to be her own money under nineteenth-century law but that of her husband, father, brother, or other male protector. At the close of 'On Needle-Work' Mary Lamb enjoys a most revolutionary vision of bourgeois women busily distributing the fruits of their husbands' capitalist gains amongst the women exploited by that system, in the name of female solidarity. How far Lamb was writing here with deliberate awareness of the revolutionary implications of her suggestions may, of course, be queried, but the essay's subversive energy is palpable, particularly at its close, though its author may try deviously to obscure it. Her letter as a whole, both through what it reveals directly and through the subtext of personal anguish apparent below its accommodating surfaces, may be considered tellingly representative of the difficulties facing the self-supporting woman at the turn of the century in her attempt to establish and preserve autonomy and self-respect.

IV

For all his superior educational training, Charles Lamb's work experiences proved, in the event, little more satisfying than his sister's; for him too the necessity of earning the family's income resulted in labours which militated against his sense of self-worth and self-respect. After his school-days were over, the

employment found for him through the patronage of Salt and
his acquaintances was initially intermittent and punctuated by
periods of unemployment. Salt first procured for him some
months' work as a clerk in the offices of his city merchant
friend, Joseph Paice; Paice, in his turn, as a director at the South
Sea House, later provided him with a further short period of
employment with that company. Finally, in 1792, when Charles
was 17, Paice's influence established him in a clerical apprenticeship at the East India Company, where he stayed for the next
thirty-three years. There is no indication in his writings that the
clerical profession was Charles' personal choice; rather, it was
the occupation for which his Christ's Hospital education had
prepared him. Debarred as he was from a university career, and
burdened, unlike other future literary figures amongst his
Bluecoat acquaintance, with family responsibilities and expectations too weighty to permit him to launch himself upon the
financially hazardous journalistic world, a clerkship provided a
milieu in which, at that time, he could still retain something of
the higher rank status into which Christ's Hospital had
introduced him whilst securing for himself and his family the
benefits of a reliable income. The skills required to fulfil a
clerk's functions, such as numeracy, a clear 'hand' and a
relatively high degree of literacy, were still rare enough in the
late eighteenth century to bestow some social prestige upon the
profession; limited to men, it was also a field in which an
aspiring employee might very probably, like Charles's brother,
further his social advance through rising to become the head of
an office.[47] Nevertheless, the clerks' working conditions in the
lower grades, and the monotony of their activities, barely
constituted an improvement upon the benighted circumstance
of the needlewoman's toil. At the East India Company, the
compound of the Accountant General's office at which Charles
had his desk was a poorly lit room overlooking a dark
courtyard, open to the public and divided into 'sets', each set
comprising a desk for about six clerks. When Thomas de
Quincey visited Lamb in the compound in the winter of 1804–5
he found him at work at a 'very lofty writing-desk', perched on

---

[47] See Richard N. Price, 'Society, Status and Jingoism: The Social Roots of
Lower Middle Class Patriotism, 1870–1900', in Geoffrey Crossick (ed.), *The
Lower Middle Class in Britain 1870–1914* (London: Croom Helm, 1977), p. 103.

a high clerk's stool, and separated from the public by a railing which enclosed him and five fellow 'quill-driving gentlemen'.[48] Here they spent anything from six to ten hours a day, and occasionally, when the company was particularly busy, eleven, twelve, or even thirteen hours, registering the proceeds of tea-sales, making out warrants, and generally auditing the accounts of what was then a vast and prosperous trading concern.[49]

The suggestion in De Quincey's description of the clerks as imprisoned, held captive at their desks by the high railing, is one which frequently recurs in Charles's references to his work in his letters. 'A prisoner to the desk', 'chained to that gally' until he has almost 'grown to the wood', he complains that the merchants and the 'drudgery' they impose 'lime twig up my poor soul & body'.[50] Writing to Wordsworth in 1815, he rails against the fatigues of his occupation with characteristic sardonic mockery:

> If I do but get rid of auditing Warehousekeeper Accts. & get no worse-harassing task in the place of it, what a Lord of Liberty I shall be. I shall dance & skip and make mouths at the invisible event, and pick the thorns out of my pillow & throw em at rich mens night caps, & talk blank verse hoity toity, and sing a Clerk I was in London Gay, ban, ban, Ca-Caliban, like the emancipated monster & go where I like up this street or down that ally.[51]

For all its whimsy, this letter with its references to Caliban's short-lived and bogus dreams of freedom, and its animosity towards the carefree rich, suggests his anger at his situation, but Charles's picturesque phraseology makes light of his sufferings even as he recounts them. Another literary clerk, writing half a century later, was to protest more directly against the 'slavery' of his employment. William Hale White uses the autobiographical persona of Mark Rutherford to denounce the conditions of clerical employment:

---

[48] *The Collected Writings of De Quincey*, ed. David Masson, 14 vols. (Edinburgh: Adam & Charles Black, 1889–90), iii. 38.

[49] For records of Charles's working hours, see, e.g. his letter to Wordsworth, 16 Apr. 1815, *Letters* ed. Marrs, iii. 141: 'I should have written before, but I am cruelly engaged and like to be, on Friday I was at the office from 10 in the morning . . . to 11 at night, last night till 9.'

[50] *Letters*, ed. Lucas, ii. 332; and *Letters*, ed. Marrs, iii. 149.

[51] *Letters*, ed. Marrs, iii. 175.

Never could there be any duty incumbent upon man more inhuman and devoid of interest than my own. . . . The whole day I did nothing but write, and what I wrote called forth no single faculty of the mind. Nobody who has not tried such an occupation can possibly forecast the strange habits, humours, fancies and diseases which after a time it breeds. . . . It is very terrible to think that the labour by which men are to live shc:ld be of this order.[52]

No such direct and sustained criticism of his situation is to be found in Charles's work. Instead, he tends to close his few epistolary complaints with regard to his labours with some such phrases as 'but I find stupid acquiescence coming over me. I bend to the yoke.'[53] The ideological pressures of his up-bringing, both at home and at school, had prepared him for an acquiescent servitude, and his use of the phrase 'I bend to the yoke', with its Christian associations, for all its irony and bitterness in this context, yet suggests his tendency to connect with a passive suffering role the fulfilment of a moral ideal.

Nor was the particular type of occupation in which he found employment one which could offer much encouragement to any incipient seeds of rebellion. Initially the clerical assistant's role had been that of a servant, part of the man of property's 'family' of retainers, and the feudal relation to the masters implicit in that position remained even after the development of capitalism and the joint stock company had depersonalized the relationship: complete obedience and deference to office hierarchies were still expected and enjoined.[54] Recent socio-historical studies of the 'blackcoated worker' describe the clerk's position during the early industrial period as one of intense and virtually unavoidable ideological ambivalence. The professional role of the clerk, like those of both the eighteenth-century servant and the traditional middle- and upper-class wife, required his personal allegiance to the employer with whom he worked in close proximity, and on whose continuing support his role and identity as an employee depended.[55] Although financially little

---

[52] 'Mark Rutherford' [William Hale White], *Autobiography and Deliverance* (Leicester: Leicester Univ. Press, 1969), pp. 247 and 250.

[53] *Letters*, ed. Marrs, iii. 141.

[54] See F. D. Klingender, *The Conditions of Clerical Labour in Britain* (London: Martin Lawrence, 1935), pp. 2–3.

[55] See David Lockwood, *The Blackcoated Worker: A Study in Class Consciousness* (London: Allen & Unwin, 1958), p. 32, and Gregory Anderson, *Victorian Clerks* (Manchester: Manchester Univ. Press, 1976), pp. 32–3.

better off than the industrial labourer, and increasingly more impoverished as the century developed, counting-house clerks worked in an environment which

> was generally conducive to their estrangement from the mass of working men and to their identification with the entrepreneurial and professional classes. . . . they usually had more education than those who went into factory employment; their work was clean and involved the exercise of brain not brawn; their dress distinguished them from ordinary employees and approximated that of the master class, with whom they worked in a close and personal relationship; their skills and future were tied up with a particular employer and enterprise.[56]

Their marginal social position, midway between the upper and lower ranks, increased the anxious status consciousness of clerks as a group; their working conditions made it difficult for them to achieve self-respect and independence, and virtually necessitated, in self-defence, the development of deferential character traits.[57]

The loss of the personal relationship with the paternalistic master, which might earlier have accorded clerks some dignity and vicarious pride, was a particularly difficult change for Charles to negotiate. Imbued with the ethos of service from birth, and identifying with what he saw as the loving devotion of his father to his own master, to whom the father had served as scrivener as well as valet, he could find no emotional compensation for his own servitude in his relation with his immediate overseers at work. Such anger as he does express against his working conditions is often vented against the petty officials in control of his 'set'. Writing to Coleridge in June 1796, for example, he rails against a refusal by an immediate superior to grant him leave of absence: 'Is it not hard, this "dread dependance on the low bred mind"?'[58] A later letter to the Wordsworths explains in similar terms Charles's comically intoxicated aggression towards a Stamp Office official who, in December 1817, had intruded upon a party given by the artist Benjamin Robert Haydon:

---

[56] Lockwood, *The Blackcoated Worker*, p. 34.

[57] See David Silverman, 'Clerical Ideologies: A Research Note', *British Journal of Sociology*, 19 (1968), p. 326, and Lockwood, *The Blackcoated Worker*, p. 211.

[58] *Letters*, ed. Marrs, i. 36.

I think I had an instinct that he was the head of an office. I hate all such people—Accountants, Deputy Accountants. The dear abstract notion of the East India Company, as long as she is unseen, is pretty, rather Poetical; but as SHE makes herself manifest by the person of such Beasts, I loathe and detest her as the Scarlet what-do-you-call-her of Babylon.[59]

Anecdotes recorded by his colleagues at the East India Company demonstrate that his anger against those officials who harassed the clerks often found direct vent during working hours too: the recollections of one of his fellow clerks, John Chambers, put on record by his executor in 1879, detail many of Charles's sharp and rebellious rejoinders to officialdom. On one occasion, for example, 'an unpopular head of department came to Lamb one day and inquired, "Pray, Mr Lamb, what are you about?" "Forty, next birthday," said Lamb. "I don't like your answer," said his chief. "Nor I your question," was Lamb's reply.'[60] His colleagues clearly relished this refusal to adopt the expected obsequiousness towards authority, and the use of his wit in such characteristic fashion as a practical and immediate weapon against petty domination must have done much to maintain Charles's ability to retain self-respect at work. But in his writings, particularly in the Elia essays, his willingness to accept in principle the 'pretty, even Poetical' abstract notion of the East India House manifests itself in Elia's apparently cheery and untroubled acquiescence in his lot.

Most of Elia's readers appear to have accepted with approval this adoption of the non-rebellious 'good child' role; no doubt his apparent acceptance of a victimized position assuaged the social guilt of some of his more privileged Victorian and Edwardian readers, and may have constituted part of his popularity. Even in a recent biography, Charles's 'sweet-tempered', obedient' 'childishness', his desire to please, and his propensity to accept 'without much question the decrees of his elders and betters' are presented as useful qualifications for his clerical office.[61] A few of his readers, however, have always found an unpalatable collusion with injustice in the reasonableness and gentle resignation of the Elia essays. In one of the

[59] *Letters*, ed. Lucas, ii. 228.
[60] Algernon Black, *Macmillan's Magazine*, 39 (Mar. 1879), 432.
[61] David Cecil, *A Portrait of Charles Lamb* (London: Constable, 1983), pp. 32–3.

volumes of her autobiographical novel *Pilgrimage*, Dorothy Richardson puts in the mouth of her *alter ego* Miriam Henderson a spirited critique of the essay 'The Superannuated Man', in which Elia describes his feelings at being finally pensioned off after thirty-three years at the desk. Although she considered the essay 'extraordinary', Miriam tells a friend, she also found

something in it that was horrible. The employers gave the old man a pension, with humorous benevolence. He is so surprised and so blissfully happy in having nothing to do but look at the green world for the rest of the time, that he feels nothing but gratitude. That's all right, from his point of view, being that sort of old man. But how dare the firm be humorously benevolent? It is no case for *humour*. It is not *funny* that prosperous people can use up lives on small fixed salaries that never increase beyond a certain point, no matter how well the employers get on, even if for the last few years they give pensions. And they don't give pensions. If they do, they are thought most benevolent. The author, who is evidently in a way a thoughtful man, ought to have known this. He just wrote a thing that looks charming on the surface and is beautifully written and is really perfectly horrible and disgusting. . . . employers ought to *know* how fearfully unfair everything is. They ought to have their complacency smashed up.[62]

Yet the essay, for all its apparent collusion, does bring about a marked change in Miriam's attitudes. It so incenses her that she looks on her own job, as a dentist's receptionist, with new eyes after reading 'The Superannuated Man', and begins to object to the ways her employers take her for granted, which she had previously accepted. The anger in her response to the essay does not therefore appear to be wholly the consequence of a habit of mind of her own which she brings to it, or a conscious ideological position previously held, but a strong reaction to the essay itself. Her reading of it has sharpened and clarified her sense of social injustice and of her own exploitation.

A close analysis of the essay suggests that, for all its apparent gratitude, it contains within itself, in an ambivalent and yet deeply felt manner, much of that anger and indignation which Miriam discovered in reaction against it. Elia, the superannuated man—and the very title of the piece suggests his bitterness—describes his period of employment as 'prison days', 'my

[62] Dorothy Richardson, *Pilgrimage*, 4 vols. (London: Virago, 1979; repr. of 1938 edn.), iii. 177–8.

captivity', 'my thraldom', in 'labyrinthine passages, and light-excluding, pent-up offices', prolonged from youth to age 'without hope of release' (ii. 193–4, 197). Now, suddenly freed, he finds himself 'in the condition of a prisoner in the old Bastile', unable to accustom himself to a new world, and missing his old chains (ii. 195). He is living in two worlds, the confinement of the past, still alive in his conceptions, and the privileged freedom of the present, and the contrast between the two, for all the humour and ornament of his language, does arouse his indignation:

Stones of old Mincing-lane, which I have worn with my daily pilgrimage for six and thirty years, to the footsteps of what toil-worn clerk are your everlasting flints now vocal? I indent the gayer flags of Pall Mall. It is Change time, and I am strangely among the Elgin marbles. . . . Man, I verily believe, is out of his element as long as he is operative. I am altogether for the life contemplative. Will no kindly earthquake come and swallow up those accursed cotton mills? (ii. 198)

Elia's approach is hardly revolutionary: he does not choose to imagine any other power than the arbitrary processes of nature as a tool to rid society of its exploitative systems. His humour also makes it possible for a reader to take much of what he has to say very lightly: Elia, the contemplative, can be seen as merely recommending indolence. At the same time, an intensity created by his unexpected juxtapositions of images and his use of evocative adverbs and adjectives draws a responsive reader into the actual experience of the superannuated man, caught between the 'everlasting flints' of the 'toil-worn' and the 'gayer flags' and Elgin marbles of the privileged. For all that he believes that humanity, as a 'contemplative' race, belongs by rights to the second world, the superannuated man finds himself at a loss, wandering 'strangely' amidst riches, for his memories of the years of toil and his sympathetic identification with those still imprisoned bewilder him; they have alienated him from wealth and the produce of wealth and made a straightforward enjoyment of his new leisure difficult. Elia appears half unconscious of his own alienation, but certain images throughout the essay, such as that of the prisoners freed from the Bastille, hint at an underlying anger, although his appreciation of the aesthetic fruits of culture and capital hold that potential rebellion in check. Nevertheless, the lives of the toiling clerks are vividly presented, and when, for example, Elia describes his misery at first commencing work and his anguish, until time and custom gradually wore his resistance down and he became 'doggedly contented, as wild animals in cages' (i. 193), he can evoke a sense of outrage in his readers. In fact, the reader's anger, once aroused, is heightened by frustration at the fact that Elia does not appear to appreciate his situation fully, and still seems to be ideologically trapped inside the world of his exploitation. However, one need not necessarily suppose, as Dorothy Richardson does, that this response also is not encoded beneath the acquiescent surface of the text.

In his everyday working life, at any rate, Charles did not evince the obsequiousness Richardson attributes to him. His first reaction on quitting his work displays nothing of that excessive gratitude towards his employers she sees in 'The Superannuated Man': he wrote a note to Henry Crabb Robinson, rejoicing in the fact that 'I have left the d—d India House for Ever!'.[63] What is more, in an earlier pre-Elian piece of journalism entitled 'The Good Clerk' Charles had denounced through parody what he called 'the astonishing narrowness and illiberality' of the eighteenth-century didactic guides which had sought to instil the virtues of deference and self-subordination into lower-rank workers (i. 129). 'The Good Clerk' is a piece of 'covered' or 'disguised Satire' in which Charles, before revealing his real purposes, sets out a list of maxims for the correct observance of clerical duties. The ideal clerk must be

clean and neat in his person . . . to do credit (as we say) to the office. . . .
He riseth early in the morning . . . that he may be first at the desk. . . .
He is temperate in eating and drinking, that he may preserve a clear head and steady hand for his master's service. . . .
He avoideth profane oaths and jesting, as so much time lost from his employ . . . making the motion of his lips, as well as of his fingers, subservient to his master's interest. (i. 127–8)

Charles's readers, by now suspecting some hoax, are then informed that these 'frugal and economical maxims' were penned as deliberate parodies, 'to divert some of the melancholy hours of a Counting House', hours which the conduct tracts

---

[63] *Letters*, ed. Lucas, ii. 465.

here mocked would wish to present to the unfortunate clerks as time dedicated to work and the fulfilment of their duties to the masters (i. 129). One example of an actual handbook for clerks, the Houlston Industrial Library's *The Clerk. A Sketch in Outline of his Duties and Description* published half a century later, does indeed, in all seriousness, pronounce it as necessary for a clerk to acquire the virtues of 'patience, perseverance, courtesy, cheerfulness' along with 'a humble distrust of self and a deferential respect for the judgement of others'. Clerks are advised in the handbook to resist the temptations of theatre attendance, because of the equivocal social standing of its audiences, and of novel-reading as it is 'as hurtful to the mind . . . as habitual dram-drinking is to the body'; they must adopt 'quiet and unassuming' clothing as denoting 'a becoming modesty of mind', and eschew eccentric, individualistic manners or speech patterns as 'provocative of contempt'.[64] In the light of these texts, Charles's behaviour patterns, his enthusiasm for the theatre, his drinking bouts, and even the quixotic eccentricities of his literary style and whimsical manner, now appear as a strategy of revolt against the orthodoxies of his employment.

Interestingly, the handbook's instructions to clerks bear markedly similar resemblances to the advice given to women in the conduct books of the late eighteenth and early nineteenth centuries. Hannah More, in her influential *Strictures on the Modern System of Female Education* (1799), exhorts women to impose upon themselves patterns of habitual restraint and deference to the male, and to instil self-mistrust and conformity to patriarchal authority in their daughters: 'They should be led to distrust their own judgement. . . . It is of the last importance to their happiness even in this life that they should early acquire a submissive temper and a forbearing spirit.'[65] An 'air of diffidence' and an obsequious demonstration of their consciousness of dependence was as necessary a personality trait for the nineteenth-century wife as it was for the aspiring clerk;[66] she

[64] Houlston's Industrial Library No. 7, *The Clerk. A Sketch in Outline of his Duties and Discipline* (London: Houlston, 1878), pp. 16, 34, and 46; quoted Price, 'Society, Status and Jingoism', p. 102.

[65] Hannah More, *Strictures on the Modern System of Female Education*, 2 vols. (London: T. Cadell & W. Davies, 1799), i. 142–3.

[66] *The Polite Lady: Or A Course of Female Education. In a Series of Letters, from a Mother to her Daughter* (2nd edn. London: Newberry & Carnan, 1769), p. 205.

too was advised to eschew 'her natural caprice, her love of self-indulgence, her vanity, her indolence—in short, her very *self*' in order to achieve her husband's approbation.[67] The comparability of the clerk's and the woman's positions, both living in close proximity with the immediate source of power in their lives, powers with which they were identified yet to which they were still in service, resulted in these tracts which similarly stress the necessity of playing the proper subordinate role, and perpetuate the existing power relation by presenting it as natural and unavoidable. Clerking itself came to be generally considered as an unmanly profession long before it was eventually categorized as a female occupation; 'born a man; died a clerk' became a catch phrase cruelly expressive of the clerk's anxieties as to his gender identity, and of the difficulty in the nineteenth century of combining masculine and subordinate roles.[68] The only way forwards towards the restoration of masculine self-respect was through promotion to the ranks of petty officialdom, a promotion which Charles himself consistently resisted. His hatred of dominance was such that he seems to have taken some pride in openly accepting, as the alternative foisted upon him, the attribution of unmanliness. One remark of his, recorded by John Chambers, tellingly indicates his refusal to adopt any of the characteristic behaviours symbolic of male dominance. According to Chambers, Charles was wont to boast to his colleagues at work that 'he thought he must be the only man in England who had never worn boots and never mounted a horse',[69] two attributes which would have played their part in differentiating the sexes at this time. He accepts a subordinate role, and, as it were, a voluntary femininity, rather than aspire towards any of the symbolic attributes of manly dominance, but does so partly in opposition to the ideologies which yoked masterfulness to the male role in the first instance.

Such symbolic rather than political resistance towards a prevailing power system has recently been characterized as

---

[67] Sarah Ellis, *The Women of England: Their Social Duties and Domestic Habits* (London: Fisher, Son & Co., 1839), p. 45.

[68] See Meta Zimmeck, 'Jobs for the Girls: The Expansion of Clerical Work for Women, 1850–1914', in Angela V. John (ed.), *Unequal Opportunities: Women's Employment in England 1800–1918* (Oxford: Blackwell, 1986), p. 158.

[69] John Chambers, quoted in William Carew Hazlitt, *The Lambs: Their Lives, Their Friends, Their Correspondence* (London: Elkin Mathews, 1897), pp. 39–40.

typical of the paradoxical stance of late eighteenth-century plebeian culture. E. P. Thompson describes what he terms as the *'rebellious* traditional culture' common to the eighteenth-century mob as one in which the workers resisted, in the name of the old paternalistic system of deference and reciprocal obligation, the economic innovations and rationalizations increasingly imposed upon them by their rulers and employers.[70] Traditional symbolic forms of protest, such as the burning of effigies, street riot, and anonymous pamphleteering, were instigated with the aim of recalling the gentry to those neglected paternalistic responsibilities rapidly losing sway as the industrial revolution, with its characteristic contractual rather than familial ties, advanced. The old order may have limited the freedom and autonomy of the worker, tied as he still was in a near feudal relation to his master, but it also provided a close system of protection. The loss of the old vertical ties of allegiance between the master and his man, at a time before new horizontal class loyalties had yet been established, imperilled plebeian security. Their protest found such forceful expression that according to Thompson it succeeded in securing 'a partial arrest of the work-discipline of early industrialism' until the close of the century.[71] In the 1790s, however, the pressures of industrial growth, allied with the repressive measures instigated against mob activity as a consequence of the fears aroused by the Gordon riots and the French Revolution, finally quelled the opposition and snapped the old relationships of reciprocity. But for those in the Lambs' position, indoctrinated from birth with a conviction of the benefits of paternalistic patronage, the sudden loss in early adulthood of that system of protection resulted in a yearning for the old order which could not easily be foregone for the ambiguous freedoms of the new world. Charles's nostalgic juxtaposition of his father and Salt's relationship with that of Lear and the faithful Kent, explored in the first chapter, bears close comparison to that harkening back towards the securer familial ties of the feudal traditions common to much eighteenth-century plebeian protest.[72] And his anarchic behaviours, his bouts of drunkenness and capricious floutings

---

[70] See E. P. Thompson, 'Eighteenth-Century English Society: Class Struggle without Class?' *Social History*, 3. (1978), 133–65.
[71] Ibid., 165.   [72] Ibid., 136–7.

of authority, also bear connection with the symbolic expressions of social discontent characteristic of the unruly mob of eighteenth-century society.

Nowhere is this strain of rebellious traditionalism more marked than in Charles's protests concerning the new time discipline. His employers at the East India House appear to have been amongst the first to do away with the long-established custom of honouring sundry saints' days throughout the year with a holiday or half-holiday. In May 1817 the company, in a bid to save money, abolished all calendar holidays, retaining only Christmas Day, Good Friday, and general fast and thanksgiving days; even those days were only to be kept free if the amount of work to be done was not unduly heavy.[73] The number of working hours the company gained by such measures may be assessed by the fact that in Christ's Hospital where, during Charles's time, all calendar holidays were kept religiously, thirty-nine days of the year, in addition to the Christmas, Easter, and summer vacations, were whole day leaves in honour of saints' anniversaries, and those of the royal family.[74] Charles deplored the loss of these traditional relaxations; as he wrote to Chambers in 1817, 'The Committee has formally abolish'd all holydays whatsoever—for which may the Devil, who keeps no holydays, have them in his eternal burning workshop.'[75] According to the propagators of the new time ethic, it was idle hands rather than industrious ones which were the peculiar property of the devil: 'see that you walk circumspectly,' preached Wesley, 'buying up every fleeting moment out of the hands of sin and Satan'.[76] The old saints' days, with their fairs and other plebeian festivities, were seen as particularly obstructive to the establishment of the radical changes in temporal consciousness associated with the work-discipline of industrialization.[77] But Charles reverses the new orthodoxy, seeing in the mechanization of human time a satanic influence. Half whimsically, half seriously, a letter sent to William and Dorothy Wordsworth exclaims

[73] See the editor's notes, *Letters*, ed. Marrs, iii. 248.
[74] Lucas, *The Life of Charles Lamb*, 2 vols. (London: Methuen, 1905), i. 47–8.
[75] *Letters*, ed. Marrs, iii. 248.
[76] Quoted in Thompson, 'Time, Work–Discipline and Industrial Capitalism', p. 62.
[77] See ibid., 53, and Hearn, *Domination, Legitimation and Resistance*, pp. 76–7.

Hang Work! . . . I am sure that Indolence indefeazible Indolence is the true state of man, & business the invention of the Old Teazer who persuaded Adam's Master to give him an apron & set him a houghing—. Pen & Ink & Clerks, & desks were the refinements of this old torturer a thousand years after under pretence of Commerce allying distant shores, promoting & diffusing knowledge, good &c.[78]

The association of work, and particularly of the East India Company, with the hosts of Satan strikes a recurring note throughout his correspondence. An 1805 letter, cut short by the demands of his employment, ends 'I come I come—, Don't drag me so hard by the hair of my head Genius of British India! I know my hour is come, Faustus must give up his soul, O Lucifer, O Mephostophelies!'[79] In 1818, the further curtailment of the East India clerks' short Saturdays exacerbated his anger against his employers, and increased the seriousness of his tone: 'by a decree past this week, they have abridged us of the immemorially-observed custom of going at one o'clock of a Saturday, the little shadow of a holiday left to us. Blast them. I speak it soberly.'[80]

  In his published works as well as his private correspondence he wages an attack upon the prevailing dissociation of leisure from godliness. In the Elia essays, 'The Superannuated Man', for example, laments the loss during his working years of the 'abundant play-time, and the frequently-intervening vacations of school days', for which he finds small recompense in the shuttered gloom of a city Sunday, the only assured holiday left to him. And a sonnet Charles published in 1819 reads:

Who first invented work, and bound the free
And holyday-rejoicing spirit down
To the ever-haunting importunity
Of business in the green fields, and the town—
To plough, loom, anvil, spade—and oh! most sad,
To that dry drudgery at the desk's dead wood?
Who but the Being unblest, alien from good,
Sabbathless Satan! . . .

    . . .
For wrath divine hath made him like a wheel—
In that red realm from which are no returnings;

[78] *Letters*, ed. Marrs, ii. 177.   [79] Ibid., iii. 220.
[80] *Letters*, ed. Lucas, ii. 228.

Where toiling, and turmoiling, ever and aye
He, and his thoughts, keep pensive working-day. (v. 55-6).

Again, the tone is frivolous, easily dismissed; the sonnet makes
light of its own distress but its very playfulness is part of its
message. The repetitive rotation of mechanical tasks and the
Sisyphean control they exert over their human operators are
seen, as in Blake's 'dark Satanic mills', as ungodly wheels of
torture. In 1820, in direct contradiction of the new morality
which would condemn the 'silent murderer, Sloth',[81] a second
sonnet praises 'divine Leisure' of which 'such foul lies are
spoke':

> They talk of time, and of time's galling yoke,
> That like a mill-stone on man's mind doth press,
> Which only works and business can redress . . .
> But might I, fed with silent meditation,
> Assoiled live from that fiend Occupation . . .
> I'd drink of time's rich cup, and never surfeit (v. 56).

Time is seen here not as a burden to be shed nor as a
commodity to be used but as a space in which to contemplate
the richness of living. Given the moral climate of his times such
lines suggest the thoroughness and consistency of Charles's
refusal to accept the ethos of work-discipline and its religiously
endorsed rationalizations; he twists his way out of the ideological
grip of the prevailing orthodoxy even though forced to live it in
practice.

But in his teens and early twenties, when he first started to
work for the East India Company, Charles had not yet
developed that degree of sardonic resistance to the conditions
of his employment evinced in his later writings and correspondence. The ideological pressures of his upbringing and
education would have made it difficult for him to withstand the
temptation to 'bend under the yoke' at best, even had his
profession not been one peculiarly resistant to any incipient
seeds of rebellion. Comparative studies of the ideological
position of clerical workers as opposed to other skilled and
unskilled workers demonstrate the nature of their employment

---

[81] Hannah More, 'Early Rising', *Works*, 7 vols. (London, 1830), ii. 42: 'Thou
silent murderer, Sloth, No more | My mind imprison'd keep'; quoted
Thompson, 'Time, Work-Discipline and Industrial Capitalism', p. 63.

to be such that to resist the required process of identification with the organizational system in which they were employed was particularly difficult. Not required in their work to exercise any craft or activity apart from those which promoted the smooth running of the system and the maintenance of its hierarchies, they could not avoid identifying with that system if they were to continue in their employment with any degree of satisfaction. To change from a collusive position in relation to his employers to one of opposition would have involved the nineteenth-century clerk in a far greater transformation of social consciousness than any equivalent change among other categories of workers.[82] Yet, if Charles did not at first outwardly rebel, it is clear from his later recollections of this early period that he felt very acutely the difference between his position and future prospects and those of his school friends who, like Coleridge and the le Grice brothers, continued with their education and went on to the universities. In the winter of 1795–6, at the age of 20, he endured a brief, and unrepeated, psychotic episode, and spent six weeks in an asylum; his biographers tend to locate the cause of his temporary derangement in an unsuccessful adolescent courtship, but the basic conditions of his working existence, and the financial necessity for its continuance, must have given him at this point cause for such complete hopelessness that it may well have had a more significant part to play in the stresses which led to his breakdown.

When insane, Charles apparently suffered from the delusion that he was the fictional character Young Norval, hero of a popular play of the period, John Home's *Douglas*. Norval, actually of royal blood but reared as a shepherd, is plagued with ambitions and yearnings beyond his circumscribed station, and spends much of the play lamenting his position:

> Once on the cold, and winter shaded side
> Of a bleak hill, mischance had rooted me,
> Never to thrive, child of another soil.[83]

---

[82] See Howard H. Davis, *Beyond Class Images: Explorations in the Structure of Social Consciousness* (London: Croom Helm, 1979), p. 173.
[83] John Home, *Douglas: A Tragedy* (London: A. Millar, 1757), p. 59. When restored to his rightful station, Norval is known as Douglas.

The disparity between his surroundings and what he feels to be
his nobler true destiny prevents him from developing any idea
of himself by which to live:

> Clouded and hid, a stranger to myself,
> In low and poor obscurity I liv'd.[84]

Charles's identification with Norval in his insanity would
appear to indicate on his part a similar bafflement, and a similar
sense of the impossibility in his daily situation at this time of
finding any satisfactory goals for his ambitions, or of expression
for his preoccupations. The experience of work for both Charles
and Mary was such that it increased their ambivalence with
regard to the power structures which dominated their lives.
While it further inculcated in them the necessity for deference
and a subordinate attitude, it also at the same time provided
them with harsh experiential lessons in the arbitrary injustices
of the differential rank and gender role systems in which they
were reared. Their subversive opposition, though veiled and
often contradictory in its expression, tellingly emerges in their
correspondence and in the semi-autobiographical writings
which deal with their working lives. As he grew older, Charles
did succeed both in his personal behaviour and in his writings
in giving indirect expression to his frustrations, but her more
limiting female role made it more difficult for Mary to break
through the imposed silence. Their rebellion remained emotional
rather than conceptually coherent, but both seem to have early
evolved an understanding of their experience which was in
opposition to the conventions of their time. Mary's essay 'On
Needle-Work' voices the protest of women prevented from
using their time and energies to acquire self-respect and
independence, while Charles's insistence upon the iniquities of
work-discipline and of the new time-consciousness questions
nineteenth-century masculine identity formations. Their writings,
taken together, provide an illumination of the dehumanizing
consequences of the time ethic of industrialization for both men
and women; while it rendered women's time valueless and

---

[84] Ibid., 64. Charles's poem 'The Tomb of Douglas' (1796), in which Douglas
is lamented as one who 'died without his fame' (v. 10), further exemplifies his
obsession with the character.

insignificant, it reduced the working man's time to mechanized labour regulated by the clock rather than the task.

In the early autumn of 1796, however, the Lambs' lives were darkened by a traumatic event, which relegated their work experience to the background of their lives, and, indeed, brought Mary's laborious career as a needlewoman to an abrupt close. Like her brother, Mary too, before 1796, had suffered from at least one mental breakdown, but now the accumulated tensions of the family situation in this most impoverished period of their existence led to an episode of manic violence which was to have long-term consequences for their sibling relationship, and for the patterns of their lives and writings as a whole. The next two chapters of this book explore the nature and consequences of this event, and the part it was to play in the Lambs' atypical response to the social formation of gender roles.

3

'We are in a manner marked'

I

On 22 September 1796 Mary Lamb, in a sudden outbreak of violent mania, brought about the death of her mother. According to a newspaper report of the incident, while preparing a meal that day,

the young lady seized a case knife laying [sic] on the table, and in a menacing manner pursued a little girl, her apprentice, round the room; on the eager calls of her helpless infirm mother to forbear, she renounced her first object, and with loud shrieks approached her parent.

The child by her cries quickly brought up the landlord of the house, but too late—the dreadful scene presented to him the mother lifeless, pierced to the heart, on a chair, her daughter yet wildly standing over her with the fatal knife.

Before concluding its account of the inquest with the Jury's verdict 'Lunacy', the report adds:

As her carriage towards her mother was ever affectionate in the extreme, it is believed that to the increased attentiveness, which her parents' infirmities called for by day and night, is to be attributed the present insanity of this ill-fated young woman.[1]

Mary's devotion to her mother, and the diligence with which she was nursing her in the months before her death, are amply testified to in Charles's letters. In June 1796 he refuses on Mary's behalf an invitation to visit Coleridge in the Lake District, explaining that 'My mother is grown so entirely helpless (not having any use of her limbs) that Mary is necessarily confined from ever sleeping out, she being her bed fellow.'[2] Her daily

---

[1] *Morning Chronicle* (22 Sept. 1796).   [2] *Letters*, ed. Marrs, i. 34.

and nightly attendance on her mother during this period seems to have formed the culmination of a lifelong affectionate care, which, according to her brother at least, was not fully reciprocated. Describing their upbringing in a letter written to Coleridge after the mother's death, Charles records that Elizabeth Lamb had very little understanding of her daughter's character and could never accept her love: 'Poor Mary, my mother . . . in opinion, in feeling, & sentiment, and disposition, bore so distant a resemblance to her daughter, that she never understood her right. Never could believe how much *she* loved her.' But Mary continued to behave with devoted care towards her mother, for all the coldness with which her affection was met; Charles adds in his letter that

every act of duty & of love she could pay, every kindness (& I speak true, when I say to the hurting of her health, & most probably in great part to the derangement of her senses) thro' a long course of infirmities & sickness, she could shew her, she ever did.[3]

His letter, written but a few weeks after his mother's death, is testimony to the strength of a sibling loyalty which not even the slaughter of the mother by the sister's hand could shake. Charles identified with his sister in the family tragedy, and shared with her the incommensurable burden of the matricidal act. An affliction of such mythic proportions could not but influence every aspect of their lives and writings, and its effects were exacerbated by the periodic return of Mary's madness, visitations which beset them both in a manner comparable to the vengeful onslaughts of the Furies upon that other pair of siblings marked by an act of matricide, Electra and Orestes.

   In these two middle chapters of my book, I shall be exploring the implications of Mary's act of matricide, and examining the part madness played in the Lambs' lives. During the first years of the nineteenth century, significant changes took place in the concept of madness and in the treatment afforded to the mad; this chapter explores the consequences for Mary and her brother of the label of 'lunatic'. The fourth chapter is concerned with the more difficult questions of Mary's relation with her mother, and of the impact the matricide had upon Charles and Mary's understanding of gender relations.

[3] *Letters*, ed. Marrs, i. 52.

II

In 1796, when Charles Lamb spent six weeks in a Hoxton madhouse, he became one of the four hundred or so a year on average admitted to private asylums in Britain during the last years of the eighteenth century: in 1813, however, Hoxton House, the institution in which it is likely he was confined, in itself alone housed 486 inmates.[4] These figures suggest the great increase in the numbers of people incarcerated for madness during the years bridging the eighteenth and nineteenth centuries, an increase which was to continue as the nineteenth century advanced. Whereas in the mid-eighteenth century the vast majority of the insane were still living at large in the community, by the mid-nineteenth century they found themselves confined in large numbers within a state-supported asylum system.[5] The causes of this unprecedented change in the social management of madness have recently occasioned much historical debate. Michel Foucault, in his seminal study *Madness and Civilization*, argues that it was the new imperatives of industrial labour which lay behind the change in the treatment of the insane; within the capitalist economy the incapacity to work became a sin to be punished by social excommunication.[6] His theories have recently been criticized as 'too schematic and doctrinaire',[7] but at least one other British social historian of madness has largely endorsed his findings. Andrew Scull's *Museums of Madness* similarly argues that

the rise of a segregative response to madness . . . can . . . be asserted to lie in the effects of the advent of a mature capitalist market economy and the associated ever more thorough-going commercialization of existence.[8]

[4] Roy Porter, *Mind-Forg'd Manacles: A History of Madness in England from the Restoration to the Regency* (London: Athlone Press, 1987), p. 8; and William Ll. Parry-Jones, *The Trade in Lunacy: A Study of Private Madhouses in England in the Eighteenth and Nineteenth Centuries* (London: Routledge & Kegan Paul, 1972), p. 43.

[5] Andrew T. Scull, *Museums of Madness: The Social Organization of Insanity in Nineteenth-Century England* (London: Allen Lane, 1979), pp. 13–14.

[6] Michel Foucault, *Madness and Civilization: A History of Insanity in the Age of Reason* (London: Tavistock, 1967), pp. 46 and 57.

[7] Porter, *Mind-Forg'd Manacles*, p. 162.

[8] Scull, *Museums of Madness*, p. 30.

According to Scull, the late eighteenth-century custom of including the mad within a general category of the idle and unemployed proved impossible to reconcile with the new disciplinarian uses to which the early nineteenth-century workhouse was fitted, in an attempt to maximize the potential work-force. Neither threats nor punishments could coerce the mad into accepting the rigours of the new work ethos; their recalcitrant presence in the workhouse constituted a distraction to the disciplining of those considered to be unemployed merely through idleness or disinclination, and they were therefore increasingly confined separately. As the old familial, paternalistic patterns of social control changed with the onset of the cash nexus, and the more centralized processes of state authority under capitalism gathered force, so control of the mad became the province of a systematized bureaucracy empowered by a new breed of specialist 'mad-doctors' who could authorize their incarceration in the increasing numbers of state-controlled or subsidized institutions.[9] Scull's analysis relates mainly to the treatment afforded to the pauper lunatic, but Foucault also suggests that the development of industrial time-discipline and the market economy could provoke a destabilizing effect upon the sanity of members of the upper and middle ranks as well, alienating them from the cycle of the seasons, and establishing 'the absolute exteriority of other people and of money, in the irreversible interiority of passion and unfulfilled desire'.[10] Charles's own confinement, as I suggested in the last chapter, may be interpreted as in part the consequence of the changes in labour relations in process during his time; his breakdown would appear to have been exacerbated by the terms of his employment at the East India House, which cut him off not only from the more cultural milieu of his Christ's Hospital days but also from those personal ties and allegiances with the 'masters' which he saw as alleviating and humanizing the labours of his father. But whatever the causes of the change in the numbers confined as mad, there can be no doubt as to its manifest reality in Britain: between 1807 and 1844 not only were the number of private licensed houses for the mad trebled, from 45 to 139, but parliamentary acts encouraged, in 1807, and enforced, in 1845,

[9] Scull, *Museums of Madness*, p. 30–54.
[10] Foucault, *Madness and Civilization*, p. 214.

the building of county asylums to house and if possible 'cure' the poorer lunatic.[11]

During the last decades of the eighteenth century, however, these changes were yet to come; an older, more erratic, but effectively more humane system was still largely in operation. Owing to a fortunate combination of her brother's concern and the timing of her act of matricide, Mary Lamb was spared the worst possible consequences of her own psychosis.[12] Once the inquest on her mother had established the cause of death as 'Lunacy', she was not required to face the ordeal of any further trial for murder. Legal ruling as to the treatment of insane offenders could still in 1796 function with a leniency surprising in a period during which the number of capital crimes exceeded two hundred, and in which children could be hanged for stealing forty shillings' worth of goods.[13] 'Lunacy', which in legal terminology referred specifically to temporary mental disorder,[14] was still accepted in law as a 'visitation of God' during which the capacity to judge between right and wrong was lost.[15] Recorded cases illustrate the comparative ease with which a plea of lunacy could result in acquittal; in 1784, for example, William Waller was acquitted on the plea of insanity for the murder of his wife, and a Miss Broadric, who murdered her lover in 1795, was found not guilty on grounds of lunacy, though evidence of insanity in her case seems to have been slender.[16] Once deemed insane, offenders were either consigned, with or without formal arraignment, to a hospital such as Bethlem, or, if sufficient surety could be given that they would be taken care of as potentially dangerous for the rest of their lives, they were restored to the protection of their families and friends.

---

[11] Scull, *Museums of Madness*, pp. 50, 60 and 113.

[12] Porter, *Mind-Forg'd Manacles*, p. 11, points out that the same clemency was not extended half a century later to the painter Richard Dadd, who was confined for over forty years for the killing of his father in a fit of insanity in 1843, and who died in Broadmoor.

[13] Nigel Walker, *Crime and Insanity in England, The Historical Perspective* (Edinburgh: Edinburgh Univ. Press, 1968), p. 52

[14] Ibid., 37: physicians distinguished the ' "interpolated" dementia of "lunacy", with its lucid intervals, from the "permanent", fixed dementia of "phrenesis or madness" '.

[15] Ibid., 56.   [16] Ibid., 64.

This second alternative, proffered in Mary's case, was gratefully accepted by Charles, who thus pledged himself to take care of his sister for the rest of her life, much to the disapproval of their older brother who thought it wiser to leave Mary to her fate in Bethlem.[17] One of the Lambs' twentieth-century biographers has suggested that the legal leniency afforded to Mary may have been the consequence of the Lamb family's early association with the Temple: both Samuel Salt and their grandmother's employer William Plumer are said to have been friends, as well as Whig colleagues, of the then Home Secretary, the Duke of Portland, and it is suggested that this influence operated in Mary's favour.[18] Recent historical studies in criminology, however, suggest that such humane proposals in the case of defendants suffering from periodic insanity were common enough in the 1780s and 1790s.[19] But by 1800, owing to the public outcry over the acquittal of a lunatic after his attempted murder of George III, a parliamentary act had been passed enforcing the detention of the criminally insane in 'strict custody' in a goal or asylum 'until His Majesty's pleasure be known'.[20] From this date on, given her past record and a clause in the 1800 Act which allowed it to function retrospectively, any action of Mary's which drew renewed public attention to her case could have had very serious consequences.

As it was, though Mary Lamb escaped the worst possible outcome of her act of matricide, for both herself and her brother its psychological effects must have been profound, particularly upon their perception of themselves and their relation to their society. The popular eighteenth-century belief was that madness was a hereditary disorder:[21] lunacy in close relatives was often cited as evidence in the defence of those pleading insanity in criminal cases.[22] Charles's period of hospitalization for madness in 1795 seems to have been mentioned in Mary's defence during the inquest on her mother, along with an account of an earlier attack which Mary had herself suffered in 1794, during

[17] See Charles's letter to Coleridge, 3 Oct. 1796, *Letters*, ed. Marrs, i. 49.
[18] Katharine Anthony, *The Lambs: A Study of Pre-Victorian England* (London: Hammond, Hammond & Co., 1948), pp. 48–9.
[19] Walker, *Crime and Insanity in England*, i. 42.   [20] Ibid., 78 and 224.
[21] See Joan Busfield, *Managing Madness: Changing Ideas and Practice* (London: Hutchinson, 1986), p. 214.
[22] Walker, *Crime and Insanity in England*, i. 59, 61, and 276.

which she was nursed at home.[23] Thomas Talfourd, Charles's first biographer, in his *Final Memorials of Charles Lamb* (1840) which first disclosed the full details of Mary's history, states that there was a strain of hereditary madness in the father's side of the family, though he gives no detail of its occurrence, and John Lamb himself seems to have escaped the illness.[24] In 1794 Charles's two-year adolescent courtship of a young Hertford-shire woman, Ann Simmons, was apparently terminated by his maternal grandmother on the grounds that the Lamb family's 'bad blood' rendered him unsuitable for matrimony.[25] After 1796, Charles's close identification with his sister led him to see them both as 'marked' by madness and matricide, and equally the object of curiosity and scandal. Certain passages in his letters indicate that this was no persecutory delusion, but that they were both frequently regarded with suspicion by neighbours who came to know Mary's history. In May 1800 he tells Coleridge that it is not 'the least of our Evils, that her case & all our story is so well known around us. We are in a manner *marked*'.[26] That month saw the first of their many subsequent household moves; leaving their lodgings in Pentonville they moved back to the City, because, as Charles explained to another correspondent,

'It is a great object to me to live in town, where we shall be much more *private*; and to quit a house & a neighborhood where poor Mary's disorder, so frequently recurring, has made us a sort of marked people. We can be no where private except in the midst of London.[27]

An awareness of the difficulties experienced by those marked out for social ostracism and scapegoating frequently finds expression in his post-1796 writings, often in bizarre forms. In his 1810 essay 'On the Inconveniences Resulting from being Hanged', a victim of the gallows, repealed at the last moment

---

[23] See the account of the inquest in *Morning Chronicle* (26 Sept. 1796), transcribed in *Letters*, ed. Marrs, i. 45.

[24] Thomas Noon Talfourd, *Final Memorials of Charles Lamb; Consisting Chiefly of his Letters not before Published, with Sketches of some of his Companions*, 2 vols. (London: Moxon, 1848), Bryan Waller Procter i. 2; ['Barry Cornwall'], *Charles Lamb: A Memoir* (London: Edward Moxon, 1866), pp. 6 and 28.

[25] Lucas, *The Life of Charles Lamb*, 2 vols. (London: Methuen, 1905), i. 81.

[26] *Letters*, ed. Marrs, i. 202.

[27] Ibid., 207.

and bearing the mark of the rope about his neck as a permanent souvenir of the occasion, explains, in nearly the same words as Charles used in his letters, that he chose to reside in the metropolis 'as the place where wounded honour (I had been told) could lurk with the least danger of exciting enquiry, and stigmatised innocence had the best chance of hiding her disgrace in a crowd' (i. 57). 'But alas!' he continues, 'the secret was soon blazoned about', and his relentless persecution by popular opinion is continued. The same fate is bemoaned by another character, called Pendulous, in Charles's farce *The Pawnbroker's Daughter*, who is similarly marked with the hangman's noose and 'stigmatized by the world' (v. 226). The concern with the plight of the socially ostracized outsider, manifest in these, and other, writings, no doubt owes its obsessive quality to Charles and Mary's own experience of victimization.[28]

The regular and frequent return of Mary's periods of insanity exacerbated their difficulties. Less than a week after the death of her mother she was restored to sanity, and was eventually released from the Islington private asylum, to which she had initially been sent, in April 1797; but in the winter of that year she suffered another attack and had to return to the Islington house. This marked the onset of a regular pattern of illness; hardly a year went by for the rest of her life in which she did not have to be nursed, either at home under the care of a hired nurse, if the attack was not too severe, or in private institutions. Propaganda aimed at accomplishing the segregation of the mad in the early nineteenth century must have exacerbated her own and her brother's anxieties concerning the wisdom of their mutual wish to keep her out of madhouses as much as possible. A characteristic warning issued by one private asylum in 1806 denounces the practice of nursing lunatics at home 'not only on account of the distress and confusion they there produce, but because there circumstances that excite a maniacal paroxysm

---

[28] For a further account of the figure of the 'marked' outsider in Charles Lamb's writings, see my essay ' "We are in a manner marked": Images of Damnation in Charles Lamb's Writings', *Charles Lamb Bulletin*, 5 (1981), 1–10; and Gerald Monsman, *Confessions of a Prosaic Dreamer: Charles Lamb's Art of Autobiography* (Durham, NC: Duke Univ. Press, 1984), pp. 22–7.

frequently exist'.[29] If the new breed of mad-doctors were to be believed, the generous and self-sacrificing instinct of those who chose to care for the insane at home could in itself have disastrous consequences for the afflicted.

Whatever the possible dangers to her sanity Mary risked through her freedom, her treatment on those occasions when she was institutionalized must often have been far more damaging to her self-respect. At the beginning of the nineteenth century, the mad were still largely seen either as inhuman monsters, beyond any treatment except that of physical restriction in chains, cages, and strait-jackets, or as people suffering from a physical disorder, to be treated by the application of leeches, cupping, and other such strenuous purges intended to drain away the tainted physical substances.[30] To induce fear in the lunatic through violent physical treatment was regarded as potentially curative: one mad-doctor writing in 1784 rationalizes this common practice with the explanation that 'fear, being a passion that diminishes excitment, may therefore be opposed to the excess of it; and particularly to the angry and irascible excitment of maniacs'.[31] A lunatic was regarded with curiosity as a freak, beyond the pale of humane concern; as late as 1815 Bethlem Hospital still gained a substantial amount of its income from the practice of exhibiting lunatics to the general public for a penny, every Sunday.[32] The mad were also considered to be impervious to the physical conditions of their confinement, and were accordingly often housed in great discomfort. For all her brother's concern, Mary could not have entirely escaped these humiliations. A recent investigation of asylum records has shown, for example, that she was once, in 1831, an inmate of Brooke House asylum in Clapton.[33] An official report of Brooke House in 1841 found it dilapidated and seriously deficient in amenities for its patients: according to the report, the female

[29] 'Brislington House: An Asylum for Lunatics' (unpub.: 1806), p. 1, quoted in Scull, *Museums of Madness*, p. 94.
[30] Parry-Jones, *The Trade in Lunacy*, p. 245.
[31] William Cullen, *First Lines in the Practice of Physics* (4th edn., London, 1784), quoted Busfield, *Managing Madness*, p. 211.
[32] Foucault, *Madness and Civilization*, p. 68.
[33] Leslie Joan Friedman, 'Mary Lamb: Sister, Seamstress, Murderer, Writer', Ph.D. thesis (Stanford, Calif., 1976), p. 388.

quarters in particular 'were most wretchedly furnished with old-fashioned lattice windows, letting the wind in so as to defy all attempts at keeping them warm'.[34]

Mary's personal experience of the manner in which the institutionalized insane were treated during the period must also have increased what anxieties she had concerning her economic and social position. The segregation of mental patients into 'private' and 'pauper' groupings was rigidly enforced, 'pauper' patients being categorized as those who received some or all of the cost of their treatment from the parish authorities. Not only were the conditions for lower-class inmates much worse than for private patients, but they were also, apparently, much more readily certified as insane, and much more likely, statistically, to be retained in the asylums as incurables.[35] The hierarchies of social rank held sway under asylum conditions as inexorably as they did in the rest of British society. A Bethlem Hospital physician, Thomas Monro, giving evidence during an 1815 parliamentary investigation into the treatment of lunatics, when asked about the use of chains and fetters in restraining the insane, reassured his audience that 'they are fit only for pauper Lunatics; if a gentleman was put into irons, he would not like it . . . it is a thing so totally abhorrent to my feelings that I never considered to put a gentleman into irons'.[36] Rationalizations were put forward to account for the discrepancy in the treatment of richer and poorer patients. Francis Willis, for example, in his *Treatise on Mental Derangement* (1823), professes himself as of the opinion that 'the man of fortune . . . will require a greater nicety in our moral treatment of him than the poor and illiterate; for he that serves, will not feel so acutely, even under his derangement, as he that is served'.[37] The vulnerability of Mary Lamb's status lay in the fact that in 1796 her family's social position placed her amongst the ranks of those who 'served' rather than 'were served'. It was only Charles's decision to spare a great part of

---

[34] R. Paternoster, *The Madhouse System* (London: 1841), quoted Parry-Jones, *The Trade in Lunacy*, p. 100.   [35] See Scull, *Museums of Madness*, p. 245.
[36] Quoted Busfield, *Managing Madness*, p. 218.
[37] Francis Willis, 'A Treatise on Mental Derangement' (1823), pp. 157–8, quoted Parry-Jones, *The Trade in Lunacy*, p. 181.

his meagre earnings for Mary's maintenance in private care that saved her from the fate of a pauper lunatic. Given her act of matricide, it must be highly unlikely that had she been so categorized she would ever have been restored to anything resembling a free and self-respecting existence.

III

Although her private treatment probably protected her to some extent, Mary must also have been affected by shifting attitudes in the conceptualization of madness, and the changes in the treatment of the mad to which they gave rise. The eighteenth-century view of the mad as either afflicted by a visitation from God, or as physically sick, changed towards the close of the century into one in which the insane were considered not so much monsters as recalcitrant children, who needed to be re-taught, by persuasive means rather than overt coercion, how to function adequately as social members.[38] Innovative institutions, such as the York Retreat, established in 1792, successfully showed that the insane could respond satisfactorily to a system which inculcated self-restraint, rather than using external corporal bondage, through offering its patients greater freedom and esteem as a reward for greater self-control. A French visitor reporting on the Retreat in 1798 saw it as treating the insane

as children who have an overabundance of strength and make dangerous use of it. They must be given immediate punishments and rewards; whatever is remote has no effect on them. A new system of education must be applied, a new direction given to their ideas; they must first be subjugated, then encouraged, then applied to work, and this work made agreeable by attractive means.[39]

[38] See William F. Bynum, Jr., 'Rationales for Therapy in British Psychiatry 1780–1835', in Andrew Scull (ed.), *Madhouses, Mad-Doctors and Madmen: The Social History of Psychiatry in the Victorian Era* (London: Athlone Press, 1981), pp. 39–40; Parry-Jones, *The Trade in Lunacy*, pp. 170–1; Scull, *Museums of Madness*, p. 43. But see Porter, *Mind-Forg'd Manacles*, p. 277, for the argument that these changes in the management of madness took effect in fact long before the close of the eighteenth century, though it was not until the 1790s that the York Institute brought them to public attention.

[39] Charles-Gaspard de la Rive, in the *Bibliothèque Britannique* (1798), p. 30, quoted Foucault, *Madness and Civilization*, p. 252. For a full account of the York Retreat, see Scull, *Museums of Madness*, pp. 67–75.

According to this so-called 'moral treatment' the insane could be conditioned by careful supervision to fear all signs of lapses from conformity in their behaviour; Blake's internalized 'mind-forg'd manacles' rather than literal bonds now became the means recommended for their treatment. Although argued for as a humane and enlightened reform, which would correct the atrocities of the past, this development in the treatment of insanity also functioned as a more efficient means of social control of the insane than their earlier neglect, and thus accorded well with the aims of the new asylums to restore the mad to useful labour within an industrialized work-force. One nineteenth-century American observer of mental asylums suggested that 'moral management' owed its successes in Britain to the habit of ingrained obedience inculcated through the English class stratification system, which, as he saw it, 'clings to the inmate of the hospital, regulates his demeanour and exerts a restraining influence over his caprices and passions.'[40]

As recent feminist critics have pointed out, 'moral treatment' corresponds interestingly to the ideological methods by which women also as a group were persuaded into accepting, and internalizing, a restricted view of themselves during this period.[41] In the late eighteenth and early nineteenth centuries, a popular genre of conduct tracts, designed to inculcate in its readers appropriate morals and values for a developing bourgeois society, emphasized the importance of self-subordination and submissiveness for women. In 1799 the influential Hannah More, for example, in her book *Strictures on the Modern System of Female Education*, warns mothers of the necessity of impressing upon their daughters 'the benefits of restraint':

An early and habitual restraint is peculiarly important to the future character and happiness of women. They should when young be inured to contradiction. . . . It is a lesson with which the world will not fail to furnish them; and they will not practise it the worse for having

---

[40] Isaac Ray, 'Observations of the Principal Hospitals for the Insane in Great Britain, France, and Germany', *American Journal of Insanity*, 2 (1846), 347; quoted Elaine Showalter, *The Female Malady: Women, Madness and English Culture, 1830–1980* (London: Virago, 1987), p. 49.

[41] Ellen Dwyer, 'A Historical Perspective', in Cathy Spatz Widom (ed.), *Sex Roles and Psychopathology* (New York: Plenum Press, 1984), p. 25; Elaine Showalter, 'Victorian Women and Insanity', in Scull, *Madhouses, Mad-Doctors and Madmen*, p. 326.

learnt it the sooner. A judicious, unrelaxing . . . curb on their tempers and passions can alone ensure their peace and establish their principles.[42]

Just as the new asylums sought to instil in men conformity to the demands of a changing economy so also they endeavoured to inculcate in recalcitrant women an acceptance of the restrictions of the increasingly limiting female gender role. 'Moral management', with its strongly paternalistic and authoritarian ethos, functioned as a particularly effective form of social re-education for women, in that the submissive and self-doubting behaviour patterns it inculcated corresponded so closely with socially approved models for all female behaviour.[43] It would appear that this correlation was apparent to contemporary observers, for while it was generally considered a serious disadvantage for a man to be certified as insane, one physician, at least, suggested that it could qualify as part of the attractions of a marriageable woman. 'Humility', Thomas Bakewell wrote in his popular *The Domestic Guide in Cases of Insanity* (1805), 'is a quality which men wish for in a wife. This complaint [insanity] cannot so properly be said to teach humility, as to implant it in the very nature'.[44] The erosion of self-confidence implanted in the victim of moral management encouraged that docility considered desirable in an early nineteenth-century wife.

Mary's writings indicate that in her case, at any rate, the prohibition of self-assertion was very strongly internalized. In her letters she refers to herself generally as 'an useless creature', and to the periods she spent in asylums as her 'banishment' or punishment. 'I have lost all self confidence in my own actions', she writes to Sarah Stoddart in 1805, and continues: 'a perception of not being in a sane state perpetually haunts me. I am ashamed to confess this weakness to you, which as I am so sensible of I ought to strive to conquer'.[45] A close reading of her correspondence with Sarah conveys the impression of a mind under such severe self-restraint that it could allow itself very

---

[42] Hannah More, *Strictures on the Modern System of Female Education*, 2 vols. (London: T. Cadell & W. Davies, 1799), i. 142–3.

[43] Showalter, *The Female Malady*, p. 79.

[44] Thomas Bakewell, *The Domestic Guide in Cases of Insanity* (London: T. Allbutt, 1805), p. 54.

[45] *Letters*, ed. Marrs, iii. 60, and ii. 186.

little freedom, particularly when it came to expressing the merest hint of criticism, or what she interpreted as criticism, of her friends. One striking incident of this restraint, and of her anguish when she feared she had lost control of it, bears movingly upon her own experience as a mental patient. In offering advice with regard to the treatment of Sarah's mother, suffering from senile dementia, Mary, in a letter of November 1805, writes:

do not I conjure you let her unhappy malady afflict you too deeply—I speak from experience & from the opportunity I have had of much observation in such cases that insane people in the fancy's they take into their heads do not feel as one in a sane state of mind does under the real evil of poverty the perception of having done wrong or any such thing that runs in their heads.

Think as little as you can, & let your whole care be to be certain that she is treated with *tenderness*. I lay a stress upon this, because it is a thing of which people in her state are uncommonly susceptible, & which hardly any one is at all aware of, a hired nurse *never*, even though in all other respects they are a good kind of people. I do not think your own presence necessary unless she *takes to you very much* except for the purpose of seeing with your own eyes that she is very kindly treated.[46]

This would appear most compassionate and humane advice, from the point of view of both mother and daughter; even the hired nurse's unkindness is remembered with a forgiving parenthetical qualification. But 'the perception of having done wrong' in writing it was soon running in Mary's head. In her next letter she tells Sarah that she has been distressed ever since:

that which gives me most concern is the way in which I talked about your Mothers illness & which I have since feared you might construe into my having a doubt of your showing her proper attention without my impertinent interference. God knows nothing of this kind was ever in my thoughts, but I have entered very deeply into your affliction with regard to your Mother, & while I was writing, the many poor souls in the kind of desponding way she is in whom I have seen, came afresh into my mind, & all the mismanagement with which I have seen them treated was strong in my mind, & I wrote under a forcible impulse which I could not at that time resist, but I have fretted so much

[46] Ibid., ii. 184–5.

about it since, that I think it is the last time I will ever let my pen run away with me.[47]

Such an extreme sensitivity to the possibility of having her words construed as a critical attack by her audience, similarly evinced in many other episodes in her correspondence,[48] indicates the extent of Mary's concern to restrain her impulsive responses to her experience lest they should contain some tinge of anger or protest against others.

Contemporary records of Mary's habitual mode of behaviour also indicate the degree to which she felt compelled in her everyday relations with others to impose an unrelenting restraint upon herself: eyewitnesses to her behaviour testify to its extreme mildness and self-repression. Wordsworth, for example, in his elegy to Charles, describes his sister as 'the meek, | The self-restraining and the ever-kind'.[49] Charles's contemporary biographers all emphasized Mary's gentleness: P. G. Patmore testifies to her 'universal loving-kindness and toleration',[50] and Barry Cornwall recalls her habitual conciliatory placidity.[51] De Quincey, in his account of his first meeting with the Lambs, maintains that the manner in which Charles teased him for his idolatrous worship of Coleridge's poetry would have led to a quarrel between them had it not been for the 'winning goodness' of 'that Madonna-like lady', Mary, 'before which all resentment must have melted in a moment'.[52] Talfourd in his *Final Memorials* portrays Mary as one who was 'to a friend in any difficulty . . . the most comfortable of advisers, the wisest of consolers'. He adds to his own account Hazlitt's testimony to her good sense; Mary, alone of all her sex, becomes the exception that proves Hazlitt's misogynistic rule: 'Hazlitt used to say, that he never met with a woman who could

---

[47] Ibid., 185–6.

[48] See, e.g. Mary's anxiety concerning her letter of Aug. 1806 to the Wordsworths on Coleridge's marital difficulties: *Letters*, ed. Marrs, ii. 238.

[49] Wordsworth, 'Written after the Death of Charles Lamb', *The Poetical Works of William Wordsworth*, ed. Ernest de Selincourt and Helen Darbishire, 5 vols. (Oxford: Clarendon Press, 1940–9), iv. 275.

[50] P. G. Patmore, *My Friends and Acquaintance*, 3 vols. (London: Saunders & Otley, 1854), iii. 200.

[51] See 'Cornwall', *Charles Lamb*, p. 128.

[52] *The Collected Writings of De Quincey*, ed. David Masson 14 vols. (Edinburgh: Adam & Charles Black, 1889–90), iii. 35.

reason, and had met with one only thoroughly reasonable—the sole exception being Mary Lamb.'[53]

But when Talfourd goes on to disclose the darker side of Mary's existence, the ineffectuality of employing an internalized 'moral management' to check a manic-depressive psychosis becomes apparent. The repressive severity of the intended control may well have exacerbated rather than alleviated the symptoms of an attack. The impossible pressures involved in perpetual self-restraint were clearly signified in Mary's double life, as Talfourd describes it. Recording her response to Hazlitt's praises, he adds:

She did not wish, however, to be made an exception, to a general disparagement of her sex; for in all her thoughts and feelings she was most womanly—keeping, under even undue subordination, to her notion of a woman's province, intellect of rare excellence, which flashed out when the restraints of gentle habit and humble manner were withdrawn by the terrible force of disease. Though her conversation in sanity was never marked by smartness or repartee; seldom rising beyond that of a sensible quiet gentlewomanly appreciating and enjoying the talents of her friends, it was otherwise in her madness.

At such times, as he recalls,

her ramblings often sparkled with brilliant description and shattered beauty. She would fancy herself in the days of Queen Anne or George the First; and describe the brocaded dames and courtly manners, as though she had been bred among them, in the best style of the old comedy . . . the fragments were like the jewelled speeches of Congreve, only shaken from their setting.

It is surely significant that even in her madness Mary could not imagine herself as living freely in the nineteenth century but had to project herself back in her imagination to an earlier period of less strenuous gender-role restraint. Talfourd, for all his apparent sympathy with Mary, obviously endorses in his account the social requirement of unremitting self-subordination for women, and concludes his depiction with approbation of the strait-jacket of propriety with which Mary constrained herself when 'well'. He informs his readers that

[53] Talfourd, *Final Memorials*, ii. 227.

not for the purpose of exhibiting a curious phenomenon of mental aberration are the aspects of her insanity unveiled, but to illustrate the moral force of gentleness by which the faculties that thus sparkled when restraining wisdom was withdrawn, were subjected to its sway, in her periods of reason.[54]

His earlier partial recognition of the excessive constraint under which she lived is lost when he considers the effect of his account upon his audience, and 'undue subordination' becomes 'wisdom'.

Recent feminist criticism of nineteenth-century women writers has suggested that during that period a woman's attempt to contain the paradoxes of the gender-role model into which she was required to fit resulted in a psychological conflict which manifested itself in her writing in the frequent doubling of a virtuous and self-controlled heroine with a 'bad', insane *doppelgänger* character, Charlotte Brontë's *Jane Eyre* presenting the most striking example of this configuration.[55] In Mary's case, however, the frustrations involved in requiring the self to live selflessly were apparent not so much in her writing as, much more devastatingly, in her life, her 'thoroughly reasonable' self-restraint being interrupted virtually annually by an outburst of 'sparkling' madness. For all the restrictions and difficulties facing women choosing a writing profession in the nineteenth century, those who did succeed in the subversive act of wielding the pen appear to have found some relief from the narrow boundaries of the required female role through the act of writing. But Mary was prohibited from turning easily to this resource not only because of her sex but also because of her career as a mental patient: for the potentially insane, writing, along with imaginative activity generally, was discouraged in the nineteenth century as a dangerous malpractice, jeopardizing mental balance.[56] It may be that little could have been done to alleviate her condition even given the most liberal and humane of social contexts: modern psycho-medical research tends to

[54] Ibid., 227–9.
[55] See Sandra M. Gilbert and Susan Gubar, *The Madwoman in the Attic: The Woman Writer and the Nineteenth-Century Literary Imagination* (New Haven, Conn., and London: Yale Univ. Press, 1979), pp. 76–8.
[56] See Norman Dain, *Concepts of Insanity in the United States, 1789–1865* (New Brunswick, NJ and London: Rutgers Univ. Press, 1964), p. 19.

confirm the significance of genetic, inheritable factors in a manic-depressive disorder, although its onset in an individual genetically at risk is still largely attributed to psycho-social causes.[57] But the repressions inculcated in the roles of both women and the mad in the nineteenth century cannot but have exacerbated her sufferings, along with those of many other unknown victims, for whom her own case serves as representative.

[57] See David L. Dunner, 'Recent Genetic Studies of Bipolar and Unipolar Depression', in James C. Coyne (ed.), *Essential Papers on Depression* (New York: New York Univ. Press, 1986), pp. 449–58.

4

A Modern Electra

I

In a letter to Sara Hutchinson of 1815, describing the Cambridge colleges she had recently visited, Mary expresses a preference for 'the little gloomy ones', and adds 'I felt as if I could live and die in them and never wish to speak again.'[1] Silence, as a way of life, has a strong part to play in the image Mary left of herself, and in no area more markedly than that which concerns her relation with her mother. Nevertheless, in order to understand as far as possible the darkness at the heart of her life and that of her brother, the least communicative hint or sign which evades their mutual silence on this score requires investigation, with what guides the late twentieth century has at its disposal. The consciousness of herself, during her sane periods, as a matricide as well as a potential lunatic must have been a heavy burden for Mary. According to recent psychoanalytic investigations of matricide, its 'effects upon the personality of the murderer are always cataclysmic': few, if any, are 'able to retain even a relative integration of the personality under the stress of the act's genesis and fulfilment'.[2] The intensity and duration of Mary's prolonged spells of depression no doubt related to her awareness of her act of matricide, as well as to the virulence of her manic-depressive condition. According to her brother, it was but the strength of their mutual tie that kept her at times from suicide: in an 1805 letter to Dorothy Wordsworth, describing Mary's despairing condition during a particularly severe attack of her illness, Charles comments that 'she lives but for me'.[3] The difficulties involved in coming to terms with

[1] *Letters*, ed. Marrs, iii. 193.
[2] Robert M. Lindner, 'The Equivalents of Matricide', *Psychoanalytic Quarterly*, 17 (1948), p. 453.
[3] *Letters*, ed. Marrs, ii. 169.

matricide, and Mary's ambivalent internalized relation to her mother, constitute some of the issues investigated in this chapter.

II

Though Mary seldom referred to her mother in her writings, it is difficult not to discern in some of the prevailing patterns of her one fictional work *Mrs Leicester's School* an attempt at working through the pains of a neglected and misunderstood childhood. As we have seen, in the tale 'The Young Mahometan', Margaret Green, the child narrator, is grievously neglected by her mother, who, following the practice of her employer, has 'wholly discontinued talking' to her (iii. 308). During her lonely wanderings about the employer's mansion, 'in as perfect a solitude as Robinson Crusoe', Margaret discovers a hidden door leading to a 'very large library', a fictional incident which no doubt mirrors Mary's discovery of Salt's library in the Temple chambers in which she was reared;[4] from then on Margaret spends all her unattended hours in this secret garden of books. She comes across a volume propounding the doctrines of Mahometanism, and adopts the tenets of this new-found creed without question, only to become tortured by the conviction that her mother and the old proprietor are doomed by their ignorance of the true faith to lurid destruction in a 'bottomless gulf'. One night, in desperation, she wakes her mother and begs her to become a Mahometan. Her nervous anxiety, misunderstood by the mother who assumes that she is delirious and sends for medical help, is alleviated by the sympathetic doctor and his wife, who remove her from her solitary environment, encourage her to talk with them about her past isolation, take her to a bustling fairground, a 'cheerful sight' with its 'many happy faces assembled together', and generally affect a cure through sociable kindness (iii. 310). But, significantly, the mother has no part to play in this cure: not

---

[4] See the Elia essay 'Mackery End, in Hertfordshire', for Charles's description of how his sister was 'tumbled early, by accident or design, into a spacious closet of good old English reading, without much selection or prohibition, and browsed at will upon that fair and wholesome pasturage' (ii. 76).

only did her neglect bring about the daughter's destabilizing obsession, but when finally confronted with Margaret's distress, she saw in it but evidence of a crazed brain. In telling her tale to her new school fellows, Margaret warns them against over-indulging an active imagination, but attributes her own confusion very cogently to the neglect she suffered: 'It must have been because I was never spoken to at all, that I forgot what was right and what was wrong' (iii. 308).

Nevertheless, for all the indications such tales provide of Mary's experience of the damage caused by maternal neglect, the loving attitude which according to her brother she always demonstrated towards her own mother before September 1796 seems to have persisted with if anything increased intensity after the matricide. After her speedy recovery from the attack which had led to Elizabeth Lamb's death, Mary apparently found herself in a curiously serene state. According to the letter written to her brother a few days after the incident, from the Islington madhouse in which she was confined, she felt assured of their mother's forgiveness. 'I have no bad terrifying dreams,' Mary writes:

At midnight when I happen to awake, the nurse sleeping by the side of me, with the noise of the poor mad people around me, I have no fear. The spirit of my mother seems to descend, & smile upon me, & bid me live to enjoy the life & reason which the Almighty has given me—. I shall see her again in heaven; she will then understand me better, my Grandmother too will understand me better, & will then say no more as she used to Do, 'Polly, what are those poor crazy moyther'd brains of yours thinkg. of always?'[5]

Her precise recollection of the grandmother's wounding words indicates Mary's painful awareness of the manner in which she was actually seen by the maternal side of her family, but she builds up in opposition to it a beatified image of a loving and understanding mother. Talfourd, in his biographical study of the Lambs, records that Mary had similarly described to Charles Lloyd how her recovery had been precipitated by a profound conviction, 'as though she had seen the reconcilement in solemn vision', 'that her mother knew her entire innocence, and

---

[5] *Letters*, ed. Marrs, i. 52.

shed down blessings upon her'.[6] Although Mary and Charles rarely referred to their mother in their writings, it would appear from the few occasions in Mary's correspondence when she does reveal glimpses of her inner world that she retained throughout life as close a sense of her mother's idealized presence as she experienced in the Islington madhouse. In September 1803, seven years after Elizabeth Lamb's death, she refers in a letter to her friend Sarah Stoddart to 'my dear Mother (who though you do not know it, is always in my poor head and heart)',[7] and two years later she consoles Dorothy Wordsworth on the death of her brother John with an account from her own experience of how the lost object of affection is internalized. 'I wished to tell you,' Mary writes: 'that you would see every object with, & through your lost brother, & that that would at last become a real & everlasting source of comfort to you, I felt, & well knew from my own experience in sorrow.'[8] The regained image of the dead, she tells the Wordsworths, in a poem included in the letter, will become 'their hearts companion'. According to Talfourd, Mary's sense of redemption from the guilt of her mother's death was so strong that she 'never shrank from alluding to her' and 'spoke of her as though no fearful remembrance was associated with the image, so that some of her most intimate friends who knew of the disaster, believed that she had never become aware of her own share in its horrors'.[9]

Nevertheless, it is clear from other contemporary sources that a sudden reminder of her mother, or too intense a recollection of her, could give Mary extreme pain, and often precipitate one of the recurring attacks of her mania. The composition of the Wordsworth letter quoted above, and the emotions it must have aroused, seems to have brought about one attack;[10] an unexpected meeting with an old admirer of her mother's had earlier led directly to another serious breakdown. Coleridge, staying with

[6] Thomas Noon Talfourd, *Final Memorials of Charles Lamb; Consisting Chiefly of his Letters not before Published, with Sketches of some of his Companions*, 2 vols. (London: Moxon, 1848), ii. 225.

[7] *Letters*, ed. Marrs, ii. 124.   [8] Ibid., 166.

[9] Talfourd, *Final Memorials*, ii. 226.

[10] Mary entered an asylum at the beginning of June 1805, and her brother records that he noticed the onset of the attack a few weeks earlier: see *Letters*, ed. Marrs, ii. 169–70.

the Lambs in April 1803, was present when Mary met with 'a Mr. Babb, an old old Friend & Admirer of her Mother'. In a letter to his wife, he attributes to this encounter Mary's breakdown of the following day, which led to a serious illness, necessitating her abrupt removal to a Hoxton asylum.[11] What is more, Talfourd seems to have been mistaken, or insufficiently informed, in his notion that Mary referred easily to her mother. The orphaned girl Emma Isola, whom the Lambs adopted in 1823, afterwards recalled that during the whole period of her residence with them no mention was made of their mother. Entirely ignorant of the manner of Elizabeth Lamb's death, she once, apparently, drew their attention to this omission:

One night, Charles and Mary Lamb and herself were seated at table. The conversation turned on the elder Lamb, when Miss Isola asked why she never heard mention of the mother. Mary thereupon uttered a sharp, piercing cry, for which Charles playfully and laughingly rebuked her; but he made no allusion to the cause.[12]

The contradictory evidence would suggest that although Mary in her conscious mind had created a beatified image of the maternal figure, to which she clung with a strong resilience and lived with constantly, nevertheless a sudden reminder of the real, historical Elizabeth Lamb could be dangerous to her vulnerable equilibrium. It also suggests a high degree of ambivalence and confusion in Mary's relation with her mother, a confusion which seems to have had a central role to play in the development of her insanity. Perhaps because of the suspected genetic factor in manic-depression it has received less attention in psychoanalytic writing than schizophrenia or the neuroses, but the few attempts made to account for the condition all stress the causal significance of disillusionment and ambivalence with regard to an early object of the affections in cases of both mania and depression. Freud, in his paper 'Mourning and Melancholia', presents the depressive as one whose disappointment with a primary love object was experienced as too disruptive to be assimilated consciously. The resultant anger and grief were

---

[11] Coleridge, *Collected Letters*, ii. 941.
[12] Thomas Purnell, in the notes to his edition of *The Complete Correspondence and Works of Charles Lamb*, 4 vols. (London: Moxon, 1870), i. p. xxix, gives this record of an interview with Emma Moxon, née Isola.

internalized, according to Freud, and directed against the subject's own self, or a part of the self: the 'shadow' of the disappointing object 'fell upon the ego', as he put it.[13] In mania, this condition of depressive self-persecution finds sudden and uncontrolled release in a burst of pent-up energy and aggression.

Post-Freudian psychoanalytic theory has provided further endorsement of the significance of the mother–child dyad in manic-depressive cases; the British 'object relations' school, in particular, has devoted much of its work to an analysis of the early, pre-Oedipal, relation with the mother, before the Oedipal antagonisms related to the recognition of the father's role intervene. According to Melanie Klein, a difficulty in early infancy in integrating the various aspects of the primary nurturer, as they appear to the baby, lies at the root of the manic-depressive syndrome. A mother may appear lovable and good when she provides the food and warmth the baby needs, but appear bad and arouse feelings of hatred when the baby's desires are not met. In order to protect the 'good' aspects of the mother from the anger and hatred directed towards her 'bad' aspects, the two imagos are split apart from one another at an unconscious level, and do not undergo the process of integration necessary for stable development, in which ambivalent feelings can be recognized, and the two polarized aspects of the love object unified and internalized as a whole. Without such integration, the unconscious will continue to harbour sadistic hatred towards the 'bad' object, which may be uncontrollably activated during an assertive manic phase, while at the same time bearing a permanent sense of acute guilt, with its concomitant depression, in relation to the idealized 'good' object.[14] How much more devastating must the depressive reaction have been, and how much more impossible to achieve the desired integration, when the mind had to confront, as in Mary's case, not simply its sadistic impulse towards the love object but the full reality of the accomplished destruction.

Ironically, through killing Elizabeth Lamb, Mary enabled

---

[13] Sigmund Freud, 'Mourning and Melancholia' (1915), *Pelican Freud Library* ed. Angela Richards (Harmondsworth: Penguin, 1984), xi. 258.

[14] Melanie Klein, 'A Contribution to the Psychogenesis of Manic-Depressive States' (1935), in ead., *Love, Guilt and Reparation and Other Works 1921–1945* (London: Hogarth Press, 1975), pp. 262–89.

herself at one level to retain undamaged her idealization of a good mother, an idealization which she had laboured to preserve during her mother's lifetime, in the face of insufficient affectionate recompense. After Salt's death in 1792 much of the daughter's energies must have been consumed in the unremitting requirement not only to earn enough through the mantua-maker's trade to support the family, but also to attend, daily and nightly, to the nursing needs of the invalid mother and senile father. During this difficult period she also seems to have accepted without demur the fact that the older brother retained his favoured, privileged position within the family even though he did nothing to help in their financial support. Antagonistic responses against the mother seem to have been expressed by Charles rather than Mary at this time. In the poems he wrote after his mother's death, Charles, with what of course may well be an excess of self-condemnation resulting from his grief, describes himself as having been 'ofttimes' a 'wayward son' to his mother (v. 22). But Mary he presents as the harmonizing force within the family which sought to resolve such conflicts: she is seen as one

> whose sweet reproof
> And meekest wisdom in times past have smooth'd
> The unfilial harshness of my foolish speech,
> And made me loving to my parents old,
> '(Why is this so, ah God! why is this so?)'   (v. 23)

The last parenthetical exclamation, expressing as it does the brother's baffled misery when he recalls the full irony of his lament, manages to escape the imposition of silence Charles as well as Mary placed upon any reference in his writings to the manner of the mother's death.

In acting as the family mediator, and accommodating herself to paternal authority, Mary was fulfilling her society's accepted ideal of female virtue. The conduct tracts of her day stressed the need for women to accept a structure of external authorities, and emphasized that it was inherent in female nature to accomplish such an accommodation. Women were informed by their male advisers that since 'Nature has not given you that unlimited range in your choice which we enjoy, she has wisely and benevolently assigned to you a greater flexibility of taste on this subject.'[15] Thomas Gisborne in his influential *Enquiry into the Duties of the Female Sex* (1797) similarly pronounced that

Providence, designing from the beginning, that the manner of life to be adopted by women should in many respects ultimately depend, not so much on their own deliberate choice, as on the determination, or at least on the interest and convenience, of the parent, of the husband, or of some other near connection; has implanted in them a remarkable tendency to conform to the wishes and example of those for whom they feel a warmth of regard, and even of all those with whom they are in familiar habits of intercourse.[16]

Interestingly, twentieth-century psychoanalytic accounts of female as opposed to male development have suggested that the structure of a female child's relation to her parents in a conventional family situation might indeed make it more in keeping with women's psychological development generally, in contrast with that of men, to identify with and accept a number of different sources of authority rather than experience them as conflicting. In the light of his reading of the work of women psychoanalysts, Freud, in 1931, recognized the importance of the pre-Oedipal stage in female development, and the primary status of the girl's attachment to the mother who reared her;[17] subsequently, Nancy Chodorow has developed these suggestions, and shown how a girl's identification with her mother, being more formative and longer-lasting than that of a male child, is not relinquished when the father also becomes important. Rather, she 'retains her preoedipal tie to her mother . . . and builds oedipal attachments to both her mother and her father upon it'. The relationship with the father does not substitute for the earlier tie with the mother, but is internalized in addition to it.[18] Mary Poovey, in her critical study of

[15] Dr John Gregory, *A Father's Legacy to his Daughters* (London: W. Strahan & T. Cadell, 1774), p. 82.

[16] Thomas Gisborne, *An Enquiry into the Duties of the Female Sex* (London: T. Cadell & W. Davies, 1799), pp. 122–3, quoted Mary Poovey, *The Proper Lady and the Woman Writer: Ideology as Style in the Works of Mary Wollstonecraft, Mary Shelley, and Jane Austen* (Chicago and London: Univ. of Chicago Press, 1984), p. 3.

[17] Freud, 'Female Sexuality' (1931), *Pelican Freud Library*, ed. Angela Richards (Harmondsworth: Penguin, 1977), vii. 367–92. In this essay Freud acknowledges his indebtedness to Jeanne Lampl-de Groot's paper 'The Evolution of the Oedipus Complex', *International Journal of Psycho-Analysis* 9 (1928), 332.

[18] Nancy Chodorow, *The Reproduction of Mothering: Psychoanalysis and the Sociology of Gender* (Berkeley, Calif.: Univ. of California Press, 1978), pp. 192–3.

Romantic women writers *The Proper Lady and the Woman Writer*, suggests that if Chodorow's arguments can be accepted then they have significant implications for a woman's psychological relation to authority; early practice in the adoption of more than one value system develops in her a tendency to 'accept a number of role models' and to accommodate herself to a variety of authority figures rather than to confront them.[19] Female conformity to the values preached by the early conduct books may well, then, have been facilitated by the psychological consequences of the conventional allocation of child care to women, though it was, of course, a particular, if all too well-established, aspect of the man-made gender role system which led to this customary child-rearing pattern, and not an ordinance of 'Nature' or of 'Providence'.

Poovey lists a number of characteristic acts of accommodation to conflicting values in the texts of Romantic women writers: the use of irony, for example, can suggest differing points of view without directly confronting any one of them. Nevertheless, she also points out that such strategies could, of course, represent an evasion on the part of the author of the tensions inherent in the life of a nineteenth-century woman.[20] A self-repressing avoidance of conflict can lead to the internalization of contradiction, and the development of depressive patterns of self-blame. Both depressive and manic-depressive disorders more commonly occur in women than in men, and recent feminist research has postulated that this gender differential is connected with the different socialization procedures meted out to the two sexes in societies which polarize gender roles. Stereotyped sex-role socialization tends to discourage manifestations of aggression more strongly in women than in men, and thus to inculcate a 'learned helplessness' in females which militates against the conscious acknowledgement and expression of anger and disillusionment.[21] The fact that Mary had so much

[19] Poovey, *The Proper Lady and the Woman Writer*, p. 254, n. 118.

[20] Ibid., 44–6.

[21] See Sue Cox and Lenore Sawyer Radloff, 'Depression in Relation to Sex Roles: Differences in Learned Susceptibility and Precipitating Factors', in Cathy Spatz Widom (ed.), *Sex Roles and Psychopathology* (New York: Plenum Press, 1984), pp. 123–43; Lenore Sawyer Radloff, 'Risk Factors for Depression: What Do we Learn from Them', in James C. Coyne (ed.), *Essential Papers on Depression* (New York: New York Univ. Press, 1986), pp. 403–20.

greater difficulty than Charles in acknowledging to herself, and in expressing, any dissension she may have consciously or unconsciously felt with regard to her mother, creating for herself instead the role of the pacifying but unappreciated mediator, may well have been in part the consequence of her society's prevailing pattern of gender role differentiation. Her long self-repression no doubt served to fuel and direct her anger when madness finally gave it its catastrophic release.

Recent psychoanalytic accounts of matricide have stressed that, like a manic-depressive psychosis, this act too has its roots in the pre-Oedipal relationship, and in an infant's inability to integrate the 'good' and 'bad' aspects of a mother figure who has aroused intense ambivalence. It is suggested that matricide may often have the paradoxical unconscious function of both avenging oneself upon the bad mother and saving the good mother from the danger of a conscious breakthrough of aggressive feelings.[22] Mary's calmness after her act of matricide may well have come from the unconscious awareness that the image of her mother was now free to undergo permanent beatification in her mind, now that no living Elizabeth Lamb remained to endanger, through her lack of adequate response, the defences of her daughter's protective affection.

Case histories of matricidal mental patients have also pointed to the repressed incestuous component in matricide.[23] The killing of the mother, whether performed by a son or a daughter, is seen as a substitution for the desired but tabooed sexual act. It may be that a yearning for homo-emotional attachments was a predominant feature of Mary's hidden inner life; while she seems to have shown little or no interest in men as sexual partners, her friendships with women were warm. In one letter to Sarah Stoddart, written after Sarah had paid the Lambs a visit, Mary, bemoaning her friend's departure, underlines the sentence *'The bed was very cold last night.'*[24]

[22] Richard Geha, 'For the Love of Medusa: A psychoanalytic glimpse into Gynecocide', *Psychoanalytic Review*, 62 (1975), 49–77.

[23] Henry Alden Bunker, 'Mother-Murder in Myth and Legend: A Psychoanalytic Note', *Psychoanalytic Quarterly*, 13 (1944), 205; Robert M. Lindner, 'The Equivalents of Matricide', *Psychoanalytic Quarterly*, 17 (1948), 461; Joel Friedman and Sylvia Gassel, 'Orestes: A Psychoanalytic Approach to Dramatic Criticism II', *Psychoanalytic Quarterly*, 20 (1951), 425.

[24] *Letters*, ed. Marrs, ii. 212.

Obviously the two had been bedfellows, and Mary, who usually found overnight visitors a disturbance, had in this case missed the company. And yet there is little in their correspondence as a whole to suggest that there was more to their friendship than the warmth customary between nineteenth-century female friends, who would usually, of course, in most households, have been required at that time of necessity to share one another's beds. In the letters Mary frequently proffers her advice concerning Sarah's many attempts to acquire for herself a husband without any suggestion that she found anything unpalatable in the idea of her friend's marriage. From the available evidence, all that can be surmised is that for Mary no adult love, apart from the tie with her brother, could replace the intensity of her ambivalent involvement with her mother. She may well have had little emotional energy to spare from what seems to have been a perpetual preoccupation, conscious and no doubt also unconscious, with that primary relationship and its catastrophic close.

In many of her stories for *Mrs Leicester's School* she appears to be struggling, in covert ways, both to tell the tale of her relation with her mother, and resolve the tensions it created. The tale of 'Ann Withers: The Changeling' is, as we have seen, centrally concerned with the dualism between a 'good' and a 'bad' mother. After the denouement, when Ann's true parenthood has been revealed, her actual biological mother, the nurse, appears to her as 'bad', as one who played a deceiving part in exchanging the babies; but the 'good' mother, Lady Harriot, is no longer hers. In the tale, however, Ann grows painfully to recognize that just as the 'good' mother's switch of affection towards her natural child, the real Harriot Lesley, indicates a superficiality in her former bond with Ann, so her own mother acted initially out of a strong feeling for her daughter, and suffered acutely when she left her behind in the Lesley household. As in 'The Young Mahometan', it is a doctor, another influence from outside the family, who helps Ann to arrive at this realization, and provides her with an insight into her own confusion that the parents themselves do not furnish. Through his counselling, Ann grasps that neither mother is wholly bad or good; she develops the strength to begin to see the ambivalence in both and accept them as such. It is, she says, because she still has not fully succeeded in doing so, and home is still too painful, that she appears as a new boarder, to tell her tale in the healing environment of Mrs Leicester's school.

'Elinor Forster', another narrative from the collection also primarily concerned with a process of painful accommodation to maternal loss, portrays a girl who mourns persistently for her dead mother, though she never mentions her name and is believed by her family to have forgotten her. Elinor seeks comfort through herself enacting the lost parent's role, taking her doll to the locked door of her mother's old room, and singing to it the lullaby with which her mother had previously soothed her, 'imitating, as well as I could, the weak voice in which she used to sing it to me' (iii. 303). A similar introjection of the idealized mother may also have had its part to play in Mary's gentle, nurturing personality, and increased the tie between herself and the brother, who became both her guardian and the object of her maternal care. But her perseverance in adopting with such sustained control during her periods of sanity a role which was the epitome of reasonableness and feminine accommodation, must have made the task of recognizing and assimilating the very different part which she had played in the mother's death that much more of an impossible proposition: only through madness could she free herself to act with uninhibited assertiveness, and, in one fatal instance, with an extreme of murderous aggression. After the death of the mother for whom it would appear she had felt such intense ambivalence, her own being, as if in helpless imitation of the internalized image of the mother, became split into 'good' and 'bad' roles, into a sane and a mad Mary, beyond conscious assimilation.

III

Interestingly, in Charles's contributions to *Mrs Leicester's School*, for which he composed three of the tales, the pattern of mother/daughter relationships closely accords with those presented by his sister. His tale 'Maria Howe', for example, is the first person narrative of a girl neglected by her parents who becomes paranoically obsessed with the conviction that her old aunt, who has provided her with most of the mothering she has received, is a witch; as with Margaret Green, it is brooding over a book, in Maria's case Stackhouse's *History of the Bible* with its lurid illustration of the Witch of Endor raising up Samuel, that induces in the child the conviction that she sees in a hitherto 'good' mothering presence a damned soul, a witch. Like Margaret, she too is cured from her obsession by the fortuitous visit of a sociable and sympathetic outsider rather than by her own parents. The pattern of Charles's response to the family tragedy in many instances appears to mirror Mary's, and suggests that he too, to some extent, shared in her propensity to split the mother imago into an idealized and a destructive one. As with Mary, his immediate reaction to the mother's death was a sustained calmness, to a degree which surprised him: he records in one of the long revealing letters he wrote to Coleridge during this period that

wonderful as it is to tell, I have never once been otherwise than collected, & calm; even on the dreadful day & in the midst of the terrible scene I preserved a tranquillity, which bystanders may have construed into indifference, a tranquillity not of despair.[25]

As he goes on to explain in the letter, his calmness had much to do with the maturing sense of responsibility which the complete dependence upon him of both father and sister afforded him at this point; however, the strength of his increased identification with his sister from the time of the mother's death points to the possibility that his tranquillity also had its roots in an unconscious release of tension similar to hers. He too had shown symptoms of repressed antagonism towards familial authority. Both Mary and her brother suffered from impediments of speech, Charles's being the more severe case.[26] According to recent psychoanalytic interpretations of the symptom, a stammerer unconsciously attributes to speech an aggressive effect, directed against the listener; the attempt to inhibit the expression of unconscious aggression results in the

[25] Ibid., i. 47.
[26] For an account of the 'catch' in Mary's speech, see Charles Cowden Clarke and Mary Cowden Clarke, *Recollections of Writers* (London: Sampson Low, 1878), p. 177. Charles Lamb's stammer is frequently referred to in anecdotal accounts of his table talk; for a biographical account, see Lucas, *The Life of Charles Lamb*, 2 vols. (London: Methuen, 1905) i. 56.

speech impediment.[27] As we have previously noted, Charles's recent biographers attribute to Elizabeth Lamb the judgemental and authoritarian mode of parenting which might induce such repressed antagonism.[28]

The curious part which his mother appears to have played with regard to Charles's confinement for madness the winter before her death may also have served to exacerbate in both brother and sister repressed hostilities and fears. A friend of Charles's, Charles Valentine Le Grice, was surprised to receive a note from Elizabeth Lamb late in 1795 informing him that the letter which she knew he had just received from her son the day before had been written in a state of madness, 'that she was sorry to say a temporary confinement was necessary, and that she desired that I would make no reply to it'. Le Grice, writing to Talfourd after Charles's death in response to the biographer's request for any information on his friend, recalls that in fact Charles's letter was 'very well written', and goes on to quote part of it from memory to demonstrate its characteristic lucidity and humour.[29] Elizabeth was clearly mistaken in her assumption, and the promptness of her response seems at least to suggest an over-sensitivity towards the manner in which her children were seen by others, if not also an over-readiness to accept the need for their confinement, at a time when in fact very few of the mad were so treated. After this incident, which suggests how strong the mother's grip still was over the lives of her children for all her invalidism, Mary, as well as Charles, may well have had every reason to fear that any further lapse of hers into insanity would have resulted in confinement.

The intensity of Charles's sympathy with his sister, and the need to provide for them both a vent for the trauma they had experienced, seem to have impelled him at times to bursts of grotesque whimsy through which he made veiled reference to Mary's situation and their history. Visitors to their household were occasionally nonplussed by Charles's habit in moments of

---

[27] See J. A. Morphew and Myre Sim, 'Gilles de la Tourette's Syndrome: A Clinical and Psychopathological Study', *British Journal of Medical Psychology*, 42 (1969), 294–5.

[28] Winifred F. Courtney, *Young Charles Lamb: 1775–1802* (London and Basingstoke: Macmillan, 1982), pp. 8 and 347–8.

[29] For a transcript of Le Grice's letter to Talfourd describing the incident, see Richard Madden, 'The Old Familiar Faces', *Charles Lamb Bulletin*, 1 (1974), 118.

hilarity of 'jumping up and slapping his sister on the shoulder', and shouting out the 'half jocular, half grotesque' rhyme:

> I had a sister—
> The devil kist her,
> And raised a blister!

According to the son of one of their last landlords, who had often witnessed the enactment, 'it was [Charles's] pretence to be proud of this triplet, as of a rhyming difficulty vanquished'.[30] He used the rhyme again in the long burlesque poem 'Satan in Search of a Wife', a parody of Hannah More's *Coelebs in Search of a Wife*, the popular evangelical tract which Charles found particularly offensive: on its first appearance he remarked that though it had 'reach'd 8 editions in so many weeks, yet literally it is one of the poorest sort of common novels with the drawback of dull religion in it. Had the Religion been high & flavour'd, it would have been something.'[31] In Charles's poem, a tailor's daughter falls in love with the Prince of Darkness when he suddenly appears to inflict a death-blow upon her father and take him off to the nether regions. Her passion being reciprocated, Satan reappears to claim his bride as she stands dreaming of his charms one night amongst the cabbages of her homely garden plot:

> the Devil stoop'd down, and kiss'd her;
> Not Jove himself, when he courted in flame,
> On Semele's lips, the love-scorch'd Dame,
> Impress'd such a burning blister.   (v.119)

In the violent act of killing the parent the Devil seduces the daughter, and claims her as his own possession, setting his fatal mark, the 'blister', upon her. In such a manner Charles appears to have seen his sister as possessed by the demon of her madness. He often describes her, in all miserable seriousness, as 'taken from me' by the recurring visitations of her mania,[32] as if her madness were a masculine rival to his own need. Her

---

[30] Thomas Westwood, 'Charles Lamb: Supplementary Reminiscences', *Notes & Queries*, 65 (May 1882); 381.

[31] *Letters*, ed. Marrs, iii. 14.

[32] See, e.g the veiled reference to Mary in Charles's poem 'The Old Familiar Faces': 'And some are taken from me' (v. 24).

marriage with the powers of darkness leaves him, who is 'wedded . . . to the fortunes of my sister',[33] a 'widow'd thing' (v. 22); the madness seems to assert a devilish and triumphant dominance over them both, and his only weapon against it is the burlesqueness of his verse, in itself at times nearly manic. The tensions of this curious rivalry may in itself have served only to increase the intensity of the sibling bond between them.

Charles's initial response to the matricide had been to see behind it the hand of God rather than of Satan: in one of his first letters to Coleridge after his mother's death he describes his sister as 'the unhappy & unconscious instrument of the Almighty's judjments [*sic*] to our house'.[34] His wording here suggests an attempt to make some sense of the horror that had befallen them through viewing it in mythical terms. The classic myth of matricide concerns, of course, the judgements which befell the unhappy house of Agamemnon, and it bears interesting resemblances to the Lambs' situation. In the myth, Electra, some years older than her brother Orestes, had saved him in infancy from the consequences of their mother Clytemnestra's harshness; similarly Mary had provided a 'good' mothering presence for Charles, cushioning him from the maternal neglect which she herself had experienced. A strong bond was thus formed in both cases between brother and sister: in all the classical accounts of the myth the 'recognition scene' which takes place between brother and sister when the exiled Orestes returns in manhood, to avenge their father's wrongs and kill his mother, is lyrically conceived, like the meeting of lovers. But one striking difference between the two cases is that in the Lambs' story a reversal of gender roles occurs: it is the sister who enacts the actual deed of vengeance, and is afterwards pursued throughout life by the avenging Furies of her madness, while it is the brother who accepts voluntarily a vicarious role in the killing, taking upon himself the burden of a shared guilt. In accepting responsibility for Mary he effectively shuts himself up for life with his sister and her ghosts, just as the Electra figure in a modern version of the myth, Eugene O'Neill's *Mourning Becomes Electra*, accepts at

---

[33] *Letters*, ed. Marrs, i. 64.   [34] Ibid., 47.

the close of the play the burden of guilt for the family tragedy, and entombs herself alive with the dead.[35]

The *Oresteia* has recently been interpreted by the French feminist theorists Hélène Cixous and Luce Irigaray as a myth centrally concerned with the overcoming of an original matriarchal order by the forces of patriarchy.[36] Orestes is finally rid of the guilt of killing a parent by Apollo's assertion that 'the mother is no parent of that which is called her child, but only nurse of the new-planted seed that grows. The parent is he who mounts'.[37] The son is thus 'rescued from madness in order to institute the patriarchal order'.[38] But the reversal of gender roles operating in the Lambs' case provides a very different resolution. A daughter cannot rid herself of matricidal guilt by a systematic degradation of the maternal and feminine role; to do so would be to annul herself. For Mary, as we have seen, the matricide, on the contrary, led to an idealization in her conscious mind of the 'good' mother, and an increased identification of her sane self with the feminine values which the idealized mother personified. Enduring within herself a double life, one passive and repressively self-restrained, the other, in its madness, forcefully actively and self-expressive, even to violence, Mary strove to distance her sane self from the act which had destroyed her mother. Similarly, her brother appears to have seen the deed as having been committed by a dominant masculine madness, satanic or divine, which had taken possession of his sister, with whose persecuted female innocence he strongly identified. The nurturing and mediating 'feminine' virtues, embodied very

[35] Eugene O'Neill, *Mourning Becomes Electra* (London: Jonathan Cape, 1932), pp. 287–8. For psychoanalytic analysis of the Orestes myth, see Melanie Klein, 'Some Reflections on The Oresteia' (1963), in *Envy and Gratitude and Other Works 1946–63* (London: Hogarth Press, 1975), pp. 275–99; and L. H. Rubinstein, 'The Theme of Electra and Orestes: A Contribution to the Psychopathology of Matricide', *British Journal of Medical Psychology*, 42 (1969), 99–108.

[36] See Hélène Cixous, 'Sorties', in ead. and Catherine Clément, *The Newly Born Woman*, trans. Betsy Wing (Manchester: Manchester Univ. Press, 1986), pp. 100–12; and Luce Irigaray, *Le Corps-à-corps avec la mère* (Ottawa: Pleine Lune, 1981), pp. 15–17, quoted and translated Margaret Homans, *Bearing the Word: Language and Female Experience in Nineteenth-Century Women's Writing* (Chicago and London: Univ. of Chicago Press, 1986), p. 2.

[37] Aeschylus, *The Eumenides*, trans. Richard Lattimore (Chicago, Ill.: Univ. of Chicago Press, 1953), p. 158.

[38] Irigaray, *Le Corps-à-corps avec la mère*, p. 17.

consistently from all accounts by Mary during her periods of sanity, are thus seen as endangered by the actively aggressive drives of her madness.

By extension, there is a tendency in both the Lambs' writings, particularly Charles's, to see assertive acts by which the self attempts to take control of its environment, rather than to accommodate itself to it, as dangerous hubris, an attempt at self-possession through imposition which may well result in a violation of the autonomy, if not the lives, of others. Sanity resides in accommodation, and the stoic acceptance of any infringements to the ego which it may require. Yet drives towards assertive self-expression, and the fulfilment of an evolutionary duty to possess and rule over the world one inhabited, were increasingly glorified during their period as the essential concomitants of masculinity. Charles's characteristic repudiation of 'the impertinence of manhood', and his refusal to concern himself with what feminist critics have recently termed as 'the myth of masculine self-possession',[39] may thus in part be seen as linked to his and his sister's attempts to come to terms with her act of matricide. Overdetermined from the outset by his identification with a father who played a wifely serving role in his relation with his master, by his early childhood bonding with Mary, and by school and work experiences atypical in comparison with those of the conventional middle-class male, Charles's predisposition to value those traits generally associated with the feminine rather than the masculine seems to have received yet sharper direction from his reactions to his mother's death. The final two chapters of this book continue this argument through a detailed analysis of the characteristic themes and styles of Charles Lamb's published writings and his correspondence.

[39] Marlon B. Ross, 'Romantic Quest and Conquest: Troping Masculine Power in the Crisis of Poetic Identity', in Anne K. Mellor, (ed.), *Romanticism and Feminism* (Bloomington and Indianapolis: Indiana Univ. Press, 1988), p. 28.

5

'The impertinence of manhood'

I

Under Coleridge's influence, Charles Lamb, by 1796, had made some tentative and initially unpublished beginnings in poetic composition. But the shock of his sister's act of matricide brought about his temporary abandonment of the practice. A postscript to the letter to Coleridge in which he first informed him of his mother's death reads 'mention nothing of poetry. I have destroyed every vestige of past vanities of that kind'.[1] The sudden plunge of his domestic world into violent madness appears to have wiped out his aspirations towards the poet's role: why this was so may have much to do with the concept of the poet prevalent during his time. Recent critical accounts of Romantic ideology have pointed to its central preoccupation with the 'grand illusion' that, through achieving an idealized 'Unity of Being', the poet could transcend his particular social and historical position.[2] The desire to establish such a transcendence is understood to be a consequence of the confusion of social and political values brought about amongst the British intelligentsia by the upheaval of the French Revolution. Disillusioned by the Terror and by France's apparent betrayal of republican principles in its occupation of Belgium and invasion of Italy, and hounded by Pitt's anti-Jacobin witch-hunt, poets such as Wordsworth and Coleridge who had earlier supported the radical cause retreated to 'the dread watch-tower of man's absolute self'.[3] From this fortress, the forces of an ordering and

---

[1] *Letters*, ed. Marrs, i. 45.

[2] Jerome J. McGann, *The Romantic Ideology: A Critical Investigation* (Chicago and London: Univ. of Chicago Press, 1983), pp. 137 and 40.

[3] Coleridge, 'To William Wordsworth', in *The Poetical Works of Samuel Taylor Coleridge*, ed. Ernest Hartley Coleridge (London: OUP, 1912), p. 405. See E. P. Thompson, *The Making of the English Working Class* (Harmondsworth:

self-possessed consciousness were to be pitted against a rapidly changing and unstable world, in order, in Coleridge's words, 'that whatever part of the terra incognita of our nature the increased consciousness discovers, our will may conquer and bring into subjection to itself under the sovereignty of reason.'[4] For Wordsworth also, 'genius' was 'the application of powers to objects on which they had not before been exercised': 'What is all this', he asks in his 1815 'Essay Supplementary to the Preface', 'but an advance, or a conquest, made by the soul of the poet?'[5] Feminist criticism has drawn attention to the heavily masculinist terms in which such aspirations were couched. The socioeconomic developments of the period, the rise of capitalism and the increase in scientific control of the natural world, are seen as having increased the onus on a poet to manifest his powers, if he was to demonstrate a masculinity equivalent to that of the capitalist entrepreneur or the scientist.[6] To be effective the language of a poet had to be a language of power, a language which would impress a new reading public with its authority and supremacy, and exert dominion over it. Charles's internalization of his father's ideology of service, and his acceptance of the 'unmanly' clerical profession, indicate that he would in any case have experienced some difficulty in adopting the masterful role of the poet as conqueror. But the trauma of his mother's death seems to have made him sharply aware of such depths of destructive irrationality that it appeared to him now but foolhardy to aspire to transcend or to control it.

Penguin, 1968), pp. 19–203, for a detailed account of the fierce repressive measures taken against British pro-revolutionary radicalism in the 1790s. For Wordsworth's and Coleridge's involvement, see also Wordsworth, *The Prelude or Growth of a Poet's Mind*, ed. Ernest de Selincourt, rev. Helen Darbishire (2nd edn., Oxford: Clarendon Press, 1959), x, and Kelvin Everest, *Coleridge's Secret Ministry: The Context of the Conversation Poems 1795–1798* (Brighton: Harvester Press, 1979), pp. 97–145.

[4] Coleridge, 'The Statesman's Manual', in *Lay Sermons* ed. R. J. White (The Collected Works of Samuel Taylor Coleridge, gen. ed. Kathleen Coburn, vi) (Princeton, NY: Princeton Univ. Press, 1972), p. 89.

[5] Wordsworth, 'Essay, Supplementary to the Preface', *The Prose Works of William Wordsworth*, ed. W. J. B. Owen and Jane Worthington Smyser, 3 vols. (Oxford: Clarendon Press. 1974), iii. 82.

[6] See, e.g. Marlon B. Ross, 'Romantic Quest and Conquest: Troping Masculine Power in the Crisis of Poetic Identity', in Anne K. Mellor (ed.), *Romanticism and Feminism* (Bloomington and Indianapolis: Indiana Univ. Press, 1988), pp. 26–34.

His correspondence with Coleridge and Wordsworth during the years which bridged the eighteenth and nineteenth centuries frequently illustrates his opposition to many aspects of the Romantic sublime endorsed by his British male contemporaries. The next part of this chapter will trace the pattern of that resistance, and its connection with his close identification with his sister. The last section goes on to explore how far he succeeded in giving expression to his own less self-centred perspective in his early pre-Elian writings. My interest throughout is in the degree to which his characteristic habits of mind may be said to represent a consistently anti-masculine sensibility.

II

According to his own testimony Charles's imagination was first excited to creative activity by Coleridge's example and influence. During the winter evenings of 1794–5, when Coleridge was virtually in hiding in London, in an attempt to avoid the consequences of his betrothal to Sarah Fricker, he and Charles met frequently at a city tavern, the Salutation and Cat. There Charles enjoyed 'those old suppers at our old . . . Inn,—when life was fresh, and topics exhaustless,—and you first kindled in me, if not the power, yet the love of poetry' (v. 2). Charles's identification with his father's servant status, along with the reinforcement this attitude of humility received through his response to his Christ's Hospital schooling, made him highly susceptible, at this early stage in his life, to hero-worship. In the young Coleridge, whose charisma was attested to by both Hazlitt and Wordsworth,[7] Charles found the intellectual hero to whom he could pledge allegiance, and at first he appears to have accepted the disciple's role with some enthusiasm. In 1795 Coleridge preached unitarianism and necessarianism, dissenting creeds then associated with the radical politics of the period: Charles adopted his beliefs with fervour. In December 1794 his mentor reported approvingly on Charles's reaction to an early illness of Mary's: 'Her illness preyed a good deal on his Spirits—though he bore it with an apparent equanimity, as

[7] See Hazlitt, The Complete Works of William Hazlitt, ed. P. P. Howe, 21 vols. (London: Dent, 1930–4) xvii. 107; Wordsworth, The Prelude, xiii. 246–68.

beseemed him who like me is a Unitarian Christian and an Advocate for the Automatism of Man.'[8]

But the death of Charles's mother brought to an abrupt close this first stage in their relation. In accordance with his necessarian convictions of the usefulness of human suffering as an education for the spirit, Coleridge initially greeted the Lambs' 'day of horrors' as an experience which would bring Charles closer to his maker: 'I look upon you as a man called by sorrow and anguish and a strange desolation of hopes into quietness, and a soul set apart and made peculiar to God!'[9] But Charles, in response, expressed, on behalf of his sister to whom he had shown the letter as well as himself, some anxiety at Coleridge's easy assumption of their spiritual exaltation. 'We are offended occasionally', he writes, with 'a certain air of mysticism' in the advice proffered:

To instance now in your last letter—you say, 'it is by the press, that God hath given finite spirits both evil and good (I suppose you mean *simply* bad men and good men) a portion as it were of His Omnipresence!' Now, high as the human intellect comparatively will soar . . . is there not, Coleridge, a distance between the Divine Mind and it, which makes such language blasphemy? . . . Man, full of imperfections, at best, and subject to wants which momentarily remind him of dependence; man, a weak and ignorant being, 'servile' from his birth 'to all the skiey influences', with eyes sometimes open to discern the right path, but a head generally too dizzy to pursue it; man, in the pride of speculation, forgetting his nature, and hailing in himself the future God, must make the angels laugh . . . Let us learn to think humbly of ourselves, and rejoice in the appellation of 'dear children' . . . seeking to know no further.[10]

This passage marks a crucial change in their relation, and it is significant that it is motivated by a response credited by Charles to his sister as much as to himself. Supported by her, Charles is not here abandoning his earlier adherence to a childlike, disciple's role, but extending it as a necessary model for Coleridge as well as himself: Coleridge should recognize not only his friend but also himself as being essentially, and permanently, in a childlike, dependent, and 'servile' role in

---

[8] *The Collected Letters of Samuel Taylor Coleridge*, ed. Earl Leslie Griggs, 6 vols. (Oxford: Clarendon Press, 1956–71), i. 147.

[9] Ibid., i. 239.   [10] *Letters*, ed. Marrs, i. 53–4.

relation to the Godhead. At the same time, the notion of the divine is set at some distance from the human condition in Charles's letter, and was in fact to exert less and less of an influence over his thoughts as he grew older, although his semi-atheistical position put him at variance with the increasing religiosity of his society.[11]

From this period on Charles reacted with suspicion to any claims of divine powers or particular spiritual approbation: he could no more credit the saintly pretensions of others that he could accept Coleridge's picture of himself as a potential saint. In February 1797 he described as 'cured' his leanings towards Quakerism, attractive to him as a faith because of the egalitarianism of its practices, because at one meeting he witnessed 'a man under all the agitations and workings of a fanatic, who believed himself under the influence of some "inevitable presence"': 'I detest the vanity of a man thinking he speaks by the Spirit, when what he says an ordinary man might say without all that quaking and trembling.'[12] His animosity towards any adoption of spurious self-inflation or the use of mystifying language also extended itself to his aesthetic judgements. In commenting in his correspondence on Coleridge's early verse, with its propensity for shadowy mystifications, he insisted upon the virtues of simplicity in style and sincerity in feeling: 'Cultivate simplicity, Coleridge, or rather, I should say banish elaborateness; for simplicity springs spontaneous from the heart.'[13] Nor were his expostulations wasted: in December 1796 Coleridge confessed to John Thelwall that his poetry 'frequently both in thought & language deviates from "nature & simplicity"', and a month later, in two consecutive letters to his publisher, Joseph Cottle, he acknowledges Charles's influence directly, confessing that he thought his friend's *'taste & judgment . . .* more correct

[11] Cf. René Fréchet, 'Lamb's "Artificial Comedy"', *Review of English Literature*, 5 (1964), 32: '[Charles] seemed to decide that religion was too abstract a thing for him, and that God was so far above man that it sounded like presumption or cant to speak about Him seriously.' Crabb Robinson in his diaries records on 5 Mar. 1826 that 'Charles Lamb's impressions against religion are unaccountably strong . . . It is the dogmatism of theology which has disgusted him and which alone he opposes' (quoted *Henry Crabb Robinson on Books and their Writers*, ed. Edith J. Morley (London: Dent, 1938), i. 302–3). In an 1817 letter, Charles himself jokingly remarks that 'I am determined my children shall be brought up in their father's religion, if they can find out what it is' (*Letters*, ed. Marrs, iii. 247.).

[12] *Letters*, ed. Marrs, i. 103.   [13] Ibid., 60 and 102.

& philosophical than my own'.[14] Recent commentators on Coleridge's poetical development have seen in the change of style which led to his so-called 'conversational' poems of the late 1790s, with their familiar tone and immediacy of emotional expression, indications of his endorsement of Charles's critiques.[15] The few verse fragments which Charles himself did compose after 1796 are similarly expressions of immediate feeling, concerned largely with his attempt to reconcile himself with the disasters which had befallen his family, and written more as personal memoranda, 'to keep present to my mind a view of things which I ought to indulge',[16] than as a return to poetry for its own sake.

But Charles continued to detect in Coleridge's poems an embattled striving to secure himself upon a transcendent plane, more exalted than that of his struggling brethren, the 'loveless ever-anxious crowd' of his 'Dejection: An Ode'.[17] 'Composed at Midnight', one of the domestic pieces of verse Charles wrote in 1797, closes with a condemnation of those poets and 'prose declaimers' who fabricate for themselves a beatific vision of the afterlife, but have 'o'er stock'd hell with devils' for their less worthy fellows. His imagined poet complacently pictures himself as elevated into a 'heaven of gold',

> far removed
> From damned spirits, and the torturing cries
> Of men, his breth'ren, fashioned of the earth,
> As he was, nourish'd with the self-same bread,
> Belike his kindred or companions once—
> Through everlasting ages now divorced
>
> . . .
>
> the saint nor pity feels, nor care,
> For those thus sentenced—pity might disturb
> The delicate sense and most divine repose
> Of spirits angelical.   (v. 24–5)

The satire of these last lines is echoed in the 'Theses Quaedam Theologicae' a letter which, in the summer of 1798, brought to a

[14] Coleridge, *Letters*, i. 278, 297, and 309.

[15] See George Whalley, 'Coleridge's Debt to Charles Lamb', *Essays and Studies*, 11 (1958), 68–85; and Mary Jacobus, *Tradition and Experiment in Wordsworth's Lyrical Ballads (1798)* (Oxford: Clarendon Press, 1976), pp. 72–3.

[16] *Letters*, ed. Marrs, i. 87.

[17] Coleridge, 'Dejection: An Ode', *Poetical Works*, p. 365.

close the sequence of Charles's early correspondence with Coleridge, and marked their quarrel over Coleridge's supposed negligence of his former pupil, Charles Lloyd, now a friend of Charles's. Responding to Coleridge's patronizing invitation reported by Lloyd—'poor Lamb . . . if he wants any *knowledge*, he may apply to me'[18]—Lamb's mocking letter to 'Learned Sir, my Friend', requests information as to the attributes of the 'Seraphim Illuminati', Coleridge's presumed ideals. His mystifying 'Angels' are envisaged by Charles as heavenly analogies to the arrogant metaphysicians and poets attacked in 'Composed at Midnight'. The questions he poses ask whether the angels 'manifest their virtues by the way of vision & theory' alone, practice being a 'sub-celestial & merely human virtue'; he wonders whether they do not sometimes sneer, and whether they have the capacity to love. Clearly intended as an attack upon Coleridge's own susceptibilities, the penultimate question demands

Whether the Vision Beatific be anything more or less than a perpetual representment to each individual Angel of his own present attainments & future capabilities, somehow in the manner of mortal looking-glasses, reflecting a perpetual complacency & self-satisfaction?

The letter is signed, with some irony now, 'Your friend and docile Pupil to instruct Charles Lamb'.[19]

But for all his failings, Coleridge remained throughout life for Charles 'an Arch angel a little damaged' as he describes him in 1816:[20] his composition of one poem alone, 'The Rime of the Ancient Mariner' would appear, from Charles's account of his response to it, to have been enough to maintain him in his friend's eyes at that elevation. What Charles appreciated in the poem, however, was not any commanding flourish of manly self-possession, but, on the contrary, its representation of the complete loss of self in a subject faced with the destructive irrationality of unconscious impulses. Charles's admiration for the poem first brought him into conflict with the poet who, by

[18] *Letters*, ed. Marrs, i. 130.
[19] Ibid., 128–9. The 'Theses' appear to be parodies of works such as Jacob Boehme's *Forty Questions of the Soul* (1620); for Boehme's influence upon Coleridge, see *Biographia Literaria*, ed. J. Shawcross, 2 vols. (London: OUP, 1907), i. 98.
[20] *Letters*, ed. Marrs, iii. 215.

1798, had become, in Charles's mocking words, Coleridge's own 'God', Wordsworth.[21] Through Coleridge, Charles had made the Wordsworths' acquaintance in 1797; in 1801, Wordsworth sent him the second edition of the *Lyrical Ballads* for comment. In a 'Note to the Ancient Mariner' added to the new edition, Wordsworth had seen fit to apologize for what he saw as faults in his collaborator's poem, complaining that 'The Poem of my Friend has indeed great defects; first, that the principal person has no distinct character . . . secondly, that he does not act, but is continually acted upon.'[22] His detraction 'hurt and vexed' Charles, who protests: 'For me, I was never so affected with any human Tale. After first reading it, I was totally possessed with it for many days.' He defends its main protagonist's lack of a distinct character on the grounds that

the Ancient Marinere undergoes such Trials, as overwhelm and bury all individuality or memory of what he was.—Like the state of a man in a Bad dream, one terrible peculiarity of which is, that all consciousness of personality is gone.[23]

Charles's identification with a sister who bore about her own neck, metaphorically speaking, the consequence of an irrational murderous act, and his experience of the disintegration of personality which such madness could entail, made the nightmarish processes of the poem vividly real to him; he recognized the psychological truth of the Mariner's passivity and complete lack of rational control, even to the extinction of personality itself. Immersed in the poem's symbolic representation of the unconscious, he abandons his own self-possession to the unchartered and uncontrollable seas upon which the Mariner's vessel drifts.

Wordsworth, on the other hand, not only resists for himself this giving up of self-possession but also discredits it, implicitly, as a potential response on the part of other readers. When

[21] *Letters*, ed. Marrs, i. 191.
[22] Wordsworth, *Lyrical Ballads*, ed. R. L. Brett and A. R. Jones (rev. edn., London: Methuen, 1965), pp. 276–7.
[23] *Letters*, ed. Marrs, i. 266. See Derek Roper, *Reviewing before the* Edinburgh: *1788–1802* (London: Methuen, 1978), p. 100, on the uniqueness of Charles's defence of the 'Marinere': Southey's attack on the poem's unintelligibility as a 'Dutch attempt at German sublimity' (*Critical Review* Dec. 1798)) 'seems to have been voiced by every contemporary critic except Charles Lamb'.

Charles turns in his 1801 letter to a direct attack on Wordsworth's own poetry and prose for the new volume, he similarly objects to Wordsworth's tendency to insist upon too marked and persistent a degree of authorial control over the type of response which he wishes his poetry to elicit from its readers. To Charles's taste, for example, the authorial voice intervenes too blatantly and didactically in 'The Old Cumberland Beggar':

it appears to me a fault in the Beggar, that the instructions conveyed in it are too direct and like a lecture: they dont slide into the mind of the reader, while he is imagining no such matter.—An intelligent reader finds a sort of insult in being told, I will teach you how to think upon this subject.[24]

The Lake poets' response to Charles's criticisms only reinforced his impression of Wordsworth's obtrusive and over-insistent management of his reader's sensibilities. In a letter to Thomas Manning, highly characteristic of the sharply humorous tones of their correspondence, Charles reported the details of his 'northern castigation':

The Post did not sleep a moment. I received almost instantaneously a long letter of four sweating pages from my reluctant Letterwriter [Wordsworth], the purport of which was, that he was sorry his 2d vol. had not given me more pleasure . . . and 'was compelled to wish that my range of Sensibility was more extended, being obliged to believe that I should receive large influxes of happiness & happy Thoughts' (I suppose from the L.B.—)

Charles recommends some of the new poems in the volume to Manning, particularly the 'Lucy' poem 'She dwelt among the untrodden ways': 'This is choice and genuine, and so are many many more. But one does not like to have 'em ramm'd down one's throat—"Pray take it—its very good—let me help you—eat faster".'[25]

His friendship with Manning, and the whimsies, puns, and ironies which marked their correspondence, furthered his ability to regard with an amused detachment the power-

---

[24] *Letters*, ed. Marrs, i. 265. See Stephen C. Gill, 'Wordsworth's Breeches Pocket: Attitudes to the Didactic Poet', *Essays in Criticism*, 19 (1969), 389–92, for a defence of 'The Old Cumberland Beggar' as 'a lecture but not propaganda'. But for the Lambs all lectures, as such, were distasteful: see *Letters*, ed. Lucas, ii. 227.

[25] *Letters*, ed. Marrs, i. 272 and 274.

mongering of his more poetical friends, though it did not detract from his admiration of some of their works.

In his response to the 1801 *Ballads* Charles characterizes Wordsworth's pedagogic tendencies with some prophetic acuteness: 'I will teach you how to think upon this subject' became a sentiment which consistently coloured Wordsworth's attitude towards his reading public. Their 1801 exchange was not to be the last instance in which his tendency to regard any lack of appreciation of his poems as a failing on the part of the audience marred his friendship with Charles. In the spring of 1808, Wordsworth, on a visit to London, had read out the recently completed 'White Doe of Rylstone' to Lamb and Hazlitt, only to be met with a deeply unsatisfactory response. By the time he came to write to Coleridge of the incident, Wordsworth had gained sufficient equanimity to lay the blame where it belonged.

As to the reception which the Doe has met with in Mitre Court I am much more sorry on Lamb's account than on my own . . . Let Lamb learn to be ashamed of himself in not taking some pleasure in the contemplation of this picture, which supposing it to be even but a sketch, is yet sufficiently made out for any man of true power to finish it for himself.[26]

Convinced of the truth of Coleridge's maxim, that 'every author, as far as he is great and at the same time *original*, has had the task of *creating* the taste by which he is to be enjoyed',[27] by 1808 Wordsworth fully accepted the poet-mentor's role: 'Every great Poet is a Teacher: I wish either to be considered as a Teacher, or as nothing.'[28] The 'great Poet' was to develop his audience's ethical powers as well as their aesthetic sensibility, 'to rectify men's feelings, to give them new compositions of feeling, to render their feelings more sane pure and permanent'.[29] Crabb Robinson, recording in his diary his own encounter with

---

[26] *The Letters of William and Dorothy Wordsworth: The Middle Years 1806–1820*, ed. Ernest de Selincourt, rev. Mary Moorman and A. G. Hill, 6 vols. (Oxford: Clarendon Press, 1969–70), ii. 221 and 222.

[27] *Prose Works of William Wordsworth*, iii. 80. Wordsworth adds: 'This remark was long since made to me by the philosophical Friend for the separation of whose poems from my own I have previously expressed my regret.' See also for a similar statement *Letters of William and Dorothy Wordsworth*, ii. 150.

[28] *Letters of William and Dorothy Wordsworth*, ii. 195.

[29] Ibid., i. 355.

Wordsworth during the 1808 London visit, reports his strictures with respectful approbation:

Wordsworth at my first *tête-à-tête* with him spoke freely and praisingly of his own poems, which I never felt to be unbecoming, but the contrary . . . He spoke at length on the connection of poetry with moral principles as well as with a knowledge of the principles of human nature. He said he could not respect the mother who could read without emotion his poem, *Once in a lonely hamlet I sojourned* . . . He wished popularity for his *Two voices are there, one is of the Sea* as a test of elevation and moral purity.[30]

But Charles continued to consider it an 'insult' to the reader to be lectured at in such a manner, and an 'impertinent' assertion of authorial power to seek such dominion over its audience.

His sister Mary, for all her habitual gentleness, shared his amused recognition of the overbearing tendencies of these 'Archangels', and their defensive self-concern. In one of her letters she relates with affectionate but mocking detail an unfortunate incident which occurred when Wordsworth paid a visit to the Lambs' lodgings in May 1815:

Godwin has just pub[li]shed a new book, I wish it may be successful but I am sure it is very dull. Wordsworth has just now looked into it and found these words 'All modern poetry is nothing but the old, genuine poetry, new [vam]ped, and delivered to us at second, or twentieth hand.' In great wrath he took a pencil and wrote in the margin 'That is false, William Godwin. Signed William Wordsworth.'[31]

While many of her letters demonstrate the affection she felt for Coleridge, she also expressed some dissatisfaction with his occasionally patronizing treatment of his old friends, and of his neglect of them once he had settled in London after his return from Malta in 1807. Neither of the Lambs attended his London lectures of 1815 for, as Mary explained in a letter to her friend Catherine Clarkson, 'we could not submit to sit as hearers to his lectures and not be permitted to see our old friend when *school-hours* were over'.[32] Subordination to didactic control, at the

---

[30] *Henry Crabb Robinson on Books and their Writers*, i. 10–11.
[31] *Letters*, ed. Marrs, iii. 161. Godwin's new volume was his *Lives of Edward and John Philips, Nephews and Pupils of Milton: Including Various Particulars of the Literary and Political History of their Times* (London, 1815).
[32] *Letters*, ed. Marrs, ii. 289.

expense of the more egalitarian and less manipulative ties of friendship, was as little to her taste as to her brother's.

But as well as criticizing the type of authority Wordsworth wished to exercise over his reader, Charles also considered his pedagogic attitude to have an adverse effect upon the capacity of his poems to evoke their subject effectively. In his 1801 letter on the *Lyrical Ballads* he comments critically upon the relation of the 'Preface' to the poems that followed it:

I could, too, have wished that The Critical preface had appeared in a separate treatise.—All its dogmas are true and just and most of them are new, *as* criticism.—But they associate a *diminishing* idea with the Poems that follow, as having been written for Experiments on the public taste, more than having sprung (as they must have done) from living and daily circumstance.[33]

Wordsworth presents himself in the 'Preface' as writing in order to create a particular effect, rather than as immersing himself in the processes of poetical representation. The effect, to Charles's mind, is not only to diminish the range of potential response in the reader, but also to belittle the immediacy of the poems themselves. They are presented as incorporated within the intentions of the poet, as owing their significance to his experimentations rather than as having an independent validity. An 1811 entry in Crabb Robinson's diary records Charles's preference, when it came to comparing the two Lakeland poets, for Coleridge's work. According to Crabb Robinson, Charles

preferred the *Mariner* to anything Wordsworth had written. Wordsworth, he thought, is narrow and confined in his views compared with [Coleridge]. He does not, like Shakespeare, become everything he pleases, but forces the reader to submit to his individual feelings.[34]

This critique of the 'egoistical sublime', expressed six years before Keats's better known but similarly worded evaluation,[35]

---

[33] *Letters*, ed. Marrs, i. 266–7. See John I. Ades, 'Friendly Persuasion: Lamb as Critic of Wordsworth', *Wordsworth Circle*, 8 (1977), 20, for the effect upon Wordsworth of Charles's comments: in subsequent editions, the 'Preface' was placed after the poems.

[34] *Henry Crabb Robinson on Books and their Writers*, i. 17.

[35] See The Letters of John Keats, ed. Hyder E. Rollins, 2 vols. (Cambridge, Mass.: Harvard Univ. Press, 1958), i. 387, where Keats contrasts 'the words-worthian or egotistical sublime' with the poet who 'has no Identity—he is continually in for—and filling some other Body'.

strikes a note generally characteristic of Charles's literary criticism. He noticed without approval a will to power in the work of his contemporaries, fuelled by the need to protect from debilitating anxieties that perpetually threatened 'myth of masculine self-possession', currently held by critical opinion to have presented such a stumbling-block to the freedom of imagination of the first generation of Romantic poets.[36] What he saw as the contrary Shakespearean capacity to lose all sense of self in the act of representing a subject, rather than to incorporate it into a manifestation of the ego's personal control, constituted Charles Lamb's test of creativity. The notes to his *Specimens of English Dramatic Poets, who lived about the time of Shakspeare* (1808) frequently assess the Elizabethan dramatists according to their ability to match the empathic imagination of their illustrious contemporary. Of George Chapman Charles comments, 'He could not go out of himself, as Shakspeare could shift at pleasure, to inform and animate other existences' (iv. 83). The funeral dirge in John Webster's *The White Devil*, v. iv, on the other hand, is singled out for admiring comparison with Shakespeare:

I never saw anything like this Dirge, except the Ditty which reminds Ferdinand of his drowned Father in the Tempest. As that is of the water, watery; so this is of the earth, earthy. Both have that intenseness of feeling, which seems to resolve itself into the elements which it contemplates. (iv. 192)

When Charles turned his critical attention to painting rather than writing, the ability of the artist to immerse his own ego entirely in the subject represented remained his ideal. His 1811 essay 'On the Genius and Character of Hogarth' praised the painter for his capacity to 'bring us acquainted with the every-day human face'; his immersion in the quotidian results in an art 'too real to admit one thought about the power of the artist who did it' (i. 86 and 75).

It would appear that Charles's preference for what he terms the art of 'Dramatic Imitation' (iv. 83) rather than the 'egotistical sublime' may have had its roots in his own characteristic

[36] Marlon B. Ross, 'Romantic Quest and Conquest: Troping Masculine Power in the Crisis of Poetic Identity', in Anne K. Mellor (ed.), *Romanticism and Feminism* (Bloomington and Indianapolis: Indiana Univ. Press, 1988), p. 28.

patterns of behaviour: at least one of his acquaintance saw him as manifesting, in his day-to-day demeanour, a disposition to 'go out of himself' as opposed to maintaining a self-centred perspective, and contrasted him with Coleridge in this respect. Sarah Flower Adams, giving an account of 'An Evening with Charles Lamb and Coleridge', remarked:

Coleridge's metaphysics seemed based in the study of his own individual nature more than the nature of others, while Charles Lamb seemed not for a moment to rest on self, but to throw his whole soul into the nature of circumstances and things around him.[37]

That it was a female commentator who made this observation may not be insignificant. The ability to see and present the quotidian in all its disjointed incongruity, without the intrusion of an organizing 'I', has recently been presented as a characteristic more common to the women poets of the Romantic period than to their male counterparts. Stuart Curran, in an essay on Romantic women poets, cites the work of Mary Robinson and Jane Taylor, amongst others, as exemplifying a 'decentered' capacity 'to document the sheer energy of life or its resolute thingness'. In such poems as Robinson's 'Winkfield Plain: or, a Description of a Camp in the Year 1800', with its vivid and detailed snapshots of camp life, 'the quotidian is absolute', he suggests.[38] Curran sees the cause of this gendered difference as originating in women's social position during the period; dispossessed of power and status in a public world increasingly becoming a male-only domain, they were less likely to succumb to the distorting habit of organizing the objects of their perception around a centred 'I', and using them as reflectors of a transcending 'Unity Of Being'. That I should here be suggesting that Charles Lamb shared such characteristically feminine traits does not detract from the validity of Curran's observations. For Charles's sex, as we have seen, did not shield him from the experience of social dispossession: his status as the child of servants; his internalization of the ideology of selfless service; his past membership of, and close identification with, that

---

[37] [Sarah Flower Adams], 'An Evening with Charles Lamb and Coleridge', *Monthly Repository*, 9 (1835), 165.

[38] Stuart Curran, 'Romantic Poetry: The I Altered', in Mellor, *Romanticism and Feminism*, pp. 190 and 192.

group marked by the label 'lunatic', perhaps the most alienated 'Other' in his society—all these factors worked to displace him from the self-centred vantage-point of the conventional nineteenth-century male of middle or upper rank. The similarities between Charles's perspective and that of Romantic women poets further endorse my central argument in this book—that differences perceived as gendered are not rooted in biology but are the consequence of access, or lack of access, to social power. But before elaborating such claims for Charles's atypicality we must first consider how far his own creative, as opposed to critical, writing did in fact exemplify such unmasculine traits.

III

In 1831, towards the close of his life, Charles Lamb complained that none of the works he published under his own name met with any critical or popular success;[39] certainly the majority of his early publications did not sell well, and were either ignored or harshly criticized in the contemporary reviews.[40] According to Julia Kristeva,

We cannot gain access to the temporal scene, that is, to the political and historical affairs of our society, except by identifying with the values considered to be masculine (mastery, superego, the sanctioning communicative word that institutes stable social exchange).[41]

As we have seen, Charles's 'temporal scene' at the beginning of the nineteenth century, preoccupied as it was with the apparent need to assert mastery over changing and potentially unstable circumstances, was one to which this comment seems particularly apposite. His own writings during that period can hardly be said to identify with masculine values; on the contrary, both the novel he published in 1798, *Rosamund Gray*, and the play *John*

---

[39] See *Letters*, ed. Lucas, iii. 328.

[40] See, e.g. the critical dismissal of his 1802 volume, *John Woodvil*, in [Thomas Brown], *Edinburgh Review*, 2 (Apr.1803), 90–6; *Annual Review*, 1 (Jan. 1803), 688–92 and [J. Ferrier], *Monthly Review*, 40 (Apr. 1803), 442–3. And see J. Fuller Russell, 'Charles Lamb at Home', *Notes & Queries*, 65 (Apr. 1882), 242, for a record of the fact that Charles made a £25 loss on the sales of the book, which he published at his own expense.

[41] Julia Kristeva, 'About Chinese Women', in *The Kristeva Reader*, ed. Toril Moi (Oxford: Blackwell, 1986), p. 155.

Woodvil which he was writing from 1798 to 1800 evince a pronounced dissatisfaction with the attributes of maleness. Written from within the conventions of the sentimental novel, *Rosamund Gray* is centrally concerned with one act of male violence which extinguishes all the female elements in the novel, and leaves its male survivors devoted to a lifetime of penance. In the idyllic pastoral opening of the tale, Allan Clare woos Rosamund, a young girl carefully reared by her benign blind grandmother, Margaret; Allan is himself lovingly nurtured by his older sister Elinor, who shares many of the characteristics of Charles's own sister.[42] Their lives are shattered by the 'systematic' villain Matravis who rapes Rosamund, not out of lust but as an act of revenge against Elinor Clare who had previously repulsed his advances.[43] Desperately calling for her granddaughter on the night of her 'ruin', Margaret dies from the shock of her absence; Rosamund herself dies in wordless bewilderment shortly afterwards; and Elinor Clare is thrown into a 'phrenzy fever' from which she also perishes. The two male survivors, Allan Clare and the nameless narrator, subsequently go through an exorcizing purification process which involves in both cases the abandonment of conventional masculine roles: Allan serves as a nurse, tending to the sick in hospitals and 'lazar houses', and the narrator seeks for comfort through a regressive immersion in the child's psychological world. Returning in manhood to the woodland scene of the disaster, he prays to be restored to that *'state of innocence'* in which he had earlier 'wandered in those shades': 'Methought, my request was heard—for it seemed as though the stains of manhood were passing from me, and I were relapsing into the purity and simplicity of childhood' (i. 26). In its preoccupation with the havoc wrought upon the female element by one act of sudden violence, and in the many similarities between Allan and Elinor's relationship and that of Charles and Mary, the tale

---

[42] An authorial aside makes veiled reference to the connection between Elinor Clare and Mary Lamb: describing Elinor's many virtues—'while her parents lived, the most attentive of daughters —since they died, the kindest of sisters'—the narrator adds 'I never knew but *one* like her' (i. 15).

[43] Charles took the name of his villain from Edward II's gaoler in Marlowe's play—Matrevis, whose heart was 'hewne from the *Caucasus'*. See *The Complete Works of Christopher Marlowe*, ed. Fredson Bowers (Cambridge: CUP, 1973), ii. 91.

seems saturated with covert reference to the Lambs' own tragedy. But in it Charles has displaced the destructive act on to a male protagonist; Matravis would appear to be the personification of that aggressive madness which he saw as taking possession of his sister, and despoiling her habitual feminine gentleness.

The 'stains of manhood' also bring about a parent's death in *John Woodvil*, and are similarly purged by a return to the state of childhood. In this historical verse drama, set in the 1660s and influenced in its style by Charles's enthusiastic reading of the Jacobean dramatists,[44] Woodvil commits indirect parricide, in that his revelation of secret haunts brings about the death of his outlawed father, an opponent of the newly restored monarchy. He succumbs to the crime through pride, as Charles explained in a letter to Manning in which he defends the play's original intended title 'Pride's Cure'.[45] In the pride of his liquor, Woodvil becomes possessed by a macho desire to prove the ties of male bonding greater than those of kin, and above 'all vows and promises, the feeble mind's religion' (v. 161); he betrays to a treacherous friend his father's whereabouts, the friend acts upon the information, and the father expires instantly on being apprehended. His son cannot forgive himself, until the moment when he relives the experience of kneeling as 'a docile infant' besides his father's knee: the memory releases tears which wash away his guilt (v. 176). In *The Romantic Movement in English Poetry*, Arthur Symons described the play as rife with references and applications to 'the tragic story which had desolated [Charles's] own household'; he saw it as Charles's attempt at 'a sort of solace and defence for Mary', in that its moral concerns the expiation of guilt through remorse.[46] But F. V. Morley, another early twentieth-century commentator on Charles's writing, pointed out that Woodvil's susceptibilities relate more closely to Charles's pre-1796 experiences than to

[44] See Charles's 'Dedication' to the 1818 volume of his Works for his explanation to Coleridge that though he never proposed to himself in writing *John Woodvil* 'any distinct deviation from common English', yet he recognized that the language of the play 'took a tinge' from his recent initiation 'in the writings of our elder dramatists' (i. 2).

[45] *Letters*, ed. Marrs, i. 177.

[46] Arthur Symons, *The Romantic Movement in English Poetry* (London: Constable, 1909), p. 164.

Mary's, and in particular to the heady tavern evenings spent with Coleridge: *'Pride's Cure* is primarily the cure of pride in the Salutation kind of friendship', according to Morley.[47] In the 1797 poem which begins 'I am a widow'd thing now thou art gone', Charles, addressing his afflicted sister during one of her enforced absences, and comparing his state with hers, had described himself as 'More sinning, yet unpunish'd, save in thee' (v. 23); it would appear that one consequence of his attempt to assimilate his mother's death and the recurring pattern of Mary's illness was a depressive preoccupation with his own failings, which he saw as not unrelated to the disaster which had befallen the family. Whether through his own person, or through the identification of the matricidal act with male aggression, masculinity and all its attributes had nothing but negative connotations for Charles; proud, rapacious, and destructive, its 'impertinence' needed to seek atonement through voluntary immersion in childlike or female roles.

The poem 'I am a widow'd thing', along with six of his other domestic pieces, formed part of the collection *Blank Verse* which Charles published with Charles Lloyd in 1798. The volume was generally derided in the critical reviews,[48] but it gained a startling notoriety through its appearance in one of James Gillray's cartoons for *The Anti-Jacobin Review and Magazine*. The episode as a whole throws an interesting light upon Charles's relation to the politics of his period. *The Anti-Jacobin Review*, along with its predecessor *The Anti-Jacobin; or, Weekly Examiner*, formed one of the more overt vehicles by which Pitt's government promulgated its witch-hunt of supposed Jacobin sympathizers. On 9 July 1798, *The Anti-Jacobin* published George Canning's poem 'The New Morality', which names Charles amongst a phalanx of British poets and radicals reviled as the presumed followers of La Réveillière-Lépaux, a member of the French Directory and one of the three 'Triumvirs' who had instigated the 'Directorial Terror' of September 1797:

> C——DGE and S—TH—Y, L——D and L—BE and Co.
> Tune all your mystic harps to praise LEPAUX![49]

---

[47] F. V. Morley, *Lamb before Elia* (London: Jonathan Cape, 1932), p. 198.
[48] See, e.g. *Monthly Magazine*, 6 (July 1798), 412: 'The childish sorrows of Mr. CHARLES LLOYD and Mr. CHARLES LAMB in their volume of "Blank Verse" are truly ludicrous.'   [49] *Anti-Jacobin: or Weekly Examiner* (9 July 1798), p. 286.

In Gillray's cartoon, which illustrated the poem on its second appearance in *The Anti-Jacobin Review*, Coleridge and Southey are caricaturized as asses, offering up their writings in homage to the Frenchman, and two amphibians squatting in the foreground of the print croak out their praises from a volume entitled 'Blank Verse by Toad and Frog'.[50] *Blank Verse* was again attacked in a footnote to an *Anti-Jacobin* review of Lloyd's novel *Edmund Oliver*:

This Mr. Charles Lloyd we conceive to be one of the twin-bards who unite their impotent efforts to propagate their principles, which are alike marked by folly and by wickedness, in a kind of baby language which they are pleased to term *blank verse*.[51]

Subsequently, in September, the *Review* printed 'The Anarchists: An Ode' which represented the same four poets, 'c———DGE, S——TH–Y, L——D, and L—BE', as singing

> Of equal rights, and civic feasts,
> And tyrant Kings, and knavish priests.[52]

In fact, however, Charles's contributions to *Blank Verse* were singularly devoid of any radical feeling, being wholly devoted to the rigours of his domestic situation, or, as in 'The Old Familiar Faces', the best-known poem in the volume, to a nostalgic yearning for the lost companions of a childhood past unsullied by subsequent devastations.[53] His co-sufferers from the *Anti-Jacobin*'s blacking campaign were unanimous in their protestations as to the inappropriateness of his inclusion. Robert Southey, commenting on the cartoon in his correspondence, remarks 'I know not what poor Lamb has done to be croaking there';[54] Lloyd, in his defensive pamphlet *A Letter to the*

---

[50] *Anti-Jacobin Review and Magazine*, 1 (Aug. 1798), facing p. 115. See David V. Erdman and Paul M. Zall, 'Coleridge and Jeffrey in Controversy', *Studies in Romanticism*, 14 (1975), 75, for the suggestion that the *Anti-Jacobin*'s attack was occasioned by George Dyer's poem, *The Poet's Fate* (1797), p. 26, a footnote to which erroneously lists Lamb and Lloyd as party to Coleridge's abortive Pantisocracy project.

[51] *Anti-Jacobin Review and Magazine*, 1 (Aug. 1798), 178.

[52] Ibid., 366.

[53] See Burton R. Pollin, 'Charles Lamb and Charles Lloyd as Jacobins and Anti-Jacobins', *Studies in Romanticism*, 12 (1973), 642, for the suggestion that prior to the assault Lamb's verses were essentially conservative in nature.

[54] Southey, *The Life and Correspondence of Robert Southey*, ed. C. C. Southey, 6 vols. (London: Longman, 1849), i. 345.

Anti-Jacobin Reviewers (1799), stresses Charles's non-participation in all radical matters;[55] and Coleridge in a footnote to the *Biographia Literaria* queries Charles's inclusion in the *Anti-Jacobin*'s castigation.[56] Numerous further comments by Charles's friends and by Charles himself testify to his lack of overt political involvement: Charles writes to Manning in 1800 that 'Public affairs . . . I cannot whip my mind up to feel any interest in. . . . I cannot make these present times present to me';[57] and De Quincey complains of Charles's complete detachment from day-to-day political events.[58] Barry Cornwall, Lamb's biographer, insists that Charles knew nothing of Lépaux, and that 'his writings had no reference whatever to political subjects';[59] and Talfourd also presents Charles as one who was 'through life, utterly indifferent to politics'.[60] In 1802 Daniel Stuart, the radical editor of the *Morning Post*, who had previously, under Coleridge's persuasions, accepted for publication a few of Charles's journalistic pieces, felt obliged to dispense with his services because, according to Stuart, 'of politics he knew nothing; they were out of his line of reading and thought'.[61]

It would appear that so all-encompassing was the *Anti-Jacobin*'s campaign that an author could be damned for the company he kept as much as for the content of his writings; Charles's friendship with Coleridge, then notorious as editor of the radical news-sheet *The Watchman*, seems to have constituted sufficient proof in the *Magazine*'s eyes of Jacobin sympathies. But the particular venom aroused in the *Anti-Jacobin*'s reviewers against the 'baby language' of *Blank Verse* points to another cause for his damnation, one more directly related to his work. In an age which so pressingly demanded from its authors an identification with masculine values, any deviation from a

---

[55] Charles Lloyd, *A Letter to the Anti-Jacobin Reviewers* (Birmingham, 1799), p. 32.

[56] Coleridge, *Biographia Literaria*, i. 49.

[57] *Letters*, ed. Marrs, i. 187.

[58] *The Collected Writings of De Quincey*, ed. David Masson, 14 vols. (Edinburgh: Adam & Charles Black, 1889–90), iii. 70–1.

[59] Bryan Waller Procter ['Barry Cornwall'], *Charles Lamb: A Memoir* (London: Edward Moxon, 1866), p. 67.

[60] Thomas Noon Talfourd, *Final Memorials of Charles Lamb; Consisting Chiefly of his Letters not before Published, with Sketches of some of his Companions*, 2 vols. (London: Moxon, 1848), i. 130.

[61] Daniel Stuart, *Gentleman's Magazine*, 9 (June 1838), 577.

manly tone of voice in writing seems to have been regarded as politically suspect. The vogue for sentimental novels and poems, popular during the second half of the eighteenth century, was now represented as the consequence of a pernicious French influence, and associated with all that was demoralizing and effeminate. Earlier, the characteristic concentration of the sentimental genre on subjective feeling, and its affirmation of the worth of feminine perceptions and values, had done much to promote the development of the proto-feminist movement of the early 1790s,[62] but its association with liberationist ideology now incited a savagely repressive reaction, in which the *Anti-Jacobin* featured largely. In Gillray's 'New Morality' cartoon, 'Sensibility' is figured as a *citoyenne* in a bonnet rouge, holding a copy of Rousseau in one hand and weeping over the carcass of a bird clutched in the other: all the while, her right foot rests on the guillotined head of Louis XVI. The suggestion is that the ethos of sensibility encouraged an excessive and overheated emotion in the individual, indulged in at the expense of any real sympathy with pain, and to the detriment of social order. According to Janet Todd in her recent study of the genre, the sentimental novel, with its preoccupation with the domestic tribulations of the middle and lower classes, was considered a pernicious levelling force; it 'appeared to favour reform by its emphasis on life's victims, and to question, if not attack, the established hierarchies of birth and gender.'[63] Charles's *Rosamund Gray*, with its espousal of feminine values, was in many ways typical of the genre, and may well have been sufficient, along with the concentration upon familial feeling and the unmanly limpidity of language in his contributions to *Blank Verse*, to link his name with the radical cause.

In opposition, however, to his contemporaries' testimony to the contrary, Winifred Courtney, in her recent biography *Young Charles Lamb*, argues that Charles's writings do show him to have taken a more active part than has hitherto been recognized

[62] See Katharine M. Rogers, *Feminism in Eighteenth Century England* (Urbana and Chicago: Univ. of Illinois Press, 1982), p. 143.
[63] Janet Todd, *Sensibility: An Introduction* (London: Methuen, 1986), p. 133. See also Alice Browne, *The Eighteenth Century Feminist Mind* (Brighton: Harvester, 1987), p. 170, for a further account of the *Anti-Jacobin*'s role in disseminating a 'distrust of sentimentalism' as an 'important strand in the conservative propaganda of the period'.

in the radical politics of his period.[64] Numerous references in
Charles's 1801 letters suggest that, in order to supplement his
limited income, he was writing for *The Albion*, a short-lived
radical newspaper, during that year; Courtney's thorough
researches have brought to light a number of hitherto uncollected
short pieces from *The Albion* which she attributes to Charles's
pen. One comparatively lengthy article, entitled 'What is
Jacobinism?' published in full as an appendix to *Young Charles
Lamb*, constitutes the strongest candidate amongst her discoveries
for inclusion in the Lamb canon: David Erdman has since
seconded her proposal that it be considered his.[65] In spite of its
title, however, 'What is Jacobinism?' does not set out to explain
Jacobin principles as such; rather, it attacks the blind crudity of
the use of categorizations and labels in general to manipulate
public opinion. Of those who encouraged the national witchhunt
for Jacobins, the *Albion* correspondent writes:

These men have set up an universal *idol*, or *idea*, under that name, to
which they find it convenient to refer *all evil* . . . To define the
boundaries and the natures of human action, to analyse the complexity
of motives, to settle the precise lines where *innovation* ceases to be
pernicious, and *prejudice* is no longer *salutary*, is a task which requires
some thought, and more candour. It is an easier occupation, more
profitable, and more fitted to the malignant dispositions of these men,
violently to force into *one class*, modes and actions, and principles
essentially various, and to disgrace that *class* with one ugly name: for
names are observed to cost the memory and application much less
trouble than *things*. . . . *Names* often associated with hostile and
unpleasant feelings, in turn engender and augment those feelings, and
the *thing* Jacobinism began to be disliked for the *name* of *Jacobin*.[66]

The piece expresses very much the sentiments one would
expect from a person in Charles's position at the time, labelled
as a Jacobin more for his choice of friends than for any manifest
political affiliations. But its protest against the crude uniformity

---

[64] Winifred F. Courtney, *Young Charles Lamb: 1775–1802* (London and
Basingstoke: Macmillan, 1982), pp. 186–202.

[65] See ead., 'New Lamb Texts from *The Albion*?', *Charles Lamb Bulletin*,
3 (1977), 75.

[66] *Albion and Evening Advertiser*, 566, (30 June 1801), 3; as transcribed in
Courtney, *Young Charles Lamb*, pp. 343–4.

of categorizations, and their use in creating an atmosphere of fear and distrust, devoid of any serious investigation of the actual characteristics of those thus scapegoated, was a telling one for the political climate of the times.

Similarly worded complaints against his age's tendency to think in terms of over-simplified categorizations figure in many of Charles's acknowledged writings of this period. In his notes to the *Dramatic Specimens*, for example, the theatre of his own age, as opposed to that of the Elizabethans, is criticized for its lazy inclination to represent a vice or a virtue through stereotypes: 'We have a common stock of dramatic morality out of which the writer may be supplied without the trouble of copying it from originals within his own breast' (iv. 115). Contemporary dramatists do not have the courage and imagination to look at the 'truth of things' (iv. 126), but satisfy their audience with dehumanized figures, representing a category rather than a complex reality. Similarly, in his essay on Hogarth, Charles complains that his age's 'extreme narrowness of system', 'that rage for classification, by which . . . we are perpetually perplexing instead of arranging our ideas' prevented the recognition of Hogarth's merits: 'we are for ever deceiving ourselves with names and theories' (i. 74). His 'Confessions of a Drunkard' likewise begins with the plea: 'O pause, thou sturdy moralist . . . and ere thy gorge riseth at the *name* which I have written, first learn what the *thing* is' (i. 133). A tendency to respond to names and their associations rather than to realities is also satirized in Charles's 1806 farce, *Mr H——*, in which the central protagonist is rejected by all his acquaintances when they discover that the name he has concealed is 'Hogsflesh', but immediately accepted back into their fellowship when a royal decree grants him 'the surname and arms of Bacon' (v. 209). By 1806 Charles had gained sufficient spirit to mock as ludicrous the manner in which an ugly name could in itself operate as a stigmatizing 'mark', but the consistency of his concern with the topic testifies to the sharpness of his recognition of the function of language within the processes of social control. His identification with his sister, as well as his own experiences, had sensitized him to the injustices perpetuated by the indiscriminate bundling of individuals under alienating categories of deviance, such as 'lunatic', 'drunkard', or 'Jacobin', a covert practice of ideological indoctrination which he saw as on the increase during his repressive times.

To obliterate the actual characteristics of persons or things through grouping them arbitrarily under demeaning classifications constitutes the crudest manifestation of the use of language as power; Charles's protests against the 'impertinence' of such practice, and his attempts to correct it, accord interestingly with recent feminist arguments as to how 'our language has trapped as well as liberated us'.[67] According to Dale Spender in *Man Made Language*:

> Language is *not* neutral. . . . Human beings cannot impartially describe the universe because in order to describe it they must first have a classification system. But, paradoxically, once they have that classification system, once they have a language, *they can see only certain arbitrary things*.[68]

Socially dominant groups have the hegemonic power to construct linguistic categories, do the naming, and thus create and control their society's concepts of 'reality' according to their own interests, labelling those not of their group as peripheral or deviant, or leaving them as unnamed and therefore invisible. Spender's researches indicate that the eighteenth and nineteenth centuries did indeed see an increase in the manipulative use of language to legitimize social hierarchies. In 1749, for example, John Kirkby in his 'Eighty Eight Grammatical Rules' made the first overt attempt to establish the male gender in grammar as 'more comprehensive' than the female, and thus to promote the usage of 'he/man' as designating the female as well as the male—that most obvious of syntactic constructions by which women as a group are rendered invisible; only patchily adopted at first, it was finally afforded legal status as the only 'correct' grammatical practice by a nineteenth-century Act of Parliament.[69] Charles Lamb's protests in his notes to the *Dramatic Specimens* against the 'blank uniformity' of his age, and 'the Decay of Symbols among us' (iv. 71) indicate his recognition, and disapproval, of the increasing attempt of 'impertinent' manhood

---

[67] Adrienne Rich, 'When We Dead Awaken: Writing as Re-Vision', in ead., *On Lies, Secrets and Silences: Selected Prose 1966–1978* (London: Virago, 1980), p. 35.

[68] Dale Spender, *Man Made Language* (London: Routledge, 1980), p. 139.

[69] Ibid., 148–50.

during his times to obliterate difference, and thus control its potentially subversive relation to the status quo, through a rigid and culturally impoverishing grid of hierarchically graded and value-laden categorizations.

But according to some feminist theoreticians, the entry into language in itself, the simple fact of naming quite apart from the subsequent proliferation of its manipulative classifications, constitutes an initial self-assertive attempt by the infant ego to control its immediate environment, and in particular to distance itself from its primary mergence with the mother. Julia Kristeva presents the father's entry into the early mother–child dyad as marking for the infant the ascendance of 'the symbolic order— the order of verbal communication', which represses the pre-verbal 'semiotic' communication between mother and child and drives it into the unconscious. 'Legislating, paternal, and restrictive', language as a system of signs imprisons the mind within its web of conceptualizations, which can never bring with it a conviction of absolute truth, dependent as it is upon the concepts of space and time which, since Kant and certainly since Einstein, have themselves been recognized as but secondary and relative configurations. For Kristeva,

It is understandable, then, that what the father doesn't say about the unconscious, what sign and time repress in the drives, appears as their truth (if there is no 'absolute', what is truth, if not the unspoken of the spoken?) and that this truth can be imagined only as a *woman*.

A curious truth: outside time, with neither a before nor an after, neither true nor false; subterranean, it neither judges nor postulates, but refuses, displaces and breaks the symbolic order before it can re-establish itself.[70]

Because language and ratiocination are seen as essentially male constructions, intuitions arising from the prelinguistic which reveal the limits of Western metaphysics, and run counter to it, figuratively take a female form. Kristeva's representation of 'absolute' truth as female, and of language or the symbolic as an obfuscating male order which, for all its logical ramifications and rationalizations, endlessly misses the mark, is curiously prefigured in one of Charles Lamb's first acknowledged pieces

[70] 'About Chinese Women', in *The Kristeva Reader*, pp. 152–3.

of non-fiction prose, his 'Curious Fragments, extracted from a commonplace-book which belonged to Robert Burton'.

It was Coleridge who first suggested to Charles the composition of the piece; staying with the Lambs in London in 1800, after their brief estrangement of 1798 had been healed,[71] he was once again encouraging his friend to write. As Charles told Manning, 'he has lugg'd me to the brink of engaging to a Newspaper, & has suggested to me for a 1st plan the forgery of a supposed Manuscript of Burton the Anatomist of Melancholy.'[72] One of the 'Curious Fragments' which Charles proceeded to compose still bore traces, however, of his earlier antagonism towards Coleridge's 'abstruse researches': the theme of the second 'Extract' is that abstract speculation distances its promulgators from a more direct perception of 'Truth' arising out of a childlike immersion within the quotidian. An elaborate pastiche of Burton's style and orthography, the passage reads:

> Philosophy running mad, madness philosophizing, much idle-learned enquiries, what truth is? and no issue, fruit, of all these noises, only huge books are written, and who is the wiser? ***** Men sitting in the Doctor's chair, we marvel how they got there . . . they care not so they may raise a dust to smother the eyes of their oppugners . . . whereas it should appear, that *Truth absolute* on this planet of ours is scarcely to be found, but in her stede *Queene Opinion* predominates, governs, whose shifting and ever mutable *Lampas*, me seemeth, is man's destinie to follow, she præcurseth, she guideth him, before his uncapable eyes she frisketh her tender lights, which entertayne this child-man . . . but and if *Very Truth* be extant indeede on earth, as some hold she it is which actuates men's deeds, purposes, ye may in vaine look for her in the learned universities, halls, colleges . . . but oftentimes to such an one as myself, an *Idiota* or common person, *no great things*, melancholizing in woods where waters are, quiet places by rivers, fountains, whereas the silly man expecting no such matter . . . on a sudden the goddesse herself *Truth* has appeared, with a shyning lyghte, and a sparklyng countenance, so as yee may not be able lightly to resist her. (i. 33–34)

Under the guise of the Anatomist, many of Charles's most characteristic preoccupations, ones which were consistently to

[71] See *The Collected Letters of Samuel Taylor Coleridge*, ed. Earl Leslie Griggs, 6 vols. (Oxford: Clarendon Press, 1956–71), i. 403–5, for the conciliatory letter with which Coleridge healed the breach.
[72] *Letters*, ed. Marrs, i. 189–90.

re-echo in his writing, here find their first playful expression. Attempts to anatomize and pin down *'Truth absolute'* through logical language are presented as a fruitless male quest; indeed, its practitioners themselves enter into the lists more in pursuit of personal power, to 'raise a dust to smother the eyes of their oppugners', than with any conviction as to the possibility of gaining their avowed goal. The child-man's weighty tomes of speculative learning are idle 'toys for the boys', while if *'Very Truth'* surfaces at all, it does so as an intuition arising from the unconscious, suddenly penetrating the conscious mind when it is least concerned with any egotistic assertion of its conceptualizing prowess. The passage, humorous and light as it is, bears close resemblance to the critiques of phallocentrism with which Kristeva, along with other feminist poststructuralists, are currently concerned. Charles's 'Curious Fragment' does indeed imagine *'Truth Absolute'*, emanating from the unconscious drives which in fact 'actuate men's deeds, purposes', as a woman, and he does show her as refusing and displacing the cumbersome but substanceless metaphysic of the symbolic order, represented in his passage by the avid and power-mongering university men. That he also personifies as female 'Queene Opinion', the shifting light by which the scholars are deluded, might be here raised as an objection to my argument: Charles could be seen as simply having a predilection towards personifying abstract nouns as female, thus giving rise to the happy coincidence of his representation of truth and Kristeva's. But 'Queene Opinion' does not stand for the symbolic order; rather, she shows it up as already deconstructed, and serves therefore as the handmaiden of *'Very Truth'*. Her excessive flightiness, her frisks and gambols, are such as to expose to the 'child-man', could he but see it, the fruitlessness of his endeavour to arrive at any truth through logical conceptualization: he is but pursuing a currently fashionable configuration, and not *'Truth Absolute'*. She plays with him to such an obvious, mocking extent that the 'Idiota or common person' can see through his web of metaphysic, of categorizations and conceptualizations, and make from it a 'light escape | Into the Beautiful'.[73]

[73] *The Complete Poems of Emily Dickinson*, ed. Thomas H. Johnson (London: Faber, 1975), p. 643.

Not surprisingly perhaps, when Charles submitted his 'Curious Fragments' to Daniel Stuart for publication in the *Morning Post* they were rejected; their stylistic quaintness alone probably made them appear unsuitable copy for a radical newspaper, for all their covert thematic subversiveness. But one recent critical commentator on Charles's writings considers his adoption of seventeenth-century language to constitute in itself a veiled critique of his age. John Coates, in a recent article in the *Charles Lamb Bulletin*, suggests that Charles constructed a historical myth of the seventeenth century as a deliberate antidote to the value systems of his own times.[74] Of his post-1800 prose style, characteristically embellished as it is with anachronistic seventeenth-century phraseology, Coates comments:

Neither the style nor the attitudes are pastiches since their quaintness is deliberately chosen as a medium as remote as possible from the downright certitudes and moral clumsiness they oppose. The style is one in which it is impossible to be brutal and it is therefore a reproach to brutality.[75]

Placing itself deliberately 'at an odd angle to the conventional writing of its period', speaking ironically or ambiguously when the expected stance was one of declamatory didacticism, Charles's style makes a protesting statement against the 'bullying' use of language current during his own times.[76] Coates criticizes as a 'gross oversimplification' the conventional view that Charles immersed himself in seventeenth-century writing and adopted its styles as a whimsical method of escape from the pressures of his difficult domestic situation; on the contrary, he argues that his interest in the writings of the earlier period, which in fact pre-dated his mother's death, and the energy and persistence with which he defended its values, were intended as a sustained and deliberate corrective of his age's heavy-handedness.[77] When Charles compares the writings of the seventeenth-century historian Thomas Fuller to those of his own contemporaries, for example, he draws attention to the

---

[74] John Coates, ' "Damn the Age! I will write for Antiquity": Lamb's Style as Implied Moral Comment', *Charles Lamb Bulletin*, 6 (1984), 154.
[75] Ibid., 150.   [76] Ibid., 148.   [77] Ibid., 155.

manner in which Fuller's antithetical style encourages in response a free activity of the mind:

The reader by this artifice is taken into a kind of partnership with the writer,—his judgement is exercised in settling the preponderance,— he feels as if he were consulted as to the issue. But the modern historian flings at once the dead weight of his own judgment into the scale, and settles the matter. (i. 116)

The didactic attitude towards the reader which Charles had earlier criticized in Wordsworth, his 'I will teach you how to think upon this subject' mentality, is here seen as an ubiquitous characteristic of the contemporary writer, to which Charles opposes the subtleties and stylistic ambiguities of the seventeenth-century authors.

The contrasts Charles draws between seventeenth-century writers and those of his own period are generally, in the 'Specimens from the Writings of Fuller, the Church Historian', as in his *Dramatic Specimens*, appended as footnotes to extracts from the earlier writings; he forbears to preach at length upon their virtues, in a manner which in itself enacts the suggestive rather than didactic style he wished to promote. Nevertheless, the disloyalty towards his period which such comments implied did not go entirely unnoticed or unreprimanded at the time; an 1809 review of the *Dramatic Specimens*, for example, objected to the notes as showing too strong an inclination 'to cavil with the taste of the present age, in a tone of much asperity'.[78] One characteristic of the age which particularly aroused Charles's ire was its changing attitude towards children and their education. Kristeva has suggested that it is a characteristic of Western reason when, in moments of crisis, it perceives its thinking processes as entrammelled within a substanceless web of signs, to 'turn towards and became haunted by childhood', a state still trailing clouds of unalienated glory, and 'wandering at the limits of the thinkable'. In her essay 'Place Names' she points to the Romantic period as one of the instances of such corrective regression.[79] Seen in this light Charles Lamb's particularly marked preoccupation with

[78] *Monthly Review*, 58 (Apr.1809), 350.
[79] Julia Kristeva, 'Place Names', in ead., *Desire in Language: A Semiotic Approach to Literature and Art* (Oxford: Blackwell, 1980), p. 27.

childhood memories and with the nature of childlike perception can be seen not simply as nostalgia but as part and parcel of his resistance to 'that rage for classification' with which his times increasingly deceived themselves. Like Coleridge and Wordsworth, he protested against the growing influence of utilitarianism on children's education, the early force-feeding with facts and classifications at the expense of more traditional imaginative reading.[80] Sarah Trimmer's periodical the *Guardian of Education* (1802–6) denounced fairy stories as 'an engine of mischief' for children,[81] and her attack was supported by a manifesto of the Society of Suppression of Vices.[82] Children's bookshops, according to Charles, were fast filling up with encyclopaedic or didactic tomes, such as Mrs Barbauld's *Early Lessons for Children*, while editions of the old fairy-tales and chap-books were no longer in print; in 1802 he wrote to Coleridge expostulating against such changes:

Knowledge insignificant & vapid as Mrs. B's books convey, it seems, must come to a child in the *shape* of *knowledge*, & his empty noddle must be turned with conceit of his own powers, when he has learnt, that a Horse is an Animal, & Billy is better than a Horse, & such like . . . Is there no possibility of averting this sore evil? Think what you would have been now, if instead of being fed with Tales and old wives fables in childhood, you had been crammed with Geography & Natural History.? Damn them. I mean the cursed Barbauld Crew, those Blights & Blasts of all that is Human in man & child.[83]

Deliberately engendering 'pert young coxcombs' (i. 143), Billy's fashionable utilitarian education encourages a child to

[80] For Coleridge's criticisms of the new development in children's education, see *Collected Letters*, i. 354; *Coleridge's Shakespearean Criticism*, ed. Thomas Middleton Raysor (London: Constable, 1930), ii. 13; and *Biographia Literaria*, i. 7–8. For Wordsworth on the same topic, see *The Prelude* (1805), v. 290–388. David V. Erdman, in 'Coleridge, Wordsworth, and the Wedgwood Fund', *Bulletin of the New York Public Library*, 60 (1956), 487–507, suggests that the Lake poets arrived at their notion of the importance of nurturing children's imagination in 1797, through their objections to Thomas Wedgwood's proposals on the reforming of children's education.

[81] Sarah Trimmer, 'On the Care which is Requisite in the Choice of Books for Children', *Guardian of Education*, 2 (1803), 407–10, quoted Virginia Haviland (ed.), *Children and Literature: Views and Reviews* (London: Bodley Head, 1974), p. 5.

[82] See George L. Barnett, ' "That Cursed Barbauld Crew" or Charles Lamb and Children's Literature', *Charles Lamb Bulletin*, 4 (1979), 5.

[83] *Letters*, ed. Marrs, ii. 81–2.

believe that he can through naming the world about him, control it, and prove himself superior to it; at the same time it brings to a premature close the child's capacity to wonder at things in themselves. As Charles puts it at the close of an 1813 essay 'Play-House Memoranda':

We crush the faculty of delight and wonder in children, by explaining every thing. We take them to the source of the Nile, and shew them the scanty runnings, instead of letting the beginnings of that seven fold stream remain in impenetrable darkness, a mysterious question of wonderment and delight to ages. (i. 160)

The tale of 'Susan Yates', one of Charles's contributions to *Mrs Leicester's School*, describes in detail through its use of the first person narrative the rich imaginative life of an isolated child, and the losses entailed by her eventual acquisition of more conventional knowledge. In her 'uninstructed solitude' Susan imagines the sound of church bells, wafted across the lonely Lincolnshire fens of her childhood home, to be the voices of angels singing; when she first visits a church and learns the true origin of the haunting sound, she regrets the loss of her original wonder (iii. 331). It was in part to counter children's early induction into an utilitarian world view that Charles entered into participation with Mary in the production of their *Tales from Shakespear* (1807), which he hopes in the 'Preface' will act as 'enrichers of the fancy' for their young audience (iii. 2); the subsequent children's books which he produced alone, such as his *Adventures of Ulysses* (1808), and *Beauty and the Beast* (1811) similarly retell old tales, and act to maintain against an 'impertinent' matter-of-fact intervention the mythologizing imagination of childhood.[84]

Charles's early publications may, then, be seen as consistently attacking the power-mongering, didactic modes of writing valued during his age. His own style, however, changed markedly during these years. Just when the majority of his contemporaries, such as Wordsworth and Coleridge, were relinquishing their former resistance to the 'Spirit of the Age'

[84] For a fuller account of Charles Lamb's resistance to utilitarian influences on children's education, and the part his writings played in the Romantics' attack on that influence, see Joseph E. Riehl, *Charles Lamb's Children's Literature*, ed. James Hogg, Salzburg Studies in English Literature, 94 (Salzburg: Univ. of Salzburg Press, 1980).

and accepting the demands it appeared to impose upon them to identify with a masculine drive towards dominance and self-control, Charles's writings also, both public and private, change in tone, but not in his case from the emotive simplicities of sentimentalism to the manly, but to an eccentric and deviant position, in deliberate opposition to the prevailing moral codes. The earnestness of tone evinced in such writings as *Rosamund Gray* and *John Woodvil*, and in much of his correspondence up to the end of the eighteenth century, was replaced by a disposition to mock at all moral attitudinizing and attempts at dominant self-assertion. One way in which this attitude finds expression in the style of his writing is in his self-appointed role as an indefatigable punster; puns abound throughout his letters, and are generally employed to debunk the pretensions of his acquaintances and the fashions of the times. His letter to Manning of 26 February 1808, to give one brief example, reads:

I have done two books . . . one . . . is Specimens of English Dramatic Poets . . . Specimens are becoming fashionable . . . They used to be called Beauties. You have seen Beauties of Shakspeare?—so have many people, that never saw any Beauties in Shakspeare. . . . I made a pun the other day & palm'd it upon Holcroft . . . I said that Holcroft said, being ask'd who were the best dramatic writers of the day, 'Hook and I'. . . . Wordsworth the great poet is coming to town. . . . He says he does not see much difficulty in writing like Shakspeare, if he had a mind to try it. It is clear then nothing is wanting but the mind. . . . Well, my dear Manning, talking cannot be infinite, I have said all I have to say . . . Here is a packet of trifles nothing worth, but it is a trifling part of the world where I live.[85]

A propensity to trifle with language in this way has recently been credited with the effect of exposing the arbitrariness of the linguistic sign system. According to Jonathan Culler:

Puns present the disquieting spectacle of a functioning of language where boundaries—between sounds, between sound and letter, between meanings—count for less than one might imagine and where supposedly discrete meanings threaten to sink into fluid subterranean signifieds too indefinable to call concepts.[86]

---

[85] *Letters*, ed. Marrs, ii. 272–5.
[86] Jonathan Culler, 'The Call of the Phoneme: Introduction', in id. (ed.), *On Puns: The Foundation of Letters* (Oxford: Blackwell, 1988), p. 3.

The proliferation of puns in Charles's slippery writings can be seen, then, as but another feature of his attack upon the arrogant blindness of those who sought to nail meaning down to words and concepts, and as a means of undermining 'impertinent' attempts to impose manipulative verbal categorizations upon the 'multitudinous moving picture' of life (i. 40). His singular habit of playing tricks upon his correspondents, very convincingly spinning some completely fictitious tale of disaster on the first page of a letter only to reveal the hoax overleaf,[87] can also be seen as part of his subversive campaign to disclose the illusions perpetrated by language, and the folly of those who credulously give themselves up to its power. Leigh Hunt in his *Autobiography* described Lamb as one who

knew how many false conclusions and pretensions are made by men who profess to be guided by facts only, as if facts could not be misconceived, or figments taken from them; and therefore, one day, when some body was speaking of a person who valued himself on being a matter-of-fact man, 'Now,' said he, 'I value myself on being a matter-of-lie man.'[88]

His matter-of-lie career culminated in the creation of the Elia persona, whose very name, as Charles pointed out, is an anagram of 'a lie'.[89]

In the earlier chapters of this book, I have explored the experiential grounds for Charles's resistance to the 'myth of masculine self-possession' and its manifestations in language: his parents' and his own social positions and the ideologies that went with them, the shock of his mother's death and the role madness played in his life and that of the stigmatized sister with whom he identified, taught him the impossibility of establishing a controlled and unified subjectivity, and the iniquity of attempting to do so through dominating others. Increasingly, he appears to have viewed the forms of social

[87] See e.g. his letters to John Mathew Gutch, July 1800, and to Manning, 29 Nov. 1800, in *Letters*, ed. Marrs, i. 211–12 and 247–8.
[88] Leigh Hunt, *The Autobiography of Leigh Hunt*, ed. J. E. Morpurgo (London: Cresset Press, 1949), p. 284.
[89] See Lucas, *The Life of Charles Lamb*, 2 vols. (London: Methuen, 1905), ii. 42, n. 1: 'Mrs Cowden Clarke records in a marginal note to her copy of Procter's Memoir [of Charles Lamb] . . . that Lamb once remarked that "Elia" formed an anagram of "a lie".'

control which proliferated during his period as a heinous farce; a certain detachment could be gained, however, through the consciousness of oneself as being played upon, and playing within, the configuration of roles and settings in which one had been placed. 'I am determined to take what snatches of pleasure, we can, between the acts of our distressful drama,' he tells Coleridge in 1800.[90] His immersion in his favourite seventeenth-century authors also furthered such a perspective; the Anatomist of Melancholy, for example, presents himself to his 'gentle reader' as an 'antic or personate actor', a 'spectator of other men's fortunes and adventures and how they act their parts, which methinks are diversely presented unto me as from a common theatre or scene'.[91] But play itself in Charles's writings becomes not simply a means of escape from harsh realities but a subtle organ of attack upon the pompous perpetrators of serious injustice. The character of his pre-1800 works indicate that such a stance was not easily arrived at, but once achieved it remained stable, and from its vantage-point he persistently attacked the masculinist dogma of his times. In what ways his best-known work, the Elia essays, took further his critique of the 'impertinence of manhood' remains to be considered in my final chapter.

[90] *Letters*, ed. Marrs, i. 215.
[91] Robert Burton, *The Anatomy of Melancholy* ed. Holbrook Jackson, 3 vols. (London: Dent, 1932), i. 15 and 18.

6

'Bridget and I should be ever playing'

I

By 1820, when Elia made his first appearance in the *London Magazine*, Charles and Mary Lamb had lived alone together for over twenty years, since the death of their father in 1799. Both frequently testify in their letters to the whole-heartedness with which they shared every aspect of their lives. In a letter to Sarah Stoddart, for example, Mary laments over her friend's comparative estrangement from her own brother, John Stoddart, and contrasts their relationship with hers and Charles's:

> you both want the habit of telling each other at the moment everything that happens,—where you go—and what you do—that free communication of letters and opinions, just as they arise, as Charles and I do.[1]

In 1805 Charles tells Dorothy Wordsworth that he conceals nothing that he does from his sister;[2] in 1824 he jokingly remarks to Procter that 'in virtue of the hypostatical union between us, when Mary calls, it is understood that I call too, we being univocal'.[3] At one point, however, Charles had made an unsuccessful attempt at extending their household; in 1819 he proposed marriage by letter to the actress Fanny Kelly, whom he had long admired. But he did so with his sister's agreement and encouragement. Mary was herself a friend of Kelly's and acted as her tutor in French, Latin, and Italian.[4] Her brother's letter makes it clear that they were indeed 'univocal' in their desire that the actress should 'consent to take your lot with us'; there was no question of an end to the sibling relationship.[5]

---

[1] *Letters*, ed. Marrs, ii. 124.   [2] Ibid., 169.
[3] *Letters*, ed. Lucas, ii. 443.   [4] See ibid., 245 and 270.
[5] Ibid., 254. His offer was refused because, as Fanny Kelly told her sister, 'I could not give my assent to a proposal which would bring me into that atmosphere of sad mental uncertainty which surrounds his domestic life' (see Lucas's notes, *Letters*, ii. 256).

And when in the next year the Elia essays began to appear, Charles celebrated in them, in a way that he had not done before in his public writings, the pleasures of his life with his sister. The *Essays*, in which Mary Lamb appears as Elia's 'cousin', Bridget Elia, are rife with references to their union of 'double singleness': 'Mackery End, in Hertfordshire' and 'Old China' are centrally concerned with Bridget; extracts from her poems, that is, Mary's, are quoted in 'Detached Thoughts on Books and Reading'; other essays, like 'Mrs Battle's Opinions on Whist', 'Dream Children', and 'The Old Margate Hoy', frequently remind the reader of her presence at Elia's side as his close companion. Altogether, about one in five of the essays makes some reference to Bridget.

Many of Charles's twentieth-century male commentators have found it necessary to explain away so marked an affection by representing it as an over-compensation for repressed feelings of hatred towards a sister who must have been, they assume, 'such a clog to him'.[6] But the closeness of their sibling tie would not necessarily have been so embarrassing for their contemporary readers: formative and warmly affectionate brother/sister relationships were a more common characteristic of early nineteenth-century lives generally than they are of modern familial relations. Late marriage, and the social segregation of the sexes before marriage, resulted in a greater degree of sibling bonding, and the lack of sexuality in the attachment led to its idealization, in a Puritanical age, as the purest love possible between the sexes. Mary Ann Hedge, for example, in *My Own Fireside* (1832), praises the brother/sister relationship as

> That tender union, all combin'd
> Of Nature's holiest sympathies;
> 'Tis Friendship in its loveliest dress
> 'Tis Love's most perfect tenderness.[7]

To modern eyes, the close relationship between William and Dorothy Wordsworth appears incestuous in its intensity, but

[6] R. A. Foakes, 'The Authentic Voice: Lamb and the Familiar Letter', *Charles Lamb Bulletin*, 2 (1975), 4.

[7] Mary Ann Hedge, *My Own Fireside* (Colchester, 1832); quoted Leonore Davidoff and Catherine Hall, *Family Fortunes: Men and Women of the English Middle Class, 1750–1850* (London: Hutchinson, 1987), p. 349.

Leonore Davidoff and Catherine Hall, in their study of middle-class family relationships at the turn of the century, suggest that it may have been no more than characteristic of the sibling ties of its period.[8] No doubt William Wordsworth's eulogistic account of the relation between the Lambs in his elegy on Charles owed much to his awareness of the significance of the bond between his own sister and himself; he praises the 'sanctity' of the Lambs' *'dual* loneliness' as 'a thousand times more beautiful' both to themselves and 'to the thoughts of others' than the single lot.[9] Of course, some sibling relationships did not entirely eschew the sexual: in 1798 James Burney, Fanny Burney's older brother, eloped with his half-sister Sarah, and set up house with her for five years;[10] later, Byron gained notoriety for his incestuous relation with his half-sister Augusta. But such scandals did little to dim the esteem with which close sibling ties continued to be regarded for much of the nineteenth century.

The brother/sister relationship was celebrated as a moral ideal in the philosophical as well as literary writings of the period. In his *Phenomenology of Spirit* (1807), Hegel presented the sibling bond as one which could provide more opportunity for the ethical enhancement of the pair involved, particularly the woman, than could marriage. Hegel's arguments are interesting for the manner in which they rationalize on moral grounds the rigid gender-role divisions of his times. He maintained that an ethical consciousness could only be developed in any given individual by participation in public affairs, in which the ethical 'shapes and maintains itself by working for the universal'. Women's particular role in reproduction disabled them, in his view, from participation in the public domain, and therefore entailed upon the male who would achieve full ethical

---

[8] Ibid., 351.

[9] Wordsworth, 'Written after the Death of Charles Lamb', *The Poetical Works of William Wordsworth*, ed. Ernest de Selincourt and Helen Darbishire, 5 vols. (Oxford: Clarendon Press, 1940–9), iv. 274 and 276.

[10] See Winifred F. Courtney, 'New Light on the Lambs and the Burneys', *Charles Lamb Bulletin*, 8 (1987), 21. See ead., *Young Charles Lamb: 1775–1802* (London and Basingstoke: Macmillan, 1982), p. 373, n. 2, for an argument against the possibility of an incestuous element in the Lambs' relation, on the grounds that 'Lamb was far too nervous of his sister's frenzies to have risked any action at all that would push her into one of her bad spells and burden both their sensitive consciences yet further.'

maturity a strict withholding of himself from excessive identification with the feminine and the domestic. A man's goal, his
quest in life, was to transcend what Hegel termed the 'nether
world' of the family and 'work for the universal'; he could not
afford to allow his sympathies to be entrammelled in the
mundane world of particularity and detail in which the female,
by nature of her reproductive role, was entombed.[11] A woman
could, however, gain a modified appreciation of the ethical at
second hand, through her vicarious involvement in the public
life of her male relatives. But the particularity of the emotional
bond between husband and wife, based as it was on individual
choice and sexual attraction, endangered this possible outcome;
the wife was as likely to pull her husband back into the 'nether
world' of unconscious attachment as to appreciate through him
the necessity for developing a sense of universalized ethical
commitments—to Husband and Child as generalized abstractions, rather than to her particular husband and her particular
child. The manner in which brother/sister relationships were
not a matter of particular, individual choice, and were withdrawn
from the reproductive cycle, made them, for Hegel, a more
viable route than marriage towards vicarious ethical development
for the female, and a safer area of involvement with women for
the male.[12]

For all his idealization of the sibling tie, however, Hegel
could hardly have sanctioned the Lambs' relationship. For
when Charles made the crucial decision to 'wed' himself, in his
own phrase, 'to the fortunes of my sister', he forfeited for them
both the Hegelian routes to ethical growth. Instead of adopting
the prescribed brother's role of dominance within the relationship, and dissociating the more significant part of his life from
domestic ties, thus providing a route towards universality for
his sister as well as himself, he rather chose to identify himself
with her fate. To side with the female entailed a loss of the
manly universal perspective, and precipitated a dangerous slide
into the uncontrollable 'nether world' of the unconscious

---

[11] Georg Wilhelm Friedrich Hegel, *Phenomenology of Spirit*, trans. A. V. Miller
(Oxford: Clarendon Press, 1977), pp. 266–90. For a feminist critique of Hegel's
arguments, see Genevieve Lloyd, *The Man of Reason: 'Male' and 'Female' in
Western Philosophy* (London: Methuen, 1984), pp. 80–5.

[12] Hegel, *Phenomenology of Spirit*, p. 74.

'Other', rendered even darker in Mary's case by the threat of insanity. The nature of Charles's alliance with his sister would also have imperilled his creative, as well as ethical, growth in the philosopher's eyes, for Hegel's condemnation of immersion in feminine particularity also featured largely in his aesthetic theories. In his *Aesthetics: Lectures on Fine Arts* he insists that the 'Ideal of Beauty' involves 'the negation of everything particular'.[13] Women, because 'they are not made for activities which demand a universal faculty', 'may have happy ideas, taste and elegance, but they cannot attain the ideal'.[14] Neither could male artists who retained too thoroughgoing an allegiance to the 'multiform particularities of everyday life' reach the heights of aesthetic achievement. Hegel's arguments provide a theoretical endorsement of the Romantic poet's insistence upon a self-possession which could safely relate to the female only through subjugating her under its own masculine control. But, as we have seen, the male poets' drive towards transcending the particular constituted, in itself, a dubious project in Charles's eyes. In his writings, particularly the *Essays of Elia*, the 'multiform particularities of everyday life' become the primary focus; his art functions to celebrate the quotidian in all its minute and fragmentary diversity, and at no times more poignantly than when his experience of immersion in everyday life is shared with 'Bridget Elia'. The following pages explore the connection between certain characteristics of the Elia essays and qualities and values generally labelled 'feminine'.

II

In 1802 Charles published in Leigh Hunt's *Reflector* a piece signed 'A Londoner', which he originally intended as an introduction to a series of connected essays; the 'Londoner' himself did not make another appearance in print, but some of Charles's twentieth-century critics have seen in the Elia essays

[13] Id., *Aesthetics: Lectures on Fine Arts*, trans. T. M. Knox, 2 vols. (Oxford: OUP, 1975), i. 157. For a feminist critique of Hegel's aesthetic theory, see Naomi Schor, *Reading in Detail: Aesthetics and the Feminine* (London: Methuen, 1987), pp. 23–41.
[14] Quoted Schor, *Reading in Detail*, p. 25.

the eventual realization, twenty years later, of Charles's intentions.[15] If the 'Londoner' can be seen as an precursor of Elia, he owed his own origins to a series of letters in praise of London which Charles sent to Manning, Wordsworth, and Robert Lloyd in the winter of 1800–1. In part written as a protest against the Lake poets' assumptions of the spiritual superiority of country as opposed to city life, Charles's letters celebrate in contrast his own attachment to the metropolis. He tells Wordsworth:

I have passed all my days in London, until I have formed as many and intense local attachments, as any of you Mountaineers can have done with dead nature . . . The Lighted shops of the Strand and Fleet Street, the innumerable trades, tradesmen and customers, coaches, waggons, play houses, all the bustle and wickedness round about Covent Garden, the very women of the Town, the Watchmen, drunken scenes, rattles;—life awake, if you awake, at all hours of the night, the impossibility of being dull in Fleet Street, the crowds, the very dirt & mud, the Sun shining upon houses and pavements, the print shops, the old Book stalls, parsons cheap'ning books, coffee houses, steams of soups from kitchens, the pantomimes, London itself, a pantomime and a masquerade, all these things work themselves into my mind and feed me without a power of satiating me. The wonder of these sights impells me into night-walks about her crowded streets, and I often shed tears in the motley Strand from fullness of joy at so much Life.[16]

In such passages Charles presents himself as readily abandoning his individual self-consciousness to the stream of particularized impressions afforded by the 'ever-shifting scenes' of the city. He is intensely involved, entirely immersed, and yet unconcerned as an individual with the outcome of these multitudinous glimpses of life in process, over which he is not tempted to impose any universalizing or self-affirming order.

Like many of the other characteristic traits in his work, his appreciation of the vivid particularities of urban life has its parallels in his sister's writings: Mary Lamb's letters frequently illustrate her pleasure in being a Londoner. In one 1802 letter to Sarah Stoddart, for example, she confesses she cannot recall from her recent visit to the Lakes 'a single circumstance I think

[15] See Ian Jack, *English Literature 1815–1832* (The Oxford History of English Literature, x) (Oxford: Clarendon Press, 1963), p. 289: 'A descendant of "The Londoner", Elia is the "picture of my humours" that had been in Lamb's mind when he wrote that essay.'

[16] *Letters*, ed. Marrs, i. 267.

will entertain you'; instead, her mind is full of the delight of their city excursions, 'driving along the Strand so fast' or 'bustling down Fleet-Market-in-all-its-glory of a saturday night'.[17] The Lambs' move to Russell Street in Covent Garden in 1817, 'a place all alive with noise and bustle', gave her particular satisfaction; she liked to listen to 'the hubbub of the carriages returning from the play' and 'the squabbles of the coachmen and linkboys'.[18] During one of their 'rest' periods in the suburbs, prescribed as a palliative for her mental instability, she found little to recompense her for the city's lost 'bustle'; 'I must confess I would rather live in Russell Street all my life, and never set my foot but on the London pavement, than be doomed always to enjoy the silent pleasures I now do', she tells one correspondent.[19] Like her brother, she was amused by the Lake Poets' insistence upon the ameliorative moral effect of mountain scenery; Charles reported to Wordsworth that during her reading of *The Excursion* Mary remarked that 'by your system it was doubtful whether a Liver in Towns had a Soul to be Saved. She almost trembled for that invisible part of us in her'.[20] Wordsworth, for his part, 'trembled for that invisible part of us in' him during his occasional visits to the 'anarchy and din | Barbarian and infernal' of the city; when, on one such visit, in September 1802, the Lambs acted as his guide to Bartholomew Fair,[21] he experienced its carnivalesque 'nether world' as typifying the 'blank confusion' of urban life. The 'swarm' of 'undistinguishable' Londoners, 'living amid the same perpetual flow | Of trivial objects, melted and reduced | To one identity,' was to him an oppressive 'hell' which stupified 'creative powers'.[22] But Mary, who, like her brother, had 'a mind that loves to be at home in Crowds',[23] found such a merged state of being exhilarating.

As if in deliberate opposition to the Wordsworthian moral ideal, Charles's paeans in praise of his city make a point of

---

[17] Ibid., ii. 90.   [18] *Letters*, ed. Lucas, ii. 217.   [19] Ibid., 273.
[20] *Letters*, ed. Marrs, iii. 96.   [21] See ibid., ii. 66.
[22] Wordsworth, *The Prelude or Growth of a Poet's Mind*, ed. Ernest de Selincourt, rev. Helen Darbishire (2nd edn., Oxford: Clarendon Press, 1959), p. 260. For a critical account of Wordsworth's reaction to Bartholomew Fair, see Peter Stallybrass and Allon White, *The Politics and Poetics of Transgression* (London: Methuen, 1986), pp. 119–24.
[23] *Letters*, ed. Marrs, i. 277.

celebrating its deformities: London 'with-the-many-sins'[24] is loved for its vices as much as its virtues. The apparent perversity of this attachment is consciously heightened in the 'Londoner' essay proper, in which the Great Wen is personified as an all-engulfing mother and anarchic Earth Goddess:

Where has spleen her food but in London? Humour, Interest, Curiosity, suck at her measureless breasts without a possibility of being satiated. Nursed amid her noise, her crowds, her beloved smoke, what have I been doing all my life, if I have not lent out my heart with usury to such scenes! (i. 40)

The City is celebrated as female and insatiably plural; her multifaceted diversity is seen as providing an alternative, and preferred, mother figure to that monolithic mountain landscape which Wordsworth hailed as his 'nurse'.[25] What is more, the City as mother does not develop the ego strength of her offspring; on the contrary, the Londoner's self-possession is lost in wonder and a glad immersion in immanence. Recent feminist critics have commented upon the Romantic poets' aptitude for appropriating the feminine element so that it serves but to bolster a dominant masculine ego:[26] for Wordsworth, for example, mother Nature appears diligently intent upon strengthening the confidence of her 'chosen son' in his creative and ethical powers, and furthering in him the development of an 'absolute self' which can transcend its particular environment if it prove unsympathetic. But the Londoner's empathic merging with the plurality of his City serves to diffuse rather than buttress the ego, and corresponds more closely to recent feminist representations of feminine subjectivity than it does to the Romantic masculine ideal. In her essay 'This Sex Which Is Not One', Luce Irigaray, for example, sees the multifaceted nature of female sexuality, and the multiple parts of the female genitalia, as providing an alternative cultural emblem to the monolithic phallus. She describes female sexuality as *'plural'*, and absorbed in a different economy from that of the male, one

---

[24] *Letters*, ed. Marrs, i. 248.

[25] See Wordsworth, 'Lines Composed a Few Miles above Tintern Abbey', *Poetical Works*, ii. 262.

[26] See Alan Richardson, 'Romanticism and the Colonization of the Female', in Anne K. Mellor (ed.), *Romanticism and Feminism* (Bloomington and Indianapolis: Indiana Univ. Press, 1988), pp. 13–25.

which 'upsets the linearity of a project, undermines the goal-object of a desire, diffuses the polarisation towards a single pleasure, disconcerts fidelity to a single discourse'.[27] Experiencing herself as several rather than single, woman is less likely to differentiate herself sharply from others and relate to them only through ownership or appropriation: instead she 'enters into a ceaseless exchange of herself with the other without any possibility of identifying either'.[28] From a very different perspective, informed not so much by the nature of female sexuality as by the consequences for women of the conventional allocation of child care to females, Nancy Chodorow, as we have seen, presents the greater intensity and duration of the female child's pre-Oedipal bond with the mother as also leading in adulthood to a greater capacity than the male's to identify and merge with others.[29] But just as masculine self-possession and the assertion of the single, phallic 'I', operate, in a phallocentric society, as prescriptive templates for both male and female achievement, so the more permeable female ego boundaries and the plurality of the female genitalia, with the alternative value-systems which they emblemize, can also potentially serve as symbolic models of behaviour for men as well as for women. Indeed, as many American and European feminists have recently stressed, they must necessarily serve to such effect if social systems based on repressive power and dominance are ever to be fully deconstructed, and not endlessly to repeat themselves with every new revolution.[30] The ready immersion of self within the quotidian which Charles exemplifies in his letters on London indicates the potential for a diffuse plurality of being in male as well as female subjectivity, a potential which, as we shall see, was to be realized more fully in his Elia essays.

Charles's love for particulars, as more vividly representative of life than universalized abstractions, is amply demonstrated

[27] Luce Irigaray, *This Sex Which Is Not One* (Ithaca, NY: Cornell Univ. Press, 1985), pp. 28–30. [28] Ibid., p. 31.
[29] Nancy Chodorow, *The Reproduction of Mothering: Psychoanalysis and the Sociology of Gender* (Berkeley, Calif.: Univ. of California Press, 1978); see above, pp. 40–1.
[30] See Adrienne Rich, 'When We Dead Awaken' in *On Lies, Secrets and Silences: Selected Prose 1966–1978* (London: Virago, 1980), p. 35; and Julia Kristeva, 'Interview—1974: Julia Kristeva and Psychoanalyse et Politique', *mf*, 5 and 6 (1981), 167.

in many of his writings. In the Elia essay 'New Year's Eve', for example, he shores up against the intimations of mortality afforded by the passing of the year the gusto of his appreciation of detail: 'the sweet security of streets', 'the delicious juices of meats and fishes, and society, and the cheerful glass, and candle-light, and fire-side conversations, and innocent vanities, and jests, and *irony itself*' (ii. 29), are juxtaposed, with conscious irony, to the eclipse of death. Occasionally, however, in his letters, he shows himself to be sufficiently entrammelled in the ideology of his times to see his propensity never to 'judge system-wise of things, but fasten upon particulars'[31] as a defect rather than a strength. Letters to Godwin and to Wordsworth apologize for his inability to respond in a suitably systematic fashion to the totalizing method of their writing: 'I can vehemently applaud, or perversely stickle, at *parts*; but I cannot grasp at a whole', he tells Godwin; 'my brain is always desultory & snatches off hints from things, but can seldom follow a "work" methodically', he explains to Wordsworth.[32] His depreciatory self-estimation corresponds closely to his contemporaries' opinion of female as opposed to male intellection: according to Hannah More, for example, 'both in composition and action [women] excel in details; but they do not so much generalize their ideas as men, nor do their minds seize a great subject with so large a grasp'.[33] The fragmentary nature of the essay, which Johnson in his 1755 *Dictionary of the English Language* defined as 'A loose sally of the mind; an irregular indigested piece; not a regular and orderly composition',[34] provided Charles with a literary genre well suited to his characteristic habits of mind. The development of the essay as a popular form in the second half of the eighteenth century has been associated with the growth in female literacy during that period; periodicals such as the *Tatler* were openly designed to appeal to a female readership and presented themselves to a great degree as magazines for women.[35] According to J. R. Green

---

[31] *Letters*, ed. Marrs, i. 163.   [32] Ibid., ii. 128 and iii. 111.

[33] Hannah More, *Strictures on the Modern System of Female Education* (London: T. Cadell & W. Davies), ii. 25.

[34] Samuel Johnson, *A Dictionary of the English Language* (London: J. and P. Knapton *et al.*, 1755).

[35] See Bertha Monica Stearns, 'Early English Periodicals for Ladies (1700–1760)', *PMLA*, 48 (1933), 41.

in the introduction to his nineteenth-century edition of Addison's essays, 'It is in this new relation of writers to the world of women that we find the key to the Essayists.'[36] While some of the male periodical writers may well have considered their adoption of the essay form as a patronizing 'writing down' to what they presumed to be the limited intellectual grasp of their new female readers, to Charles the genre provided an opportunity to 'fasten upon particulars' which was natural to his way of thinking.

The eighteenth-century and early nineteenth-century periodical essay characteristically took the form of a pseudonymously signed 'letter' addressed to the editor of the periodical: as Jon P. Klancher explains in his book *The Making of English Reading Audiences 1790–1832*, the correspondence page in a twentieth-century newspaper 'remains a faint vestige of what once constituted a periodical's whole mode of public discourse'.[37] In some of his pre-Elian journalism, Charles used the pseudonymous epistolary voice to develop an ironic form of dramatic monologue which was later to influence the formation of his Elia persona. Typically, in these character sketches, a fictitious personality or 'type' discloses his character traits in a spirit of self-congratulation, while at the same time unconsciously exposing to the reader the self-deception and selfishness to which his complacent egotism blinds him.[38] For Charles, the form was useful in that it allowed him to represent the 'impertinence of manhood' and its pretensions in a manner which did not cut across his refusal to adopt a judgemental position. The character is free to account for his life in his own terms, without the intrusion of a didactic authorial voice, yet his readers discern his condition, and in the process may recognize similar patterns of self-deception in themselves, but

[36] John Richard Green (ed.), *Essays of Joseph Addison* (London: Macmillan, 1880), p. ix.

[37] Jon P. Klancher, *The Making of English Audiences 1790–1832* (Madison, Wis.: Univ. of Wisconsin Press, 1987), p. 21.

[38] See Allie Webb, 'Charles Lamb's Use of the Character', *Southern Quarterly*, 1 (1963), 273–84, for the historical context of Charles's character portrayals. Lamb's character sketches, like much of his writings, were influenced by his favourite seventeenth-century reading: see Melvin R. Watson, *Magazine Serials and the Essay Tradition, 1746–1820*, (Baton Rouge, La.: Lousiana State Univ. Press, 1956), p. 79, for an account of the sketches as a 'mixture of seventeenth-century method and eighteenth-century manner'.

all in a spirit of ironic play rather than heavy-handed condemnation. In the 1811 essay 'Edax on Appetite', for example, Edax
complains at length of the burdens imposed upon his humane
and loving spirit by his excessive appetite. He recollects his
school-days, and

> the horror I used to feel, when in some silent corner retired from the
> notice of my unfeeling playfellows, I have sat to mumble the solitary
> slice of gingerbread allotted me by the bounty of considerate friends,
> and have ached at heart because I could not spare a portion of it, as I
> saw other boys do, to some favourite boy;—for if I know my own
> heart, I was never selfish,—never possessed a luxury which I did not
> hasten to communicate to others; but my food, alas! was none; it was
> an indispensable necessary. (i. 120)

'Reminiscences of Juke Judkins, Esq., of Birmingham' (1826)
provides a fuller portrayal of the Edax type. Judkins reveals
himself to be a miser of the first order, although his prodigious
conceit and complacency blind him to the self-condemnatory
nature of his autobiography.[39] As ironic forms it has been
suggested that these dramatic monologues influenced later
nineteenth-century writings, such as Browning's poems or
Dickens's use of unconscious self-disclosure in establishing
character.[40] In them, through the use of the first person, Charles
dramatizes with obvious enjoyment the moral deformities of
the humanity which flowed by him on the London streets
without divorcing his voice from theirs; he is merged with
them, and yet his exposure of the particular roles they play in
the 'pantomime or masquerade' of human relations may help to
shake them, through laughter, out of their act.

But these occasional pieces, whether or not they proved
effective, would hardly have been sufficient in themselves to
establish Charles's reputation as an essayist. As he recognized
in an only recently published review of Hazlitt's *Table Talk*, 'a
series of Miscellaneous Essays, however well executed in the

---

[39] For a further account of Judkins's unintentional self-revelations, see
Charles I. Patterson, 'Charles Lamb's Insight into the Nature of the Novel',
PMLA, 67 (1952), 381.

[40] See Geoffrey Tillotson, 'The Historical Importance of Certain *Essays of Elia*',
in James V. Logan, John E. Jordan, and Northrop Frye (eds.), *Some British
Romantics: A Collection of Essays* (Columbus, Ohio: Ohio State Univ. Press,
1966), pp. 95–6; and Peter A. Brier, 'Lamb, Dickens and the Theatrical Vision',
Charles Lamb Bulletin, 2 (1975), 65–70.

parts, if it have not some pervading character to give a unity to it, is ordinarily as tormenting to get through as a set of aphorisms, or a jest-book.'[41] In 1820 his involvement with the newly established *London Magazine* gave him the opportunity to develop such a pervasive persona. Recommended to John Scott, the first editor of the *London*, by Hazlitt,[42] Charles found amongst its contributors a congenial 'body corporate' which established in him a sense of loyalty towards the periodical, resulting in the production, over the next six years, of a series of essays under the signature 'Elia'.[43] Through them he became, for the first time, in his middle forties, a popular writer in his own day, and on them his subsequent reputation as an author largely rests. Throughout the nineteenth and early twentieth centuries Elia was esteemed for the manner in which his conversational mode of address furthered the familiar style in essay writing. Many of the essays owed their origins to passages from Charles's actual correspondence; the germs of such essays as 'Distant Correspondents', 'A Dissertation upon Roast Pig', 'Amicus Redivivius', 'Barrenness of the Imaginative Faculty in the Productions of Modern Art', and 'A Death-Bed' are to be found in his personal letters, to be later reworked from memory for periodical publication.[44] Addressed directly to the readers, as opposed to the periodical editor, the epistolary style

[41] Roy Park (ed.), *Lamb as Critic* (London: Routledge & Kegan Paul, 1980), p. 300.

[42] See Thomas Noon Talfourd, *Final Memorials of Charles Lamb; Consisting Chiefly of his Letters not before Published, with Sketches of some of his Companions*, 2 vols. (London: Moxon, 1848), ii. 1. By all accounts an exemplary editor, and one who particularly appreciated Charles's work, Scott's involvement in a bitter feud with *Blackwood's Magazine* culminated in February 1821 in a duel and his subsequent death. John Taylor became his successor as editor of the *London*. See Josephine Bauer, *The London Magazine 1820–29* (Copenhagen: Rosenkilde and Bagger, 1953) and T. R. Hughes, ' "The London Magazine" (1820–1829)' (unpub. Oxford Univ. diss., 1931).

[43] For accounts of the 'gentle anarchy' of the *London* circle, in which Charles found himself much at home, see Bryan Waller Procter ['Barry Cornwall'], *Charles Lamb: A Memoir* (London: Edward Moxon, 1866), p. 156; Jack, *English Literature 1815–1832*, p. 287; and Tim Chilcott, *A Publisher and his Circle: The Life and Work of John Taylor, Keats's Publisher* (London: Routledge & Kegan Paul, 1972), p. 143–8.

[44] For the original epistolary version of each of these essays, see *Letters*, ed. Marrs, iii. 252 ('Distant Correspondents'); *Letters*, ed. Lucas, ii. 317–18 ('A Dissertation on Roast Pig'); ii. 405–6 ('Amicus Redivivus'); iii. 97–8 ('Barrenness of the Imaginative Faculty in the Productions of Modern Art'); iii. 67 ('A Death-Bed').

of the essays assumes, and thereby, if it succeeds with a reader, creates, a relaxed and sympathetic response. But Elia's apparent innocuousness and his open admission of his many failings also have the effect of seductively drawing the disarmed reader in to participate empathically in singular processes at work in his essays.

In 'A Character of the Late Elia' supposedly written 'by a friend' and later republished by Charles as the 'Preface' to the second volume of Elia's collected essays, Charles describes Elia as one who was forever 'making himself many', and 'shadowing forth' under the guise of a first-person narrator the experiences of disparate characters (ii. 151).[45] His personal correspondence indicates that Charles experienced himself as a conglomeration of parts rather than a whole; in 1822 he explained himself to Wordsworth as 'made up of queer points' and of 'many parts', and connects this with his capacity to merge with others to such an extent that to lose an acquaintance entailed the loss of a part of himself.[46] Dead authors as well as contemporaries made up his multiple parts: 'I love to lose myself in other men's minds', Elia exclaims in the essay 'Detached Thoughts on Books and Reading' (ii. 172) This desire to merge with others, this 'feminine forgetfulness of one's self', as Walter Pater put it,[47] is manifested in the Elia essays in a manner which invites the reader's participation. Experiencing himself as many, Elia incorporates within himself, under his own signature, a variety of disparate 'types' which frequently represent the darker aspects of the human personality. These are not externalized or projected out on to a scapegoated 'other' but recognized as the 'shadow' parts of a multiple self. The Elia essay 'The Convalescent', for example, is a veiled presentation, in the first person, of the hypochondriac type, and the last of Elia's series of 'Popular Fallacies', 'That a Sulky Temper is a Misfortune', is disputed by a persona with markedly paranoid characteristics. But in these essays, as opposed to Charles's earlier character sketches such

[45] See A. G. van Kranendonk, 'Notes on the Style of the Essays of Elia', *English Studies*, 14 (1932), 9, and Wayne McKenna, *Charles Lamb and the Theatre* (Gerrards Cross: Colin Smythe, 1978), pp. 8–9, for further analyses of the dramatic element in Elia's adoption of roles.

[46] *Letters*, ed. Lucas, ii. 319.

[47] Walter Pater, *Plato and Platonism, The Works of Walter Pater*, vi (London: Macmillan, 1910), p. 281.

as 'Edax on Appetite', the 'type' undergoes a change during the course of his monologue, in a manner which highlights one of the particular techniques of the Elia essays as a whole. In a comment on the *Essays of Elia* in *A Room of One's Own* Virginia Woolf draws attention to 'that wild flash of imagination, that lightning crack of genius' which frequently puncture the essays, upsetting their logical linearity and 'wholeness' and leaving them 'flawed and imperfect', but increasing their suggestive force.[48] No change occurs in the personality of 'Edax' during his monologue, but the self-enclosed worlds of the 'Convalescent' and the 'Popular Fallacies' paranoid are shattered by revelations which break in upon their accounts and leave them at the close of the piece with their pretensions punctured. These pieces provide examples of what Friedrich Schlegel, categorizing the types of irony in his essay 'On Incomprehensibility' (1800), has called 'dramatic irony', 'that is, when an author has written three acts, then unexpectedly turns into another man and now has to write the last two acts'.[49]

In 'The Convalescent' the essayist begins by presenting himself as suffering from an inflation of self-aggrandizement during a bout of illness. 'How sickness enlarges the dimensions of a man's self to himself!' he exclaims: the patient 'has put on the strong armour of sickness, he is wrapped in the callous hide of suffering; he keeps his sympathy, like some curious vintage, under trusty lock and key, for his own use only' (ii. 184). But a letter from his editor requesting an article cuts across the egotism of Elia's convalescent state, and returns him to reality:

The hypochondriac flatus is subsiding; the acres, which in imagination I had spread over—for the sick man swells in the sole contemplation of his single sufferings, till he becomes a Tityus to himself—are wasting to a span; and for the giant of self-importance, which I was so lately, you have me once again in my natural pretensions—the lean and meagre figure of your insignificant Essayist. (ii. 186–7)

Similarly, at the opening of the last 'Popular Fallacy', the essayist presents himself as having reached a paranoid peak of self-gratification by persuading himself of the disloyalty of his friends. In this heady state, it is possible to

Think the very idea of right and fit fled from the earth, or your breast the solitary receptacle of it, till you have swelled yourself into at least one hemisphere; the other being the vast Arabia Stony of your friends and the world aforesaid. To grow bigger every moment in your own conceit, and the world to lessen: to deify yourself at the expense of your species; to judge the world—this is the acme and supreme point of your mystery—these the true PLEASURES OF SULKINESS. (ii. 274)

But this inflation also, like the Convalescent's, abruptly subsides before the close of the piece, with the friendly entrance upon the scene of the very acquaintances whom Elia had earlier been denouncing; their arrival demolishes 'the whole flattering superstructure which pride had piled upon neglect' (ii. 274).

Such pieces seem written with the intention of demonstrating the ease with which egotism and the will to power, the 'impertinence of manhood', can be blown up into a species of madness when nursed in isolation; in each case the 'hypochondriac flatus' (ii. 186) is punctured by a call back to the sanity of community and friendship. Puncturing an oppressive system was an act with which Charles could empathize even in its most violent and self-destructive forms. An 1811 essay on the Gunpowder Plot, which he republished as part of the Elia essay 'Guy Faux', recognizes in Faux's plot the desperate acting out of a strangled appeal for justice, and concludes with an appeal to 'every honest Englishman' to pre-empt the need for such violent acts: Charles asks his readers to 'hold the *lantern* to the dark places of corruption,' and 'apply the *match* to the rotten parts of the system' (ii. 243). The lightening flash of recognition which cuts through the rotten parts of the multiple system of the self in such pieces as 'The Convalescent' and 'That A Sulky Temper is a Misfortune' has perhaps its immediate real-life correlative for Charles not so much in the Gunpowder Plot as in the blow with which Mary in her madness struck at the oppressions weighing upon her own existence, unconsciously projected on to the person of her mother. Charles writes as if in a deliberate attempt to demonstrate to his sister that the knife may be applied to 'bad' objects through the healing agency of the text, rather than through a more uncontrollably physical acting out. In these Elia essays, the 'bad' object is not externalized as a Government or parental figure, but located, owned, and punctured within the self.

The pattern of inflation followed by puncture recurs as a shaping motif in many of the Elia essays. The first of the Elia essays opens with a sequence in which the reader, imagined as a busy, preoccupied capitalist, is drawn away from 'thy passage from the Bank—where thou hast been receiving thy half-yearly dividends' to explore a superannuated, near-by edifice, whose 'importance is from the past', the South Sea House (ii. 1 and 7). Its deserted labyrinthine passages, peopled in the past by a host of characters whom Elia calls up from the shades, act as an emblem of the fate of the vast inflated bubble of present-day enterprise, equally regardless in its pretentious busy-ness of its own puncturing nemesis, yet to come. In essay after essay Elia recalls his past and sets it as a counterpoint to present preoccupations, to illustrate their relativity. The coexistence of 'the child Elia—that "other me," there, in the back-ground' (ii. 28) with the adult persona frequently serves as a foil to reveal and puncture the 'impertinence of manhood'. The essay 'Poor Relations', for instance, constitutes a particularly subtle example of the phenomenon. In the experience of reading this essay there is no single moment at which the knife can be said to go in, but the final phrase suddenly holds up 'the lantern' to reveal the operation as having been performed, the cancer as having been exposed, all unbeknownst to the reader anaesthetized by Elia's seemingly innocuous prose. The essay opens with a spiralling string of cruelly humorous phrases through which Elia appears to associate himself with the rich man's embarrassed and disdainful attitude towards his Poor Relations—an attitude implicit in the name itself. Denied an unquestioning acceptance into the domestic circles to which by blood they belong, 'poor relations', like the drunkard or the Jacobin, are damned by name, and consequently in reality; their families are unready to consider 'what the *thing* is' as opposed to 'the *name*' (i. 133). But in the second half of the piece, Elia recollects his personal acquaintance as a child with an impoverished relative:

The earliest impressions which I received on this matter, are certainly not attended with anything painful, or very humiliating, in the recalling. At my father's table (no very splendid one) was to be found, every Saturday, the mysterious figure of an aged gentleman . . . A sort of melancholy grandeur invested him. (ii. 161)

Impressed by the dignity and presence of the old man, the child also notices that when on one unfortunate occasion he is inadvertently treated patronizingly, he reacts with strong feeling and is clearly acutely sensitive to his position and the opprobrium it may bring upon him. The essay had opened with the words 'A Poor Relation—is the most irrelevant thing in nature . . . an odious approximation . . . a preposterous shadow, lengthening in the noontide of your prosperity . . . a perpetually recurring mortification'; it closes, after the description of the old man, with the sentence 'This was—a Poor Relation' (ii. 157–8 and 163). The idea of what it means to be a Poor Relation, rather than what it is to have a Poor Relation, has by now been so strongly impressed upon the reader's mind that it comes as a shock to be reminded of the easy, slighting mockeries with which he or she had thoughtlessly acquiesced at the commencement of the essay. The general effect of the whole is to bring about a recognition and rebuttal of a dehumanizing attitude in the self, without arousing in the reader feelings of either bitter self-contempt at the original barbarism or complacent pride in the amelioration.[50]

In these essays Elia takes upon himself the role of one who aggrandizes the self through projecting its shadow parts on to a scapegoated other, and then turns the tables against that persona to reveal the 'thing of darkness' as lodged within his own breast. As he says in 'Witches, and other Night Fears', speaking of the monsters of superstition generally, 'the archetypes are in us, and eternal' (ii. 68). According to Julia Kristeva in her essay 'Women's Time' such a withdrawal of projections constitutes a necessary step in the deconstruction of all hierarchical and divisive social roles; the 'struggle, the implacable difference, the violence' between apparently polarized groups has to be 'de-dramatized' and acknowledged instead as a clash of contradictory forces at work within the subject. The 'violence' has to 'be conceived in the very place where it

[50] For a similar account of 'Poor Relations', see Violet Khazoum, 'The Novel and Characters in the *Essays of Elia*', *Studies in English Literature*, 16 (1976), pp. 574–5.

operates with the maximum intransigence, in other words, in personal and sexual identity itself, so as to make it disintegrate in its very nucleus'.[51] In this passage, Kristeva is thinking primarily of the need to deconstruct gender difference; she presents the construction of polarized male and female roles as the primary act of projection which initiates the dehumanizing process whereby the Other is externalized and categorized as alien to the self. For the sociologist Jean Lipman-Blumen also the sex-gender system is

the blueprint for *all* other power relationships . . . Gender roles are the model for power relationships between generations, socio-economic classes, religious, racial and ethnic groups, as well as between imperial powers and their colonies, and between less developed and post-industrialized societies . . . As long as this key power relationship between men and women remains in the traditional balance, *all* institutions are protected from change.[52]

Binary divisions, involving an imbalance of power, between white and black, upper and lower class, old and young, the governors and the governed, are seen as constructed according to the pattern established by the early inculcation of differential gender roles; once that hierarchical division has been accepted, it is difficult for the subject to free itself from the concept of human relations as a power-struggle between opposing groups. Liberation from such destructive patterns can only be achieved by the recognition that contradictory drives, both active and passive, are perpetually at work within the individual, and need to be accepted as such, without value-laden splitting. Only through an artificial violence, involving the projection out on to another of conflicting attributes, is the false myth of unproblematic subjective coherence constructed.

As part of Charles's aim to undermine the walls raised between one group and another, and the limitations to human potential which such divisions entail, some of the Elia essays do deal specifically with the problem of gender difference. The essay 'Modern Gallantry', for example, expresses with uncharacteristic directness Elia's anger at the hypocrisy of those men

---

[51] Kristeva, 'Women's Time', *The Kristeva Reader*, p. 209.
[52] Jean Lipman-Blumen, *Gender Roles and Power* (Englewood Cliffs, NJ: Prentice Hall, 1984), pp. 5 and 48.

who would disguise the injustices of gender inequality under a veneer of 'gallantry'. The modern gallant may pride himself on his deferential appreciation of his lady, but Elia cannot give credence to this 'conventional fiction' of male esteem for the female until social conditions, as they affect all men and women, are drastically changed: 'I shall begin to believe that there is some such principle influencing our conduct, when more than one-half of the drudgery and coarse servitude of the world shall cease to be performed by women' (ii. 80). In other more characteristic essays, Elia's open recognition of his own feminine attributes works to deconstruct the 'conventional fiction', or, as Kristeva terms it, the 'metaphysic', of gender difference. The sentence with which Elia opens the essay 'Old China'—'I have an almost feminine partiality for old china' (ii. 247)—declares at once his enjoyment of the particularities of quotidian domesticity, and his acknowledgement of the feminine traits in himself revealed by that partiality. Moreover, when he proceeds to describe the scenes painted on the old teacups, it becomes clear that they please particularly because in themselves they demonstrate a freedom, as naïve art, from conventional frames of representation. 'Seen through the lucid atmosphere of fine Cathay', 'lawless' figures, 'under the notion of men and women, float about, uncircumscribed by any element, in that world before perspective—a china teacup'. Elia's affection for them dates from infancy, from before the period of memory, and he refuses to allow any acceptance of adult conventions to diminish his appreciation. In the world represented on the teacup, modern systematizing structures such as the theory of perspective, in itself but a historically constructed convention without absolute validity,[53] become irrelevant; the rules and divisions by which adult society organizes and constrains sense data are revealed as but relative fabrications. Elia draws particular attention to the teacup art's freedom from conventional gender differentiation, and the pleasure that gives him: 'I love

[53] See E. H. Gombrich, *Art and Illusion: A Study in the Psychology of Pictorial Representation* (London: Phaidon Press, 1960), p. 209: ' "We do not always realize," writes Sir Herbert Read, "that the theory of perspective developed in the fifteenth century is a scientific convention; it is merely one way of describing space and has no absolute validity".'

the men with women's faces, and the women, if possible, with still more womanish expressions' (ii. 248).

But nowhere, perhaps, is Elia's attempt to show how the individual subject can be made up of both masculine and feminine elements more effectively illustrated than in the essay 'Mrs Battle's Opinions on Whist'. Mrs Battle, with a masculine absoluteness, is dedicated to the battle in play of cards: 'It was her business, her duty, the thing she came into the world to do' (ii. 33). She scorns frivolous players and the decorations of the play, while Elia, taking the more feminine role, tries to point out to her that the colour and ornament of the cards may have their part to play in the gratifications she draws from her favourite pursuit. Defending her insistence upon 'the rigour of the game', Mrs Battle presents card-playing as a harmless means of satiating the competitive drive, without demurring at the unfeminine implications of confessing to such a need:

To the puny objectors against cards, as nurturing the bad passions, she would retort, that man is a gaming animal. He must be always trying to get the better in something or other:—that this passion can scarcely be more safely expended than upon a game at cards: that cards are a temporary illusion; in truth, a mere drama; for we do but *play* at being mightily concerned, where a few idle shillings are at stake, yet, during the illusion, we are as mightily concerned as those whose stake is crowns and kingdoms. They are a sort of dream-fighting; much ado; great battling, and little bloodshed; mighty means for disproportioned ends; quite as diverting, and a great deal more innoxious, than many of those more serious *games* of life, which men play, without esteeming them to be such. (ii. 37)

For all her use of the masculine pronoun in this passage, Mrs Battle is the warring animal in the essay: she will not countenance such idle frivolities as playing without a stake, '*for love*'. It is her need to play the warrior's role in life which is appeased by the utilitarian ends to which she devotes cards, and not Elia's, who is content, rather, to play at times for the sake of play itself.[54]

The essay closes with the depiction of a free-floating moment

[54] See John E. Stevens, 'Charles Lamb, the Romantic Humorist', *Charles Lamb Bulletin*, 3 (1978), 120, for a further account of the contrasts drawn in this essay between Mrs Battle's utilitarian stance and Elia's Romanticism.

in which Elia is joined in a game 'for love' by his cousin
Bridget, a moment out of time with no before or after:

That last game I had with my sweet cousin (I capotted her)—(dare I tell
thee, how foolish I am?)—I wished it might have lasted for ever,
though we gained nothing, and lost nothing, though it was a mere
shade of play: I would be content to go on in that idle folly for ever. . . .
Bridget and I should be ever playing. (ii. 37)

For the Lambs such moments of peace had, of course, their own
significance, but in these essays Charles's work reaches out to
enfold the reader also in the embrace of such a moment. In the
above quotation, for example, Elia, in his direct approach to the
reader, does dare to disclose his foolish childlikeness, trusting
in and thereby creating a playful childlike or mothering
response: the reader is guided towards ways of experiencing
which have conventionally been viewed as unmanly and
systematically undervalued as such. Robert D. Frank, in a
critical study of the Elia essays, has pointed to the manner in
which Elia's open admission of folly or feminine weakness in
such essays as 'Old China' and 'Mrs Battle's Opinions on Whist'
gains his readers' confidence: 'since we feel that he has no
designs on us, we relax, unaware that we are preparing
ourselves to participate sympathetically in his meditation'.[55]
The route along which the reader is drawn in these essays is
one which takes him or her away from the conventional paths
of gender differentiation; sympathizing with Mrs Battle, a
female reader gains access to masculine components in the self,
while a male reader, if he identifies with her warlike disposition,
is accepting it as an attribute of the female as much as the male.

   The subversiveness of this deviant route may not, of course,
be consciously recognized by the reader; Hazlitt's comments
upon the essay provide one example of a contemporary reader
who was drawn into the wayward play of the text without
apparently discerning its gender-role implications. In such
essays as 'On Effeminacy of Character', Hazlitt presents himself
as an unequivocal promoter of masculine values:

There is nothing more to be esteemed than a manly firmness and
decision of character. I like a person who knows his own mind and

[55] Robert D. Frank, *Don't Call Me Gentle Charles!: An Essay on Lamb's* Essays
of Elia (Corvallis: Oregon State Univ. Press, 1976), p. 124.

sticks to it; who sees at once what is to be done in given circumstances and does it. . . . There is stuff in him, and it is of the right practicable sort.[56]

Not surprisingly, perhaps, Hazlitt's favourite amongst the Elia essays was 'Mrs Battle's Opinions on Whist'; he particularly appreciated the clarity of its language, 'undefiled' by Elia's customary use of ornate turns of expression.[57] But the unusual manliness of discourse that Hazlitt admires in the essay is Mrs Battle's rather than Elia's; in providing the reader with a record of her reported speech, Elia adopts a direct, no-nonsense form of address suited to her rationalistic stance. It is Mrs Battle, with her 'fine eighteenth-century countenance', who here, for all her biological femininity, embodies the manly principles Hazlitt advocates, though he does not choose to reflect upon that fact. In such a manner Elia plays with all his readers, provoking them gently and barely perceptively into a change of attitude, and a widening of conceptual horizons. Enacting a variety of apparently disparate roles, and presenting each as so many aspects of the self, Elia draws the reader in to sympathize and identify with his various aspects, and find for them as many answering parts in themselves.

III

The *Essays of Elia*, then, meet Schlegel's demand 'that events, men, in short the play of life, be taken as play and be represented as such'.[58] In the 'Preface by a Friend of the late Elia' Elia's persistent childlikeness and his resentment of 'the impertinence of manhood' is presented as the 'key to explicate some of his writings' (ii. 153). The childlike phenomenon of play constitutes the key to the method of the Elia essays as well as their content. As we saw at the close of the last chapter, it also formed part of the Lambs' courageous endeavour to extract as

[56] Hazlitt, *The Complete Works of William Hazlitt*, ed. P. P. Howe, 21 vols. (London: Dent, 1930–4) viii. 253.

[57] Ibid., 245.

[58] Friedrich Schlegel, *Dialogues on Poetry and Literary Aphorisms*, trans. Ernest Behler and Roman Struc (University Park, Pa. and London: Pennsylvania State Univ. Press, 1968), p. 89.

much joy as they could out of their troubled lives. Through his Elia persona Charles draws the reader also into the sanity of play. In the essay 'New Year's Eve', Elia casts a retrospective glance back over the 'play' of his life as a whole in a manner which allows him to accept even the more painful chapters of his past as features of the game:

I play over again *for love*, as the gamesters phrase it, games, for which I once paid so dear. I would scarce now have any of those untoward accidents and events of my life reversed. I would no more alter them than the incidents of some well-contrived novel. (ii. 28)

In commenting on this passage in a suggestive essay on 'Lamb's Women', Gillian Beer has drawn attention to the connection between it and the theories of play put forward in the writings of the psychoanalyst D. W. Winnicott.[59] In his book *Playing and Reality* Winnicott presents the creativity of the artist as a continuation into adulthood of children's play, and stresses in particular the important function of such play in the acceptance of reality. Imaginative play is located in a 'potential space' between the inner world of the subject and its apprehensions of outer reality, between self and Other. Winnicott aims to show that

the task of reality-acceptance is never completed, that no human being is free from the strain of relating inner and outer reality, and that relief from this strain is provided by an intermediate area of experience . . . which is not challenged (arts, religion, etc.) This intermediate area is in direct continuity with the play area of the small child who is 'lost' in play.[60]

Through the use of symbols in creative play, such as the '*fort-da*' game which Freud describes in 'Beyond the Pleasure Principle', children at once signify their developing awareness of their separateness from others and lack of omnipotent control over their environment, and also begin, through the active manifestation of their powers in constructing the game, to reconcile themselves to the indignities of this position.[61] In just

[59] Gillian Beer, 'Lamb's Women', *Charles Lamb Bulletin*, 6 (1984), 142.
[60] D. W. Winnicott, *Playing and Reality* (Harmondsworth: Penguin, 1974), p. 15.
[61] See Freud, 'Beyond the Pleasure Principle' (1920), *Pelican Freud Library*, ed. Angela Richards (Harmondsworth: Penguin, 1984), xi. 283–7. In the 'fort-da'

such a way Elia describes himself in 'New Year's Eve' as creating in recollection a narrative from his life, by which even its more difficult phases become facets in the richness of the whole, and form a pattern like that of art. Winnicott's argument supports Schiller's declaration that 'man only plays when he is in the fullest sense of the word a human being, and *he is only fully a human being when he plays.*'[62] But we need not rely solely upon twentieth-century psychoanalysts for accounts of the 'intermediate area' of play and its relation to art and to life: one of the Elia essays, 'On the Artificial Comedy of the Last Century', describes 'the happy breathing-place' between objective reality and the subjective imagination afforded by creative play in terms very similar to Winnicott's. In this essay Elia attacks the burdensome insistence of early nineteenth-century theatre audiences upon seeing stage performances as straightforward representations of objective reality; unable to free themselves from moral attitudinizing, they allocate blame to dramatic characters in a manner which blinds them to what Charles sees as the playfulness of Restoration comedy. Its pleasures for him lie in the very deliberateness of its artifice, the way in which its actors, through playing to the gallery, indicate that they are enacting their roles 'under the life, or beside it; not *to the life*' (ii. 164). By means of this 'secret correspondence with the company before the curtain' (ii. 140), the actors, openly dispensing with any semblance of reality, invite the audience to join in the game. But the theatre-goers of Elia's day were not prepared to allow even drama a space for play:

We have no such middle emotions as dramatic interests left. . . . We substitute a real for a dramatic person and judge him accordingly. . . . We dare not contemplate an Atlantis, a scheme, out of which our coxcombical moral sense is for a little transitory ease excluded. . . . We would indict our very dreams. (ii. 141, 144)

game, a child, through throwing away and then reclaiming a small object, symbolically enacts its mother's departure and return; the game expresses the child's awareness of the mother's separateness, and at the same time is consolatory, because it allows the child to pass from the passive position of being overpowered by the mother's absence to an active one where he inflicts the same fate upon an object.

[62] Friedrich Schiller, *On the Aesthetic Education of Man in a Series of Letters*, (1793), ed. and trans. Elizabeth M. Wilkinson and L. A. Willoughby (Oxford: Clarendon Press, 1967), p. 107.

His contemporaries must exert an 'impertinent' and 'detestable coxcombry of moral judgement upon every thing'; like the utilitarian schoolteacher criticized in the Elia essay 'The Old and the New Schoolmaster', nothing comes to them 'not spoiled by the sophisticating medium of moral uses' (ii. 53). But, for Elia, participation in the 'intermediate experience' of the theatre refreshes his perception of reality and helps him to accept its confinements:

I confess for myself that . . . I am glad . . . now and then, for a dream-while or so, to imagine a world with no meddling restrictions . . . I come back to my cage and my restraint the fresher and more healthy for it. I wear my shackles more contentedly for having respired the breath of an imaginary freedom. (ii. 142)

Located between the anarchic inner world of the self and the strictures of everyday decorum, the 'middle' ground of play allows a shared respite which eases the 'task of reality-acceptance'.

In her book *The Fool: His Social and Literary History* Enid Welsford examines the function of the Fool in culture; she concludes that the clown's play acts as

a social preservative by providing a corrective to the pretentious vanity of officialdom, a safety-valve for unruliness, a wholesome nourishment to the sense of secret spiritual independence of that which would otherwise be the intolerable tyranny of circumstance.

Under the 'dissolvent influence' of the Fool's personality 'the iron network of physical, social and moral law, which enmeshes us from the cradle to the grave, seems—for the moment—negligible'.[63] Welsford cites Elia as an exemplar of the Fool at work, or rather at play. Elia, as an entity, personifies the 'middle' ground of play, and provides it for his readers. In his essays our attention is frequently alerted to the spirit of play at work in everyday life to ameliorate its astringencies. The essay 'Captain Jackson', for example, presents the retired Captain as one who, though 'steeped in poverty up to the lips' (ii. 193), succeeded through a 'riotous imagination' in overcoming the reality of privation, for his family as well as himself. Welcoming

---

[63] Enid Welsford, *The Fool: His Social and Literary History* (London: Faber, 1935), p. 317.

guests with an air of benevolent affluence to spartan meals, his manner transformed the matter laid before them:

You saw with your bodily eyes indeed what seemed a bare scrag . . . remnant hardly sufficient to send a mendicant from the door contented. But in the copious will—the revelling imagination of your host—the 'mind, the mind, Master Shallow,' whole beeves were spread before you—hecatombs—no end appeared to the profusion. (ii. 190)

Continued exposure to their father's 'magnificent self-delusion' maintained in his daughters' minds, a happy, if materially unsubstantiated, sense of the family's worth; he 'conjured up handsome settlements before their eyes, which kept them up in the eye of the world too, and seem at last to have realised themselves; for they both have married since, I am told, more than respectably' (ii. 192). Playing 'the Bobadil at home' became in this case an alchemy which masters fortune and transmutes its baser materials.[64]

Elia also encourages his readers to take the sting out of potentially disturbing encounters with others by seeing people's behaviour generally as but part of their act, part of the games people play. In the essay 'A Complaint of the Decay of Beggars in the Metropolis' he attacks the efforts of Society for the Suppression of Mendicity, formed in 1818, to clear the street of London of its vagrant population. The Society saw London's beggars as an irritating eyesore and waged a campaign to put them all to work, or into workhouses. Elia defends their existence as having its part to play in the colourful pantomime of the city's life, and in answer to the Society's objections that the mendicants frequently wheedled small change out of the passing citizens' pockets through impostures and lying tales, he suggests to his readers that the token given be seen, at worst, as but payment for a lively piece of acting:

Shut not thy purse-strings always against painted distress. Act a charity sometimes . . . When they come with their counterfeit looks, and mumping tones, think them players. You pay your money to see a

---

[64] Bobadil was a braggart in Jonson's play *Every Man in his Humour*. For a further analysis of the manner in which Captain Jackson 'transmutes reality by the power of words', see Kathryn Sutherland, 'The Coming of Age of the Man of Feeling: Sentiment in Lamb and Dickens', *Charles Lamb Bulletin* 7 (1986), 200.

comedian feign these things, which, concerning these poor people, thou canst not certainly tell whether they be feigned or not. (ii. 120)

In such a manner, the Elia essays frequently present social interaction as taking place in the 'intermediate area' of play, as the 'actors' juggle with the restrictive codes and recalcitrant materials of their environment in the pursuance of their personal needs.

To see human behaviour as play requires a sustained sense of irony, and irony is an attribute to which Elia frequently lays claim. In the essay 'Imperfect Sympathies' he compares his own habits of mind with those of 'Scotchmen' whom he humorously typifies as dogmatic and literal thinkers. The Caledonian mind, according to Elia's categorization, cannot accept indirect expressions or 'understand middle actions'. 'Surmises, guesses, misgivings . . . partial illuminations, dim instincts, embryo conceptions, have no place in his brain, or vocabulary. . . . Between the affirmative and the negative there is no borderland with him' (ii. 60). But the contrasting 'order of imperfect intellects' in which Elia's is included 'have no pretences to much clearness or precision in their ideas, or in their manner of expressing them'; their minds are 'suggestive' rather than 'comprehensive' (ii. 59). Wandering in 'the twilight of dubiety', they are 'unhappily blest' with a vein of irony which they must extinguish before they can make themselves comprehendible to the 'clock-work' mechanics of the literal mind. Elia's twentieth-century critics have compared the type of mind he describes as his own in 'Imperfect Sympathies' with Keats's description of 'negative capability'.[65] The 'anti-Caledonian' is 'capable of being in uncertainties, Mysteries, doubts, without any irritable reaching after fact & reason'.[66] The 'dubiety' of half-knowledge is Elia's natural location, and in essay after essay he indicates an acceptance of the darkness that limits human vision.

[65] See e.g. Park, Lamb as Critic, pp. 11–12; and Frank, Don't Call Me Gentle Charles! p. 32. D. S. Perry ('Hazlitt, Lamb and the Drama', Ph.D. thesis (Princeton, NJ, 1966), pp. 315–19) has argued that it may have been with Lamb that the notion of 'negative capability' originated. He suggests that Hazlitt acquired the idea from Lamb, and included it in lectures which subsequently influenced Keats (see Hazlitt, Works, xx. 375). His arguments remain largely hypothetical, however.

[66] The Letters of John Keats, ed. Hyder E. Rollins, 2 vols. (Cambridge, Mass.: Harvard Univ. Press, 1958), i. 193.

In the essay 'A Quaker's Meeting', for example, religious faith, the centre of the Quaker proceedings as far as its participants are concerned, has no part to play in Elia's account of the meeting; he retains the uncommitted perspective of negative capability even as he immerses himself in the Quaker experience. The essay opens with a celebration of the manner in which, during the Quaker gathering, 'Silence, her sacred self' 'is multiplied and rendered more intense by numbers, and by sympathy'. Elia continues, in Silence's praise: 'She too hath her deeps, that call unto deeps. Negation itself hath a positive more and less; and closed eyes would seem to obscure the great obscurity of midnight' (ii. 45). But in this arresting passage, the expected significance of Quaker worship is subverted. The worshippers are not portrayed as closing their eyes and preserving a silence in order to contemplate with assurance a 'light within'; rather, their closed eyes represent a defensive action in the face of a 'great obscurity' which no light can penetrate. The thin membranes of the eyelid only 'seem to obscure' the surrounding darkness; silence, 'eldest of things—language of old Night—primitive Discourser' (ii. 46), speaks of imponderabilities which language cannot fathom. The void into which the silence opens is not filled, in Elia's account, by any superhuman presence; rather, the shadow of an ironic 'dubiety' falls between his experience of the meeting and its intended significance. Yet the human context of this 'negative' ritual still gives it, for Elia too, a 'positive more and less'. The 'burthen of the mystery' is shared in the communicative silence of the Quaker meeting; the atmosphere of intense wordless sympathy which Elia prizes opens up for the participants an area of serious play in which they share a mute acceptance of the limits of consciousness.

To 'take playfulness seriously' is, for Schlegel, a way to 'apprehend what is at the centre', but irony with its ambivalent relation to certitude—the manner in which it 'coquettes with infinite arbitrariness'—at the same time threatens always to dislodge the very notion of a meaningful 'centre'.[67] This tension between serious play and the irony which makes space for it and yet threatens it with dissolution is pivotal to the *Essays*.

[67] Schlegel, 'Ideas' (1800) and 'Athenäum Fragments' (1798), in Wheeler, *German Aesthetic and Literary Criticism*, pp. 57 and 52.

Elia's attachment to 'that dangerous figure—irony' as he calls it in the 'Preface' (ii. 152), means that the 'happy breathing-place' of play always hangs in a delicate balance, and is perpetually in danger of being revealed as an insubstantial location, and deconstructed into nothingness in the process of the essay itself. Mary Jacobus, in a recent article on Romantic prose, analyses such essays as 'Dream-Children; A Reverie' to show how Elia's 'ironic self-dissolution' opens up 'dizzying vistas of non-being'.[68] In 'Dream-Children' Elia presents himself as recalling his past in the company of his two children, only to find the mirage of their presence fading away from him into oblivion before the close of the piece:

while I stood gazing, both the children gradually grew fainter to my view, receding, and still receding till nothing at last but two mournful features were seen in the uttermost distance, which, without speech, strangely impressed upon me the effects of speech; '. . . We are nothing; less than nothing, and dreams. We are only what might have been, and must wait upon the tedious shores of Lethe millions of ages before we have existence, and a name'—and immediately awaking, I found myself quietly seated in my bachelor arm-chair where I had fallen asleep, with the faithful Bridget unchanged by my side . . . (ii. 103)

The 'play' has 'unravelled' itself, as Jacobus puts it, and left behind it a black hole into which Elia's very existence is in danger of being sucked. The close of the essay not only reveals Elia's fantasy as pertaining to that order of wish-fulfilment which, through its distance from reality, alienates dreamers from life rather than reconciles them to its astringencies; it also cuts so sharply into Elia's fabrications that his genial, playful persona is itself rendered substanceless. It is Charles Lamb, in his bachelor armchair, with Mary at his side, who is left behind, in emptiness and loss, at the close, whilst the tricksy Elia seems to have followed his dream children into oblivion.

'Irony', according to Schlegel, 'is something one simply cannot play games with'.[69] The tension between the 'genial

---

[68] Mary Jacobus, 'The Art of Managing Books: Romantic Prose and the Writing of the Past', in ead., Romanticism, Writing, and Sexual Difference: Essays on The Prelude (Oxford: Clarendon Press, 1989), p. 157.

[69] Schlegel, 'On Incomprehensibilities', in Wheeler, German Aesthetic and Literary Criticism, p. 37. For an account of Schlegel's theory of irony, and its

impulse' to communicate, without which Charles said he could not write,[70] and the ironic compulsion to expose such communication as based upon a substanceless web of arbitrary constructions, provides the paradoxical subtext to the Elia essays as a whole. Both impulses have been categorized as feminine attributes. Irony, as a mode of discourse, is at an opposite extreme from the straightforward manly style of communication approved by Hazlitt. The impulse to 'tell it slant' rather than to comment or criticize directly, is characterized by Gilbert and Gubar in *The Madwoman in the Attic* as the means by which nineteenth-century woman writers 'managed the difficult task of achieving true female literary authority by simultaneously conforming to and subverting patriarchal literary standards'.[71] Geniality, for which Elia's writings have been abundantly praised during his own days and since, is an offshoot of that wish to merge with others, to dissolve in an atmosphere of mutual trust and affection the barriers between self and Other, which, as we have seen, has been presented as a trait more marked in female than male development. But the way in which both responses accommodate themselves to the reader's expectations, rather than confront them directly, has its negative aspects: as Mary Poovey has pointed out, indirectness can prove debilitating, however imaginatively satisfying it may be, in that it deflects criticism from the social institutions it intends on one level to attack, and masks resignation to a situation experienced as unalterable.[72]

Elia, in accordance with the ideology within which Charles was reared, presents himself as the servant of his readers,[73] and frequently accommodates himself to their ways of thinking.

relation to British Romanticism, see Anne K. Mellor, *English Romantic Irony* (Cambridge, Mass.: Harvard Univ. Press, 1980), pp. 7–30.

[70] *Letters*, ed. Lucas, ii. 426.

[71] Sandra M. Gilbert and Susan Gubar, *The Madwoman in the Attic: The Woman Writer and the Nineteenth-Century Literary Imagination* (New Haven, Conn., and London: Yale Univ. Press, 1979), p. 73.

[72] Mary Poovey, *The Proper Lady and the Woman Writer: Ideology as Style in the Works of Mary Wollstonecraft, Mary Shelley, and Jane Austen* (Chicago and London: Univ. of Chicago Press, 1984), pp. 242–3.

[73] See e.g. 'Ritson *versus* John Scott the Quaker' (not repr. in the collected volumes of the Elia essays), where Elia reassures his readers that 'the town may be troubled with something more in his own way the ensuing month from its poor servant to command. ELIA' (i. 219).

Essayists generally, necessarily more dependent than other writers on the immediate approval of their public for their livelihood, needed to identify themselves with their readers' interests and write in close proximity to them.[74] Charles had always found it impossible to write in isolation; on one occasion, in 1806, when he tried the experiment of renting a room apart from his and Mary's lodgings in which to write, he found he could not do so without her company; he seems to have needed her mothering presence to give him the secure space in which to 'play' creatively.[75] According to his biographer Patmore, 'Lamb was not a man whose mind was sufficient to itself . . . the *home* of his spirit was the face of the common earth, and in the absence of human faces and sympathies, it longed for them with a hunger that nothing else could satisfy.'[76] 'How I like to be liked, and *what I do* to be liked!' Charles confides to Dorothy Wordsworth in 1821, with reference to Elia's growing popularity.[77] His refusal to pose as a teacher or superior to his readers left him with likeability as the only kind of influence he could allow himself to exert with his audience, and one congenial to his affiliative inclinations. To influence others through presenting oneself as likeably similar to them has been seen as one of the few routes to power available to women within patriarchal social structures,[78] but this process of psychological identification, once established, cannot easily be broken without endangering the possibility of influence. The closeness of Elia's confidential tie with his readers creates in them, as we have seen, a mothering and protective response, but it was a relation which made it difficult for him to cut directly across any of their more limiting ideological prejudices. In the composition of an essay, his subtle use of a puncturing irony does frequently allow him to expose the blind spots in

[74] See Thomas McFarland, *Romantic Cruxes: The English Essayists and the Spirit of the Age* (Oxford: Clarendon Press, 1987), pp. 54–5.

[75] See *Letters*, ed. Marrs, ii. 220.

[76] Patmore, *My Friends and Acquaintance*, i. 28.

[77] *Letters*, ed. Lucas, ii. 288. See also an 1830 letter, in which Charles tells another correspondent: 'I like to be liked, but I don't care about being respected. I don't respect myself' (ibid., iii. 266.)

[78] See Irene H. Frieze, Jacquelynne E. Parsons, Paula B. Johnson, Diane N. Ruble, and Gail L. Zellman, *Women and Sex Roles: A Social Psychological Perspective* (New York: Norton, 1978), pp. 309–16.

conventional thought-patterns without overtly criticizing the reader; at other times, however, Elia genially falls in with the most arbitrary and indeed shocking prejudices of his times without questioning them. Blatant and unquestioned anti-semitism and racism were common enough phenomena in early nineteenth-century London life:[79] both are confessed to by Elia with blithe and unembarrassed confidentiality in the essay 'Imperfect Sympathies'. The irony of the contradiction, that a persona which this study has presented as one formed to deconstruct the processes of scapegoating should here be unconcernedly servicing prejudice in its most overt and destructive forms, is of an order virtually to puncture and unravel the arguments of this chapter as a whole. Unless very strongly provoked by personal experience, as he seems to have been in the writing of 'Modern Gallantry', for example, Elia refrains from commenting directly and systematically on his society's limitations, and even occasionally falls in with them. The personal is not generally politicized in his writings: his disposition, one is tempted to say, is too feminine and insufficiently feminist.

Instead the debilitating shadow of the unresolved contradictions in Elia's position fell upon his progenitor. Elia was liked, but at such a cost that eventually Charles began to find him nauseating: when in 1831 he contributed some pieces to the *Englishman's Magazine* he asked its editor Edward Moxon to 'leave out the sickening Elia at the end'.[80] Many critical pages have been devoted to the question of how far Elia can be identified with Charles himself. The general consensus seems to be that the persona reflected some, but not all, of Charles's characteristic habits of mind.[81] Charles's pre-Elian critical writings and his letters show him responding with greater sharpness and directness to social injustice than could be accommodated within the Elia essays. The popularity of his *alter ego* appears at times to grate upon him; in an autobiographical note he describes himself as 'the true Elia . . . and

---

[79] See M. Dorothy George, *London Life in the Eighteenth Century* (1st edn., 1925; Harmondsworth: Penguin, 1966), pp. 135 and 144.

[80] *Letters*, ed. Lucas, iii. 318.

[81] See e.g. David Cecil, *A Portrait of Charles Lamb* (London: Constable, 1983), p. 150; and Jack, *English Literature 1815–1832*, pp. 288–9.

rather better known from that name without a meaning, than from anything he has done or can hope to do in his own' (i. 21). The 'genial impulse' behind Elia became harder for him to maintain as the 1820s progressed, and within the essays themselves the ironic perspective which was its counterpoint threatened more and more overtly to dissolve the persona. From first to last the Elia essays hint at the possibility of this undoing. The first essay 'The South-Sea House', after its reconstruction of the lives of the old clerks, closes with the sentence 'Reader, what if I have been playing with thee all this while—peradventure the very *names*, which I have summoned up before thee, are fantastic' (ii. 7). 'That We Should Rise with the Lark', one of the last of the 'Popular Fallacies' which bring to a close the second volume of the *Essays of Elia*, is written entirely from an alienated perspective. Elia is in retreat from the play of life which has proved an idle folly:

The mighty changes of the world already appear as but the vain stuff out of which dramas are composed. We have asked no more of life than what the mimic images in play-houses present us with. Even those types have waxed fainter. (ii. 270)

Fred V. Randel, commenting on this passage in his recent study of the Elia essays, points out that the theatrical metaphor is here used in its traditional guise as a denigration of life—that life is nothing but a play; as such it reverses Elia's previous celebratory use of it as creating the 'happy breathing-place' necessary for a full acceptance of reality.[82] To encounter life with buoyant gusto, to 'rise with the lark', is represented in this essay as a naïve abuse of energy:

It is flattering to get the start of a lazy world; to conquer death by proxy in his image. But the seeds of sleep and mortality are in us; and we pay usually in strange qualms, before night falls, the penalty of the unnatural inversion. (ii. 269–70)

'Disappointment', Elia says, 'struck a dark veil' between him and the 'dazzling illusions' of the world: the genial impulse to merge seems in his depression to have proved insufficiently rewarding and too draining, leaving him without the energy or

---

[82] Fred V. Randel, *The World of Elia: Charles Lamb's Essayistic Romanticism* (Port Washington, NY: Kennikat Press, 1975), p. 161.

inclination to continue with the game. Only the bitter play of irony itself, as a withdrawn and solipsistic utterance, is left to him. The 'gentle-hearted Charles' of Coleridge's 'This Lime-Tree Bower my Prison' 'to whom | No sound is dissonant which tells of Life' becomes in 'That We Should Rise with the Lark' more akin to the disenchanted 'flâneur' of Baudelaire's *Le Spleen de Paris*:

Lost in this mean world, jostled by the crowd, I am like a weary man whose eye, looking backwards, into the depth of years, sees nothing but disillusion and bitterness, and before him nothing but a tempest which contains nothing new.[83]

Commenting on this passage in his study of Baudelaire, Walter Benjamin sees its expression of disillusionment as the depressive consequence of Baudelaire's prolonged immersion in the 'narcotic' 'glitter' of the urban crowd. The city loiterer abandons himself to the crowd; empathizing with it, he surrenders himself to an intoxication which, according to Benjamin, is 'the intoxication of the commodity around which surges the stream of customers'.[84] He suffers, in Baudelaire's words, 'the holy prostitution of the soul which gives itself wholly, poetry and charity, to the unexpected that appears, to the unknown that passes'.[85] Baudelaire was familiar with Charles Lamb's works; it has been suggested that he drew both the title and the inspiration of *Le Spleen de Paris* from 'The Londoner', with its query 'Where has spleen her food but in London?'[86] Sucking at the 'measureless breasts' of an indifferent city, the Londoner yearns to abandon himself obliviously to a relation which can appear as but delusively nourishing. The Elia persona also seems to share a similar wish to nestle into the passing reader's affections and succour itself there, only to become disenchanted by suspicions of meanness, or meaninglessness, in the object to which it seeks to attach itself. Benjamin terms this experience

---

[83] Charles Baudelaire, *Œuvres*, ed. Yves-Gérard Le Dantec, 2 vols. (Paris: Bibliothèque de la Pléiade, 1931–2), ii. 641, quoted Walter Benjamin, *Charles Baudelaire; A Lyric Poet in the Era of High Capitalism* (London: Verso, 1983) pp. 153–4.

[84] Benjamin, *Charles Baudelaire*, p. 55.

[85] Baudelaire, *Œuvres*, i. 421; quoted Benjamin, *Charles Baudelaire*, p. 56.

[86] See Daniël A. de Graaf, 'Baudelaire en Charles Lamb: Invloed van de *Essays of Elia* op *Spleen de Paris*', *Vlaamse Gids*, 50 (1966), 587–95.

'the disintegration of the aura in the experience of shock'; the self, riddled with jostling identifications, suffers the shock of its own loss at the moment in which it falls apart. Charles's use of personae and irony, and his stress upon the balancing properties of play, protect him to some extent from this dissolution; when he imagines his readers as unsympathetic, he can 'retire, impenetrable to ridicule, under the phantom cloud of Elia' (ii. 29). And, for all the bleakness of such essays as 'That We Should Rise with the Lark', the moments of lost trust in the humanity of the faceless crowd of readers or Londoners are rare in his writing. Nevertheless, the 'Popular Fallacy' indicates that the feminine loss of ego-boundaries which mergence entails was often experienced by him as painful.

It would be possible to read 'That We Should Rise with the Lark' as but one example of Elia's incorporation of different facets of the darker aspects of the human personality. Just as in the last section we read another 'Popular Fallacy', 'That a Sulky Temper is a Misfortune', as the personification of a paranoiac type, so this essay too could be interpreted as spoken by a 'type', caught up in this instance in the insidious seductions of the death-wish. But nothing deflects or punctures the depressive withdrawal of Elia in 'That We Should Rise with the Lark', and its ironic note of retreat is one frequently to be found in Charles's later correspondence. In 1824 he tells Bernard Barton that he is suffering from 'an oyster-like insensibility to the passing events . . . My day is gone into Twilight and I don't think it worth the expence of candles'.[87] An 1830 letter to Wordsworth repeats the dismissive metaphors of 'To Rise with the Lark': 'The seasons pass us with indifference . . . they are hey-pass re-pass [as] in a show-box . . . Let the sullen nothing pass.'[88] According to Patmore, who was personally acquainted with Charles during the last years of his life, when alone

his thoughts were apt to brood and hover . . . over dangerous and intractable questions, on which his strong common sense told him there was no satisfaction to be gained, but from which his searching spirit could not detach itself.[89]

---

[87] *Letters*, ed. Lucas, ii. 413.   [88] Ibid., iii. 241.
[89] Patmore, *My Friends and Acquaintance*, i. 52.

Charles's writings express, in a way that Keats's seldom do, the more painful aspects of negative capability, with its osmotic lack of mental boundaries; unable to cut out any sombre or disquieting reflection, his mind seems too permeable to retain an elastic bounce, and confront life with gusto. As Keats's letters suggest, the lack of a distinct identity, which he presents as one of the concomitants of 'negative capability', results in a tendency to be overwhelmed by the more forceful and pressing personalities of others, be they 'a Iago or an Imogen'.[90] Charles was aware of the dangers in his and Mary's liability to be 'dragged along in the current of other peoples thoughts, hampered in a net', with their minds 'positively discharged into their greater currents'.[91] During the 1820s, the accumulated fatigues of his clerical work, added to the strain of maintaining his output of Elia essays, left him particularly susceptible to such obsessive identifications. In a letter to Bernard Barton he describes his reaction to the conviction and death-sentence of the banker and forger Henry Fauntleroy in 1824:

I tremble, I am sure, at myself, when I think that so many poor victims of the Law at one time of their life made as sure of never being hanged as I in my presumption am too ready to do myself. What are we better than they? Do we come into the world with different necks? . . . I am shocked sometimes at the shape of my own fingers, not for their resemblance to the ape tribe (which is something) but for the exquisite adaptation of them to the purposes of picking, fingering, &c. No one that is so framed, I maintain it, but should tremble.[92]

The 1825 essay 'The Last Peach' similarly records his uncontrollable identification with the convicted 'F——'. 'Suspensarus', as he signs himself, is tormented by the sight of his own fingers because 'they seem so admirably constructed for—pilfering' (i. 285).[93]

---

[90] Keats, *Letters*, i. 387.   [91] *Letters*, ed. Marrs, iii. 215 and 216.

[92] *Letters*, ed. Lucas, ii. 447.

[93] See also, for a further illustration of Charles's obsession with Fauntleroy, *Memories of Old Friends, being Extracts from the Journals and Letters of Caroline Fox*, quoted in the notes to *Letters*, ed. Lucas, ii. 448. Soon after Fauntleroy was hanged, an advertisement appeared in the daily papers which read 'To all good Christians! Pray for the soul of Fauntleroy'. 'At one of Coleridge's soirées it was discussed for a considerable time; at length Coleridge, turning to Lamb, asked "Do you know anything about this affair?" "I should think I d–d–d–did'" said Elia, "for I paid s–s–s–seven and sixpence for it!"'

Charles's morbid identification with such characters as Fauntleroy amounted in the mid-1820s to a nervous illness, which incapacitated him from work, and brought about his early release from the East India Company. But his freedom, and his and Mary's permanent removal from London to the country suburbs, only exacerbated his depression. He missed London, his 'old Jerusalem', and the 'fine indifferent pageants of Fleet Street': 'In dreams I am in Fleetmarket', he tells Wordsworth, 'but I wake and cry to sleep again'.[94] The greater frequency and duration of Mary's manic-depressive attacks during the 1820s and 30s were also extremely debilitating for them both: Charles appears increasingly to have sought relief from depression in alcohol, but it is clear from his vivid depiction of the sad plight of the alcoholic in the 1813 essay 'Confessions of a Drunkard' that he must have known drink could do little to aid him. In the essay the Drunkard warns his readers that 'It is inexpressible how much this infirmity adds to a sense of shame, and a general feeling of deterioration': 'Life itself, my waking life, has much of the confusion, the trouble, and the obscure perplexity, of an ill dream. In the daytime I stumble upon dark mountains' (i. 139 and 138). The anguished cry of the Drunkard, 'Who shall deliver me from the body of this death?' is frequently repeated in Charles's own letters.[95]

In the event, death itself delivered him, with compassionate abruptness, in December 1834. Out walking on the 22nd he tripped over a stone and bruised his face; erysipelas developed, a gangrenous infection which, according to the medical dictionaries, was, in the pre-penicillin era, a serious disease in persons over sixty and tantamount to a death sentence. Charles was only

---

[94] *Letters*, ed. Lucas, iii. 241–2.

[95] See 'Confessions of a Drunkard', *Works*, i. 137, *Letters*, ed. Marrs, ii. 35, and *Letters*, ed. Lucas, ii. 385 and 414, for Charles's use of this biblical quotation (Rom. 7: 24.) The question of whether or not the 'Confessions' were autobiographical has been much discussed (see *Quarterly Review*, 27 (1822), 120–1; Morley (ed.), *Henry Crabb Robinson on Books and their Writers*, i. 128; Charles Cowden Clarke and Mary Cowden Clarke, *Recollections of Writers*, pp. 56–7). Charles himself denied it (see *London Magazine* (Aug. 1822), quoted in Lucas's notes, *Works*, i. 432), and the general consensus seems to be that though Charles frequently had to be escorted home from any convivial occasion, a very little drink incapacitated him. This does not suggest that he was at any time a hardened alcoholic, though he clearly had sufficient experience to empathize strongly with the condition.

59 but his body lacked the strength to resist the infection; he weakened rapidly and died on the 27th, in the Edmonton lodgings for mental patients run by the Waldens. Mary lived on for a further twelve years, financially well provided for through her brother's care, but rarely sane.

But even in their darkened last years, the capacity to live in the present did not entirely desert them. Charles's last letter to Manning records Mary's struggles to be content when well: 'We play piquet, and it is like the old times a while'.[96] Their neighbour, the schoolmistress, who had assumed that Charles as well as Mary was an insane patient in the Waldens' care, was apparently often drawn to her window by his 'cheery voice' as he emerged from the next-door house; 'he would accost passers-by', she recollected, 'and walk and talk with them down the street'.[97] The Londoner's impulse to merge was still predominant, in his suburban exile. Nor was Mary's mediating loving-kindness entirely obliterated by the increasing encroachments of her insanity, even after her brother's death. At one point, it became clear to her friends that the Waldens were ill-treating her and they sought to remove her elsewhere, but she refused to leave at first, because of her concern for the children of the household: according to Procter, Mary explained to him that 'whilst the children were young, she was desirous of staying, to mediate between them and the mother (whose temper she says amounts to a disease)'.[98]

IV

'Everything in heaven & earth, in man and in story, in books & in fancy, acts by Confederacy, by juxtaposition, by circumstance & place', Charles had told a correspondent in 1801.[99] The circumstances of the Lambs' lives—their social position as the children of servants, their occupations, the afflictions of matricide and madness—worked to over-determine in both of

---

[96] Letters, ed. Lucas, iii. 410 and 409.

[97] H. F. Cox, 'Charles Lamb at Edmonton', The Globe (1875), quoted Lucas, Life of Charles Lamb, 2 vols. (London: Methuen, 1905), ii. 253.

[98] Procter in a letter to Talfourd, 22 June 1841, quoted Lucas, Life of Charles Lamb, ii. 285.

[99] Letters, ed. Marrs, ii. 36.

them a feminine relation towards the power structures of their society. In particular, the strength of the sibling bond between them created a shared flexible identity in which each daily played alternating motherly and childlike roles. Their dual accounts, in Mary's correspondence and the Elia essay 'Mackery End, in Hertfordshire', of a visit they made together to a country farmhouse may serve as a final testimony to this characteristic interplay. Mackery End was farmed by the Lambs' maternal relations and during their childhood they were frequently sent to holiday there; in 1815 they returned to the farm for the first time as adults, but Charles, no doubt fearful of the harsh welcome they might receive given the manner of their mother's death, at first attempted to dissuade Mary from making their presence known. In a letter describing the visit, Mary records his protective anxiety over the possibility of her hostile reception.[100] Charles must have remembered Mary's letter when he came to write his *London Magazine* essay; the atmosphere as well as the recorded detail of the two accounts of the visit are very similar. But in his narrative the protective role is Bridget's; childish shyness rather than prudent reserve is presented as the cause of Elia's hesitations, while 'Love, stronger than scruple, winged my cousin in without me' (ii. 78). Remembering the kindness of the welcome they in fact received from their mother's relatives, Elia concludes his essay by pledging that

when I forget all this, then may my country cousins forget me; and Bridget no more remember, that in the days of weakling infancy I was her tender charge—as I have been her care in foolish manhood since—in those pretty pastoral walks, long ago, about Mackery End, in Hertfordshire (ii. 79).

The reciprocity of the Lambs' relationship, and their perpetual interchange of mother/child, or leader/follower, roles, promoted an awareness of the dual, if not multiple, aspects of the apparently single subject. In Mary's case this doubling had of course its tragic aspects: her assertive, 'masculine' element, so much repressed by the circumstance of her birth and the effects of her mental illness, as well as the gender role divisions of her period,

---

[100] *Letters*, ed. Marrs, iii. 159.

appears only to have found full expression in madness. But her writing seeks to mediate between warring elements, of class and generation, and to create places of sanctuary, like Mrs Leicester's school, for the women and girls for whom she wrote. Charles's work too, particularly the Elia essays, perpetually encodes the possibility of a balanced and playful interchange between the various contradictory parts of the individual psyche. The greatness of art 'manifests itself in the admirable balance of all the faculties' (ii. 187), Elia wrote in the essay 'Sanity of True Genius'. The Elia essays invite the reader to share in the sanity of play in which the multiplicity of the subject in its many guises can be accepted without projection, and the unbalanced urge to power by any one facet of the self held in check, along with the concomitant drive to dominate others. Central to the establishment of this difficult balance are the feminine values of mediation and empathy, and their capacity to deconstruct those egoistic tendencies towards self-aggrandizement and the control of the Other which became so strongly identified with the masculine ideal during the Romantic period. Through the formation of their lives of 'double singleness' the Lambs had established an alternative pattern of gender relations, one which was not dependent upon the artificial segregation of rigidly polarized masculine and feminine roles. The vantage-point of this lived experience afforded them a view of the flexible nature of subject identity: in themselves, as well as in relation to the other, each was aware of at least a double singleness. At times their writings disclose the pain and confusion entailed by such an acknowledgement of the plurality of being, when it is at odds with prevailing ideologies; but at other times their work celebrates the liberations which such a recognition brings, and extends them to the reader.

Select Bibliography

AARON, JANE, ' "We are in a manner marked": Images of Damnation in Charles Lamb's Writings', *Charles Lamb Bulletin*, 5 (1981), 1–10.

ALLSOP, THOMAS, *Letters, Conversations and Recollections of S. T. Coleridge*, 2 vols. (London: Moxon, 1836).

ANDERSON, G. A., (ed.), *The Letters of Thomas Manning to Charles Lamb* (London: Martin Secker, 1925).

ANDERSON, GREGORY, *Victorian Clerks* (Manchester: Manchester Univ. Press, 1976).

ANTHONY, KATHARINE, *The Lambs: A Study of Pre-Victorian England* (London: Hammond, Hammond & Co., 1948).

ARIÈS, PHILIPPE, *Centuries of Childhood* (Harmondsworth: Penguin, 1973).

BARNETT, GEORGE L., ' "That Cursed Barbauld Crew" or Charles Lamb and Children's Literature', *Charles Lamb Bulletin*, 4 (1979), 1–18.

BEER, GILLIAN, 'Lamb's Women', *Charles Lamb Bulletin*, 6 (1984), 138–43.

BENJAMIN, WALTER, *Charles Baudelaire; A Lyric Poet in the Era of High Capitalism* (London: Verso, 1976).

BRIGGS, ASA 'The Language of "Class" in Early Nineteenth-Century England', in Asa Briggs and John Saville (eds.) *Essays in Labour History* (London: Macmillan, 1960), pp. 43–73.

BROWNE, ALICE, *The Eighteenth Century Feminist Mind* (Brighton: Harvester, 1987).

BUNKER, HENRY ALDEN, 'Mother-Murder in Myth and Legend: A Psychoanalytic Note' *Psychoanalytic Quarterly*, 13 (1944), 198–207.

BUSFIELD, JOAN, *Managing Madness: Changing Ideas and Practice* (London: Hutchinson, 1986).

CECIL, DAVID, *A Portrait of Charles Lamb* (London: Constable, 1983).

CHODOROW, NANCY, *The Reproduction of Mothering: Psychoanalysis and the Sociology of Gender* (Berkeley, Calif.: Univ. of California Press, 1978).

CIXOUS, HÉLÈNE, 'Sorties', in Hélène Cixous and Catherine Clément, *The Newly Born Woman*, trans. Betsy Wing (Manchester: Manchester Univ. Press, 1986), pp. 63–132.

COATES, JOHN, ' "Damn the Age! I will write for Antiquity": Lamb's Style as Implied Moral Comment', *Charles Lamb Bulletin*, 6 (1984), 147–58.

COLERIDGE, SAMUEL TAYLOR, *Biographia Literaria*, ed. J. Shawcross, 2 vols. (London: OUP, 1907).

—— *The Poetical Works of Samuel Taylor Coleridge*, ed. Ernest Hartley Coleridge (London: OUP, 1912).

—— *The Collected Letters of Samuel Taylor Coleridge*, ed. Earl Leslie Griggs, 6 vols. (Oxford: Clarendon Press, 1956–71).

—— 'The Statesman's Manual', in *Lay Sermons*, ed. R. J. White (The Collected Works of Samuel Taylor Coleridge, gen. ed. Kathleen Coburn, vi) (Princeton, NJ: Princeton Univ. Press, 1972).

—— *On the Constitution of the Church and State*, ed. John Colmer (The Collected Works of Samuel Taylor Coleridge, gen. ed. Kathleen Coburn, x) (Princeton, NJ: Princeton Univ. Press, 1976).

COURTNEY, WINIFRED F., *Young Charles Lamb: 1775–1802* (London and Basingstoke: Macmillan, 1982).

—— 'New Light on the Lambs and the Burneys', *Charles Lamb Bulletin*, 8 (1987), 19–27.

COWDEN CLARKE, CHARLES, and COWDEN CLARKE, MARY, *Recollections of Writers* (London: Sampson Low, 1878).

COYNE, JAMES C. (ed.), *Essential Papers on Depression* (New York: New York Univ. Press, 1986).

CULLER, JONATHAN (ed.), *On Puns: The Foundation of Letters* (Oxford: Blackwell, 1988).

CURRAN, STUART, 'Romantic Poetry: The I Altered', in Anne K. Mellor (ed.), *Romanticism and Feminism* (Bloomington and Indianapolis: Indiana Univ. Press, 1988), pp. 185–207.

DAVIDOFF, LEONORE, and HALL, CATHERINE, *Family Fortunes: Men and Women of the English Middle Class, 1750–1850* (London: Hutchinson, 1987).

DAVIS, HOWARD H., *Beyond Class Images: Explorations in the Structure of Social Consciousness* (London: Croom Helm, 1979).

DE QUINCEY, THOMAS, *The Collected Writings of Thomas de Quincey*, ed. David Masson, 14 vols. (Edinburgh: Adam & Charles Black, 1889–90).

ERDMAN, DAVID V. and ZALL, PAUL M., 'Coleridge and Jeffrey in Controversy', *Studies in Romanticism*, 14 (1975), 75–83.

EVEREST, KELVIN, *Coleridge's Secret Ministry: The Context of the Conversation Poems 1795–1798* (Brighton: Harvester Press, 1979).

FOAKES, R. A., 'The Authentic Voice: Lamb and the Familiar Letter', *Charles Lamb Bulletin*, 2 (1975), 1–10.

FOUCAULT, MICHEL, *Madness and Civilization: A History of Insanity in the Age of Reason* (London: Tavistock, 1967).

FRANK, ROBERT D., *Don't Call Me Gentle Charles!: An Essay on Lamb's Essays of Elia* (Corvallis: Oregon State Univ. Press, 1976).

FRIEDMAN, JOEL, and GASSEL, SYLVIA, 'Orestes: A Psychoanalytic Approach to Dramatic Criticism II', *Psychoanalytic Quarterly*, 20 (1951), 423–33.

FRIEDMAN, LESLIE JOAN, 'Mary Lamb: Sister, Seamstress, Murderer, Writer', Ph.D. thesis (Stanford, Calif., 1976).

FRIEZE, IRENE H., PARSONS, JACQUELYNNE E., JOHNSON, PAULA B., RUBLE, DIANE N., and ZELLMAN, GAIL L., *Women and Sex Roles: A Social Psychological Perspective* (New York: Norton, 1978).

GEHA, RICHARD, 'For the Love of Medusa: A Psychoanalytic Glimpse into Gynecocide', *Psychoanalytic Review*, 62 (1975), 59–73.

GILBERT, SANDRA M., and GUBAR, SUSAN, *The Madwoman in the Attic: The Woman Writer and the Nineteenth-Century Literary Imagination* (New Haven, Conn., and London: Yale Univ. Press, 1979).

HAZLITT, WILLIAM CAREW, *The Lambs: Their Lives, Their Friends and Their Correspondence* (London: Elkin Mathews, 1897).

HAZLITT, WILLIAM, *The Complete Works of William Hazlitt*, ed. P. P. Howe, 21 vols. (London: Dent, 1930–4).

HEARN, FRANCIS, *Domination, Legitimation, and Resistance: The Incorporation of the Nineteenth-Century English Working Class* (Westport, Conn.: Greenwood Press, 1978).

HECHT, J. JEAN, *The Domestic Servant Class in Eighteenth-Century England* (London: Routledge & Kegan Paul, 1956).

HEGEL, GEORG WILHELM FRIEDRICH, *Aesthetics: Lectures on Fine Arts*, trans. T. M. Knox (Oxford: OUP, 1975).

—— *Phenomenology of Spirit*, trans. A. V. Miller (Oxford: OUP, 1977).

HOMANS, MARGARET, *Bearing the Word: Language and Female Experience in Nineteenth-Century Women's Writing* (Chicago and London: Univ. of Chicago Press, 1986).

HOME, JOHN, *Douglas: A Tragedy* (London: A. Millar, 1757).

HUNT, LEIGH, *The Autobiography of Leigh Hunt*, ed. J. E. Morpurgo, 2 vols. (London: Cresset Press, 1949).

IRIGARAY, LUCE, *This Sex Which Is Not One* (Ithaca, NY: Cornell Univ. Press, 1985).

JACK, IAN, *English Literature 1815–1832*, (The Oxford History of English Literature, x. ed. F. P. Wilson and Bonamy Dobrée) (Oxford: Clarendon Press, 1963).

JACOBUS, MARY, *Tradition and Experiment in Wordsworth's Lyrical Ballads (1798)* (Oxford: Clarendon Press, 1976).

—— *Romanticism, Writing, and Sexual Difference: Essays on* The Prelude (Oxford: Clarendon Press, 1989).

KEATS, JOHN, *The Letters of John Keats*, ed. Hyder E. Rollins, 2 vols. (Cambridge, Mass.: Harvard Univ. Press, 1958).

KELLY, JOAN, 'The Doubled Vision of Feminist Theory', in Judith L. Newton, Mary P. Ryan, and Judith R. Walkowitz (eds.), *Sex and Class in Women's History* (London: Routledge & Kegan Paul, 1983).

KHAZOUM, VIOLET, 'The Novel and Characters in the Essays of Elia', *Studies in English Literature*, 16 (1976), 563–77.

KLEIN, MELANIE, 'A Contribution to the Psychogenesis of Manic-Depressive States' (1935), in ead., *Love, Guilt and Reparation and Other Works 1921–1945* (London: Hogarth Press, 1975), pp. 262–89.

—— 'Some Reflections on *The Oresteia*' (1963), in *Envy and Gratitude and Other Works 1946–63* (London: Hogarth Press, 1975), pp. 275–99.

KLINGENDER, F. D., *The Conditions of Clerical Labour in Britain* (London: Martin Lawrence, 1935).

KRISTEVA, JULIA, *Desire in Language: A Semiotic Approach to Literature and Art* (Oxford: Blackwell, 1980).

—— 'Interview—1974: Julia Kristeva and Psychanalyse et Politique', *mf*, 5 and 6 (1981), 164–7.

—— *The Kristeva Reader*, ed. Toril Moi (Oxford: Blackwell, 1986).

LAMB, CHARLES and LAMB, MARY, *The Works of Charles and Mary Lamb*, ed. E. V. Lucas, 7 vols. (London: Methuen, 1903–5).

—— *The Letters of Charles and Mary Anne Lamb*, ed. Edwin W. Marrs, Jr., 3 vols. (Ithaca, NY and London: Cornell Univ. Press, 1975–8).

—— *The Letters of Charles Lamb: To which are added those of his sister Mary Lamb*, ed. E. V. Lucas, 3 vols. (London: Dent and Methuen, 1935).

LINDNER, ROBERT M., 'The Equivalents of Matricide', *Psychoanalytic Quarterly*, 17 (1948), 453–70.

LIPMAN-BLUMEN, JEAN, *Gender Roles and Power* (Englewood Cliffs, NJ: Prentice Hall, 1984).

LLOYD, GENEVIEVE, *The Man of Reason: 'Male' and 'Female' in Western Philosophy* (London: Methuen, 1984).

LOCKWOOD, DAVID, *The Blackcoated Worker: A Study in Class Consciousness* (London: Allen & Unwin, 1958).

LOWN, JUDY, 'Not so much a Factory, More a Form of Patriarchy: Gender and Class during Industrialization', in Eva Gamarnikow, *et al.* (eds.), *Gender, Class and Work* (London: Heinemann, 1983).

LUCAS, E. V., *The Life of Charles Lamb*, 2 vols. (London: Methuen, 1905).

McFARLAND, THOMAS, *Romantic Cruxes: The English Essayists and the Spirit of the Age* (Oxford: Clarendon Press, 1987).

McGANN, JEROME J., *The Romantic Ideology: A Critical Investigation* (Chicago and London: Univ. of Chicago Press, 1983).

McKENNA, WAYNE, *Charles Lamb and the Theatre* (Gerrards Cross: Colin Smythe, 1978).

MELLOR, ANNE K., *English Romantic Irony* (Cambridge, Mass.: Harvard Univ. Press, 1980).

MONSMAN, GERALD, *Confessions of a Prosaic Dreamer: Charles Lamb's Art of Autobiography* (Durham, NC: Duke Univ. Press, 1984).

MORE, HANNAH, *Strictures on the Modern System of Female Education*, 2 vols. (London: T. Cadell & W. Davies, 1799).

MORLEY, F. V., *Lamb before Elia* (London: Jonathan Cape, 1932).

MORPHEW, J. A., and SIM, MYRE, 'Gilles de la Tourette's Syndrome: A Clinical and Psychopathological Study', *British Journal of Medical Psychology*, 42 (1969), 293–301.

NEFF, WANDA FRAIKEN, *Victorian Working Women: An Historical and Literary Study of Women in British Industries and Professions 1832–1850* (London: Allen & Unwin, 1929).

PARK, ROY, (ed.), *Lamb as Critic* (London: Routledge & Kegan Paul, 1980).

PARRY-JONES, WILLIAM LL., *The Trade in Lunacy: A Study of Private Madhouses in England in the Eighteenth and Nineteenth Centuries* (London: Routledge & Kegan Paul, 1972).

PATMORE, P. G., *My Friends and Acquaintance*, 3 vols. (London: Saunders & Otley, 1854).

PATTERSON, CHARLES I., 'Charles Lamb's Insight into the Nature of the Novel', *PMLA*, 67 (1952), 375–82.

PERKIN, HAROLD, *The Origins of Modern English Society 1780–1880* (London: Routledge & Kegan Paul, 1969).

PINCHBECK, IVY, *Women Workers and the Industrial Revolution 1750–1850* (1st edn., 1930; London: Virago, 1981).

POLLIN, BURTON R., 'Charles Lamb and Charles Lloyd as Jacobins and Anti-Jacobins', *Studies in Romanticism*, 12 (1973), 633–47.

POOVEY, MARY, *The Proper Lady and the Woman Writer: Ideology as Style in the Works of Mary Wollstonecraft, Mary Shelley, and Jane Austen* (Chicago and London: Univ. of Chicago Press, 1984).

PORTER, ROY, *Mind-Forg'd Manacles: A History of Madness in England from the Restoration to the Regency* (London: Athlone Press, 1987).

PRANCE, CLAUDE A., *Companion to Charles Lamb: A Guide to People and Places 1760–1847* (London: Mansell, 1983).

PRICE, RICHARD N., 'Society, Status and Jingoism: The Social Roots of Lower Middle Class Patriotism, 1870–1900', in Geoffrey Crossick (ed.), *The Lower Middle Class in Britain 1870–1914* (London: Croom Helm, 1977), pp. 89–112.

PROCTER, BRYAN WALLER ['Barry Cornwall', pseud.], *Charles Lamb: A Memoir* (London: Edward Moxon, 1866).

RANDEL, FRED V., *The World of Elia: Charles Lamb's Essayistic Romanticism* (Port Washington, NY: Kennikat Press, 1975).

RICHARDSON, ALAN, 'Romanticism and the Colonization of the Female', in Anne K. Mellor (ed.), *Romanticism and Feminism* (Bloomington and Indianapolis: Indiana Univ. Press, 1988) pp. 13–25.

RIEHL, JOSEPH E., *Charles Lamb's Children's Literature*, ed. James Hogg, Salzburg Studies in English Literature, 94, (Salzburg: Univ. of Salzburg Press, 1980).

ROBERTS, DAVID, *Paternalism in Early Victorian England* (London: Croom Helm, 1979).

ROBINSON, HENRY CRABB, *Henry Crabb Robinson on Books and their Writers*, ed. Edith J. Morley, 3 vols. (London: Dent, 1938).

ROGERS, KATHARINE M., *Feminism in Eighteenth Century England* (Urbana and Chicago: Univ. of Illinois Press, 1982).

ROSS, MARLON B., 'Romantic Quest and Conquest: Troping Masculine Power in the Crisis of Poetic Identity', in Anne K. Mellor (ed.), *Romanticism and Feminism* (Bloomington and Indianapolis: Indiana Univ. Press, 1988), pp. 26–51.

RUBINSTEIN, L. H., 'The Theme of Electra and Orestes: A Contribution to the Psychopathology of Matricide', *British Journal of Medical Psychology*, 42 (1969), 99–108.

SCHOR, NAOMI, *Reading in Detail: Aesthetics and the Feminine* (London: Methuen, 1987).

SCULL, ANDREW T., *Museums of Madness: The Social Organization of Insanity in Nineteenth-Century England* (London: Allen Lane, 1979).

—— (ed.), *Madhouses, Mad-Doctors and Madmen: The Social History of Psychiatry in the Victorian Era* (London: Athlone Press, 1981).

SHOWALTER, ELAINE, *The Female Malady: Women, Madness and English Culture, 1830–1980* (London: Virago, 1987).

SILVERMAN, DAVID, 'Clerical Ideologies: A Research Note', *British Journal of Sociology*, 19 (1968), 326–33.

SOUTHEY, ROBERT, *The Life and Correspondence of Robert Southey*, ed. C. C. Southey, 6 vols. (London: Longman, 1849–50).

SPENDER, DALE, *Man Made Language* (London: Routledge, 1980).

STALLYBRASS, PETER, and WHITE, ALLON, *The Politics and Poetics of Transgression* (London: Methuen, 1986).

STEVENS, JOHN E., 'Charles Lamb, The Romantic Humorist', *Charles Lamb Bulletin*, 3 (1978), 113–29.

STONE, LAWRENCE, *The Family, Sex and Marriage in England 1500–1800* (London: Weidenfeld & Nicolson, 1977).

SUTHERLAND, KATHRYN, 'The Coming of Age of the Man of Feeling: Sentiment in Lamb and Dickens', *Charles Lamb Bulletin*, 7 (1986), 196–210.

TALFOURD, THOMAS NOON, *Final Memorials of Charles Lamb; Consisting Chiefly of his Letters not before Published, with Sketches of some of his Companions*, 2 vols. (London: Moxon, 1848).

THOMPSON, DENYS, 'Our Debt to Lamb', in F. R. Leavis (ed.), *Determinations: Critical Essays* (London: Chatto & Windus, 1934).

—— *Reading and Discrimination* (London: Chatto and Windus, 1934).

THOMPSON, DOROTHY, 'Women, Work and Politics in Nineteenth-Century England: The Problem of Authority', in Jane Randall (ed.), *Equal or Different: Women's Politics 1800–1914* (Oxford: Blackwell, 1987), pp. 57–64.

THOMPSON, E. P., *The Making of the English Working Class* (Harmondsworth: Penguin, 1968).

—— 'Time, Work-Discipline, and Industrial Capitalism', in M. W. Flinn and T. C. Smout (eds.), *Essays in Social History* (Oxford: Clarendon Press, 1974), pp. 39–77.

—— 'Eighteenth-Century English Society: Class Struggle without Class?' *Social History*, 3 (1978), pp. 133–65.

TILLOTSON, GEOFFREY, 'The Historical Importance of Certain *Essays of Elia*', in James V. Logan, John E. Jordan, and Northrop Frye (eds.), *Some British Romantics: A Collection of Essays* (Columbus, Ohio: Ohio State Univ. Press, 1966), pp. 89–116.

WALKER, NIGEL, *Crime and Insanity in England, i. The Historical Perspective* (Edinburgh: Edinburgh Univ. Press, 1968).

WEISNER, THOMAS S., 'Sibling Interdependence and Child Caretaking: A Cross-Cultural View', in Michael E. Lamb and Brian Sutton-Smith (eds.), *Sibling Relationships: Their Nature and Significance across the Lifespan* (Hillsdale, NJ: Lawrence Erlbaum Associates, 1983), pp. 305–27.

—— and GALLIMORE, RONALD, 'My Brother's Keeper: Child and Sibling Caretaking', *Current Anthropology*, 18 (1977), 169–90.

WELSFORD, ENID, *The Fool: His Social and Literary History* (London: Faber, 1935).

WHALLEY, GEORGE, 'Coleridge's Debt to Charles Lamb', *Essays and Studies*, 11 (1958), 68–85.

WHEELER, KATHLEEN (ed.), *German Aesthetic and Literary Criticism: The Romantic Ironists and Goethe* (Cambridge: CUP, 1984).

WILSON, D. G., 'Charles Lamb and Bloomsbury', *Charles Lamb Bulletin*, 4 (1979), 21–4.

WINNICOTT, D. W., *Playing and Reality* (Harmondsworth: Penguin, 1974).

WOLLSTONECRAFT, MARY, *Vindication of the Rights of Woman*, ed. Miriam Brody Kramnick (Harmondsworth: Penguin, 1975).

—— *The Wrongs of Woman: or, Maria. A Fragment* in *Mary, A Fiction and The Wrongs of Woman* (London: OUP, 1976).

WORDSWORTH, WILLIAM, *The Poetical Works of William Wordsworth*, ed. Ernest de Selincourt and Helen Darbishire, 5 vols. (Oxford: Clarendon Press, 1940–9).

—— *The Prelude or Growth of a Poet's Mind*, ed. Ernest de Selincourt, rev. Helen Darbishire (2nd edn., Oxford: Clarendon Press, 1959).

—— *The Prose Works of William Wordsworth*, ed. W. J. B. Owen and Jane Worthington Smyser, 3 vols. (Oxford: OUP, 1974).

Index

Adams, Sarah Flower 146
Albion, The 154
  'What is Jacobinism?' 154–5
Allsop, Thomas 14–15
Anti-Jacobin Review and Magazine
  150–3

Barbauld, Anna Laetitia 162
Baudelaire, Charles 201
Beer, Gillian 190
Benjamin, Walter:
  on Baudelaire 201–2
Birrell, Augustine 8
British Ladies' Magazine 52, 68, 69
Brontë, Charlotte:
  Jane Eyre 113
Browning, Robert 178
Burke, Edmund:
  Reflections on the Revolution in France
  30
Burney, James 169
Burton, Robert 166
  Charles Lamb's pastiches of 57, 158
Byron, George Gordon, Lord 169

Canning, George:
  'The New Morality' 150
Carlyle, Thomas 9
Chambers, John 84, 89
Chodorow, Nancy:
  The Reproduction of Mothering 5,
  40–1, 122–3, 175
Christ's Hospital 24, 42, 80, 91, 100
  and Charles Lamb 58–66
Chudleigh, Mary Lee, Lady 25
Cixous, Hélène:
  on the *Oresteia* 131
Coates, John 160–1
Coleridge, Samuel Taylor:
  Aids to Reflection in the Formation of a
  Manly Character 3
  and anti-Jacobinism 133, 151–2
  and anti-utilitarianism 162
  and Charles Lamb 7, 66, 133–40,
  144, 146, 158, 201

  and Christ's Hospital 58, 63, 66
  and Mary Lamb 67, 118–19, 143–4
  On the Constitution of the Church and
  State 4
  and Romantic ideology 133–4
  'The Rime of the Ancient Mariner'
  139–40
  The Statesman's Manual 134
Courtney, Winifred F.:
  Young Charles Lamb 153–4, 169 n.
Cowden Clarke, Mary 14, 38
Culler, Jonathan 164
Curran, Stuart 146–7

Dadd, Richard 101 n.
Davidoff, Leonore, and Hall,
  Catherine 54, 169
de Beauvoir, Simone 68
de l'Enclos, Ninon:
  and Mary Lamb 67–8
De Quincey, Thomas:
  on Charles Lamb 80–1, 152
  on Charles and Mary Lamb 2
  on Mary Lamb 111
Dickens, Charles:
  and anti-utilitarianism 55
  and Charles Lamb 178
Dyer, George 66

East India Company:
  and Charles Lamb 22, 80–7, 91–3,
  100, 204
Edgeworth, Maria 58
Erdman, David V. 154, 162 n.

Field, Mary:
  and John Lamb jnr. 36, 44
  and Mary Lamb 44, 117
  and the Plumers 37–8, 43
Fleetwood, William 25
Foucault, Michel:
  Madness and Civilization 99–100
Frank, Robert D. 188
Freud, Sigmund:
  on manic depression 119–20

Freud, Sigmund (*cont.*):
  on play 190–1
  on women 122
Friedman, Leslie Joan 68 n., 105 n.

gender:
  and child caretaking 38–41
  and clerical work 52–3, 82, 88–9
  and domestic service 16, 24–7
  and education 51, 57–68, 71–2
  and 'English' 6, 11–12
  and the essay genre 176–7, 198
  and language 156–9
  and madness 17, 108–9, 113, 123–4
  and marriage 76–8
  and matricide 130–2
  and mergence 5, 40–2, 174–5, 202,
    203, 205, 206–7
  and needlework 68–79
  and power relations 16, 25–6, 31–5,
    88–9, 95–6, 121–3, 147, 163–6,
    174–5, 184–6, 197, 198, 206–7
  and the quotidian 146–7, 171, 175–6
  and Romanticism 3–4, 132, 134–5,
    145–7, 163–4, 174
  and sensibility 152–3
  and sibling relationships 2, 169–71
  and social change 2–4, 53–4, 73, 75,
    132, 134, 152–3
  and time discipline 52, 57, 70, 75
  and work segregation 72–6
Gilbert, Sandra M., and Gubar, Susan
  197
Gillray, James:
  and anti-Jacobinism 150–3
Gisborne, Thomas:
  *Enquiry into the Duties of the Female
    Sex* 122
Godwin, William 32, 143

Haydon, Benjamin Robert 83
Hays, Mary 51 n., 74
Hazlitt, William:
  and Charles Lamb 178–9
  'On Effeminacy of Character' 188–9,
    197
  on Mary Lamb 67–8, 111–12
  on 'Mrs Battle's Opinions on Whist'
    189
Hedge, Mary Ann 168
Hegel, Georg Wilhelm Friedrich:
  Aesthetics: Lectures on Fine Arts 171
  on sibling relationships 169–71

Hogarth, William:
  Charles Lamb on 31, 34, 145
Home, John:
  Douglas 94–5
Hunt, Leigh 171
  on Charles Lamb 165
  on Christ's Hospital 60–1

Irigaray, Luce:
  on the *Oresteia* 131
  'The Sex Which Is Not One' 174
Isola, Emma 67
  and Mary Lamb 119

Jacobus, Mary 6, 196
Johnson, Samuel 49, 176

Keats, John:
  and the 'egoistical sublime' 144–5
  and 'negative capability' 194, 203
Kelly, Fanny 31
  and Charles Lamb 167
Kelly, Joan 76 n.
Kennedy, J. M.:
  on Charles Lamb 9–10
  on Mary Lamb 13
Klancher, Jon P. 177
Klein, Melanie:
  on manic depression 120
Kristeva, Julia:
  'About Chinese Women' 147, 157,
    159
  'Place Names' 161
  'Women's Time' 184–6

LAMB, CHARLES:
  and alcohol 20–1, 204
  and anti-Jacobinism 150–5
  and anti-semitism 199
  and anti-utilitarianism 55–7, 162–3,
    187
  and child caretaking 38–42
  and childhood 53–7, 148–9, 161–3,
    183
  and Christ's Hospital 58–66
  and clerical work 52–3, 80–96
  and Coleridge 66, 133–40, 144, 146,
    158, 201
  critical reception of 6–13, 55, 84–5,
    149–50, 160–1, 179, 199
  death of 3, 204–5
  and depression 202–4

and the Elia persona 165, 172,
177–202
and Elizabeth Lamb 35–6, 127–8
and the essay genre 176–8, 198
and gender roles 4–5, 15–16, 31–5,
41–2, 52–9, 65, 82, 88–9, 95–6,
131–2, 134–5, 145–50, 153,
170–1, 175–6, 184–9, 197, 205–7
and geniality 196–7
and hoaxes 165
and irony 176, 177–8, 181, 194–8
and John Lamb 23–35
and John Lamb jnr. 35–6
and language 6, 154–61, 163–5,
179–80
and London 172–5, 201–2, 204
and madness 17, 94–5, 99, 128
and marriage 103, 167
and Mary Lamb 2–3, 13–14, 16,
38–42, 98, 128–32, 136, 148–50,
167–73, 182–3, 187–8, 204, 205,
206–7
and matricide 128–33, 135–6, 182–3
and mergence 5–6, 39–42, 175,
203–4
and 'negative capability' 194–5, 203
and officialdom 30–1, 83–4
and particularity 171, 172–7
and play 166, 187–96, 200
and puns 164–5
and religion 136–7
and Romantic ideology 3–4, 132–47,
161–4, 173–4
and servant roles 23–35, 197–8
and seventeenth-century writing
12, 145, 149, 155, 160–1, 177 n.
and social ostracism 17, 103–4
and social rank 21–3, 30, 34–5, 38,
44–6, 52–3, 56, 59–62, 80, 82–3,
89–91, 93–4
and stammering 36, 59, 127–8
and the stocks 20–1
and time and work discipline 20–1,
54–7, 91–3
and the Waldens 1, 205
and William Wordsworth 139–45,
161, 169, 173
WORKS:
Adventures of Ulysses 163
'An Autobiographical Sketch' 199
Beauty and the Beast 163
Blank Verse (with Charles Lloyd)
150–3

'Composed at Midnight' 138–9
'Confessions of a Drunkard' 155,
204
'Curious Fragments, extracted from
a commonplace-book which
belonged to Robert Burton' 56,
158–160
'Edax on Appetite' 178, 181
Essays of Elia 'A Complaint of the
Decay of Beggars in the
Metropolis' 193–4
'A Death-Bed' 179
'A Dissertation upon Roast Pig'
179
'A Quaker's Meeting' 195
'Amicus Redivivius' 179
'Barrenness of the Imaginative
Faculty in the Productions of
Modern Art' 30, 179
'Blakesmoor in H-shire' 44–6
'Captain Jackson' 192–3
'Christ's Hospital Five and Thirty
Years Ago' 63–5
'Detached Thoughts on Books and
Reading' 168, 180
'Distant Correspondents' 179
'Dream-Children: A Reverie' 36,
38, 168, 196
'Imperfect Sympathies' 194, 199
'Mackery End, in Hertfordshire'
36, 38, 168, 206
'Modern Gallantry' 13, 185–6, 199
'Mrs Battle's Opinions on
Whist' 168, 187–9
'New Year's Eve' 176, 190–1
'Old China' 5, 168, 186–8
'On the Artificial Comedy of the
Last Century' 191–2
'Poor Relations' 183–4
'Popular Fallacies—XIV. That a
Sulky Temper is a Misfortune'
180–2, 202
'Popular Fallacies—XVI. That We
Should Rise with the Lark'
200–2
'Preface, by a Friend of the late
Elia' 5, 180, 189, 196
'Sanity of True Genius' 207
'The Convalescent' 180–2
'The Old and the New School-
master' 192
'The Old Benchers of the Inner
Temple' 24, 26, 28, 55–7

CHARLES LAMB (*cont*.):
  WORKS (*cont*.):
    Essays of Elia (*cont*.):
      'The Old Margate Hoy' 168
      'The Praise of Chimney-
        Sweepers' 11
      'The South-Sea House' 183, 200
      'The Superannuated Man' 85–7,
        92
      'Witches, and other Night
        Fears' 184
    'Guy Faux' 182
    'If from my lips . . .' 41
    John Woodvil 147–50, 159, 164
    'Leisure' 93
    Mr. H- 155
    Mrs Leicester's School (with Mary
      Lamb) 32, 43, 207
    'Arabella Hardy: The Sea
      Voyage' 32–4, 64
    'Maria Howe: The Witch Aunt'
      126–7
    'Susan Yates: First Going to Church'
      163
    'On the Genius and Character of
      Hogarth' 31, 34, 145, 155
    'On the Inconveniences Resulting
      from being Hanged' 103–4
    'Play-House Memoranda' 163
    'Recollections of Christ's
      Hospital' 60–3, 66
    'Reminiscences of Juke Judkins,
      Esq., of Birmingham' 178
    Review of Hazlitt's *Table-Talk*
      178–9
    Rosamund Gray 147–9, 153, 164
    'Satan in Search of a Wife' 129
    'Specimens from the Writings of
      Fuller, the Church Historian'
      160–1
    *Specimens of English Dramatic Poets,
      who lived about the time of
      Shakspeare* 12–13, 31, 145,
      155–6, 161
    'Table-Talk', 29
    Tales from Shakespear (with Mary
      Lamb) 32, 163
    'The Good Clerk' 87–8
    'The Last Peach' 203
    'The Londoner' 171–2, 174
    'The Old Familiar Faces' 151
    The Pawnbroker's Daughter
      104

'Theses Quaedam Theologicae'
  138–9
'Work' 92–3
'Written on Christmas Day, 1797'
  121, 150
Lamb, Elizabeth:
  and Charles Lamb 35–6, 127–8
  and John Lamb 23, 36–8
  and John Lamb jnr. 35–6
  and Mary Lamb 35–8, 46, 48, 97–8,
    115–21, 124–6, 128, 131
Lamb, John:
  and Charles Lamb 23–35
  and Elizabeth Lamb 23, 36–8
  and *King Lear* 29–30, 34, 90
  as 'Lovel' 25–6, 28–9
  and madness 103
  *Poetical Pieces on Several
    Occasions* 27–8, 36
  and Samuel Salt 23–30
Lamb, John jnr.:
  and Charles Lamb 35–6
  and Elizabeth Lamb 35–6
  and Mary Lamb 35–6, 121
LAMB, MARY:
  as 'Bridget Elia' 36, 38, 168, 171, 188,
    196, 206
  and Charles Lamb 2–3, 13–14, 16,
    38–42, 98, 128–32, 136, 148–50,
    167–73, 182–3, 187–8, 204, 205,
    206–7
  and Coleridge 118–19, 143–4
  as counsellor 14–15
  critical reception of 13–15
  and domestic service 23–4, 37–8, 46,
    51
  education of 24, 36, 51, 67–8, 116 n.
  and Elizabeth Lamb 35–8, 46, 48,
    97–8, 115–21, 124–6, 128, 131
  and feminism 69–79
  and gender roles 3, 5, 38, 40–2, 48–9,
    52, 68–79, 95, 109–14, 121–4,
    130–2, 204–7
  and John Lamb jnr. 35–6, 121
  and *John Woodvil* 149–50
  and London 172–3
  and manic depression 1, 96, 104, 109
  and marriage 76–8
  and matricide 1, 97–8, 101–2,
    115–26
  and mergence 5, 40–1, 121–3, 173,
    203
  and needlework 51, 68–79

and *Rosamund Gray* 148–9
and Sarah Stoddart 15, 48–9, 77, 109–111, 124–5, 167
and self-repression 5, 109–14, 121–4
and social ostracism 17, 103–4
and social rank 38, 42–4, 46–50, 69, 78–9, 106–7
treatment of as lunatic 104–7
and the Waldens 1, 205
and William Wordsworth 118, 143, 173
on women's time 52, 70, 74–5
WORKS:
Mrs Leicester's School (with Charles Lamb) 32, 43, 207
'Ann Withers: The Changeling' 46–9, 125–6
'Charlotte Wilmot: The Merchant's Daughter' 43–4
'Elinor Forster: The Father's Wedding Day' 126
'Margaret Green: The Young Mahometan' 44, 46, 116–17, 127
'On Needle-Work', 5, 51–2, 68–79, 95
Poetry for Children (with Charles Lamb) 'Breakfast', 41
Tales from Shakespear (with Charles Lamb) 32, 163
Le Grice, Charles Valentine 62, 65, 128
Leavis, F. R. 10, 11–12
Lipman-Blumen, Jean 185
Lloyd, Charles:
and anti-Jacobinism 151
Blank Verse 150–1
and Charles Lamb 139
London Magazine 40, 167, 179

McFarland, Thomas 13–14, 198 n.
madness:
and asylums 99–100, 104–7
changes in the concept of 107–8
and industrialization 99–101, 108
and the law 101–2
manic depression 119–20
and matricide 115, 124
and 'moral management' 107–9
and social isolation 17, 103–4
and social rank 106–7
and women 17, 108–9, 113, 123–4
Manning, Thomas 22, 141
Martineau, Harriet 2

Mellor, Anne K. 196–7 n.
Monsman, Gerald 104 n.
More, Hannah:
Coelebs in Search of a Wife 129
Strictures on the Modern System of Female Education 88, 108, 176
Morley, F. V. 13, 149–50
Morning Chronicle, The 160
Munro, Thomas 106

Oresteia, The 98, 130–1

Pater, Walter 180
Patmore, P. G.:
on Charles Lamb 198, 202
on Mary Lamb 111
Plumer, William:
and the Lamb family 23, 102
his mansion and the Lambs 43–6, 62
Poovey, Mary:
The Proper Lady and the Woman Writer 54, 122–3, 197
Porter, Roy 107 n.
Procter, Bryan Waller ['Barry Cornwall, pseud.]:
on Charles Lamb 152
on Charles and Mary Lamb 42
on Mary Lamb 111, 205

Randel, Fred V. 200
Richardson, Dorothy:
on 'The Superannuated Man' 85, 87
Riehl, Joseph E. 163 n.
Robinson, Henry Crabb:
on Charles Lamb 7, 144
on Mary Lamb 14
and William Wordsworth 142–3
Ross, Marlon B. 132 n., 134 n., 145 n.
Rousseau, Jean-Jacques 153
Émile 64

Salt, Samuel:
and John Lamb 23–30
Lamb family's dependence on 42, 48–9, 59, 80, 102, 116, 121
Schiller, Friedrich 191
Schlegel, Friedrich 181, 189, 195–6
Scott, John:
and the *London Magazine* 179
Scull, Andrew:
Museums of Madness 99–101, 107

Shakespeare, William:
  Charles Lamb on 144–5
  King Lear 29–31
Showalter, Elaine 72
  The Female Malady 108–9
social change:
  and childhood 53–4, 161–2
  and gender roles 2–4, 53–4, 73, 75,
    132, 134, 152–3
  and industrialization 5, 20–1,
    49–50, 55–7, 89–93, 95–6
  and language 155–7
  and madness 99–101
  and Romanticism 3–4, 132–4, 163–4
  and sentimentalism 152–3
social rank:
  and clerical work 80, 82–3, 93–4
  and domestic service 16, 23–35,
    37–8
  and education 59–62
  · and madness 106–7
  and needlework 51, 72–3
South Sea Company 35, 183, 200
Southey, Robert:
  and anti-Jacobinism 151
  on Charles Lamb 6, 22
  on Charles and Mary Lamb 3, 42–3
Spender, Dale:
  Man Made Language 156
Stoddart, Sarah:
  and John Stoddart 48, 167
  and Mary Lamb 15, 48–9, 77,
    109–11, 124–5, 167
Stuart, Daniel:
  and *The Morning Post* 152, 160
Swinburne, Algernon 8
Symons, Arthur 8, 149

Talfourd, Thomas Noon:
  on Charles Lamb 7
  on Mary Lamb 14, 103, 113–14,
    117–19
Thompson, E. P. 90, 134 n.

'Time, Work-Discipline and
  Industrial Capitalism' 21, 56–8,
  75
Thompson, Denys 10–11
Todd, Janet 153
Trimmer, Sarah 162

Wakefield, Priscilla 74
Watts, Isaac 60
Weisner, Thomas S. 39–40
Wellek, René 12–13
Welsford, Enid 192
White, William Hale ['Mark
  Rutherford', pseud.] 81–2
Willis, Francis 106
Winnicott, D. W.:
  Playing and Reality 190–1
Wollstonecraft, Mary:
  *The Wrongs of Woman: or Maria.
  A Fragment* 51
  Vindication of the Rights of Women, A
  71, 74
Woolf, Virginia 181
Wordsworth, Dorothy:
  and Mary Lamb 118
  and William Wordsworth 168–9
Wordsworth, William:
  and anti-utilitarianism 162
  'Character of the Happy Warrior' 4
  and Charles Lamb 7, 139–45, 161,
    169, 173
  and Dorothy Wordsworth 168–9
  'Essay Supplementary to the
    Preface' 134
  and London 173
  Lyrical Ballads 140–2, 144
  and Mary Lamb 111, 118, 143, 173
  'Note to the Ancient Mariner' 140
  'Ode to Duty', 4
  and Romantic ideology 133–4, 174
  The Excursion 173
  'The Old Cumberland Beggar' 141
  'The White Doe of Rylstone' 142